**Deschutes
Public Library**

D0554365

THE DESEGREGATION OF PUBLIC LIBRARIES
IN THE JIM CROW SOUTH

THE DESEGREGATION
OF
PUBLIC LIBRARIES
IN THE
JIM CROW SOUTH

Civil Rights and Local Activism

WAYNE A. WIEGAND | SHIRLEY A. WIEGAND

Louisiana State University Press ▐▐▐ Baton Rouge

Published with the assistance of the Michael H. and Ayan Rubin Fund

Published by Louisiana State University Press
Copyright © 2018 by Louisiana State University Press
All rights reserved
Manufactured in the United States of America
FIRST PRINTING

DESIGNER: Michelle A. Neustrom
TYPEFACES: Whitman, text; Meltow San 200
PRINTER AND BINDER: Sheridan Books, Inc.

Several paragraphs from chapter 1 first appeared in Wayne A. Wiegand, *Part of Our Lives: A People's History of the American Public Library* (New York: Oxford University Press, 2015), and are reproduced by permission of Oxford University Press.

Several paragraphs from chapters 7 and 8 first appeared in Wayne A. Wiegand, "Forgotten Heroes in Civil Rights History," *American Libraries* 48 (June 2017): 3–7.

Portions of chapter 9 and the epilogue first appeared in Wayne A. Wiegand, "'Any Ideas?' The American Library Association and the Desegregation of Public Libraries in the American South," *Libraries: Culture, History, and Society* 1, no. 1 (March 2017): 1–22, copyright © 2017 by the American Library Association's Library History Round Table. This article is used by permission of The Pennsylvania State University Press.

LIBRARY OF CONGRESS CATALOGING-IN-PUBLICATION DATA

Names: Wiegand, Wayne A., 1946– author. | Wiegand, Shirley A., author.
Title: The desegregation of public libraries in the Jim Crow South : civil rights and local activism / Wayne A. Wiegand and Shirley A. Wiegand.
Description: Baton Rouge : Louisiana State University Press, [2018] | Includes bibliographical references and index.
Identifiers: LCCN 2017038119| ISBN 978-0-8071-6867-7 (cloth : alk. paper) | ISBN 978-0-8071-6868-4 (pdf) | ISBN 978-0-8071-6869-1 (epub)
Subjects: LCSH: African Americans and libraries—Southern States—History—20th century. | Discrimination in public accommodations—Southern States—History—20th century. | Public libraries—Southern States—History—20th century. | Civil rights movements—Southern States—History—20th century.
Classification: LCC Z711.9 .W54 2018 | DDC 027.475—dc23
LC record available at https://lccn.loc.gov/2017038119

The paper in this book meets the guidelines for permanence and durability of the Committee on Production Guidelines for Book Longevity of the Council on Library Resources. ∞

To the black youths
who risked their lives to desegregate
Jim Crow public libraries
in the American South.

A sadly belated "Thank you."

CONTENTS

ILLUSTRATIONS

following page 100

ACKNOWLEDGMENTS

Our thanks to Christine Pawley, who painstakingly went through an earlier draft of this book and gave wise counsel and advice that substantially improved it; Chris Dodge, who compiled the index; the anonymous reader for Louisiana State University Press, who not only carefully screened the manuscript but also prodded us to take a broader perspective; and especially our editor, Rand Dotson, who showed amazing patience with sometimes fussy authors and who certainly made this into a better book.

We also thank former students and colleagues with whom we've discussed ideas and conclusions that found their way into our narrative; Karen Muller of the American Library Association Library, who screened the American Library Association Executive Board minutes for mention of amicus briefs filed by the association between 1954 and 1965; the American Library Association, for a Diversity Grant that Wayne used in May 2012 for research into newspaper databases at the Library of Congress; Emory University's Manuscript, Archives, and Rare Book Library for a short-term fellowship in October 2012, and especially Randall Burkett, who made Wayne's weeklong stay there so profitable; librarians at the University of Wisconsin–Madison, and especially Michele Besant of the School of Library and Information Studies; archivists at the Wisconsin Historical Society, where Wayne perused the records of the Louisiana Section of the Congress on Racial Equality, which was so heavily involved in desegregating rural Louisiana public libraries; Marquette University Law School, and especially Dean Joseph Kearney, for supporting this project, and Patricia Cervenka and other law school librarians who helped retrieve research materials at so many stages of this project; Florida A&M University Law School, for supporting this project in so many ways while Shirl was visiting professor there from 2008 through 2011; librarians at Florida State University, and especially the School of Information's Goldstein Library director, Pamala Doffek, and her staff, many of whom helped this project in so many ways; librarians and archivists at the Library of Congress (where

Wayne spent weeks going through newspaper databases—especially the ProQuest African American newspapers—and several days going through the papers of the National Association for the Advancement of Colored People in the Manuscripts Reading Room); archivists at the University of Illinois at Urbana-Champaign (where Wayne consulted the American Library Association Archives); librarians and archivists at the Virginia State Library in Richmond, the University of South Carolina Library in Columbia, the University of Georgia in Athens, the Louisiana State University in Baton Rouge, the Alabama State Department of Library and Archives in Montgomery, and the Mississippi Department of Library and Archives in Jackson, where Wayne perused microfilmed newspapers from small towns within each state; librarians and archivists at the Civil Rights Museum in Albany, Georgia, where director Lee Formwalt showed Shirl documents relating to the desegregation of the public library and where Wayne and Shirl perused copies of local newspapers; archivists at the National Archives and Records Service in Philadelphia; librarians at the Auburn Avenue Research Library on African American Culture in Atlanta, who kindly copied and mailed to us a transcript of an oral history interview with Annie McPheeters, longtime director of Atlanta's black public libraries; and indirectly the National Endowment for the Humanities, for a Fellowship for University Teachers for Wayne in 2008–9 that funded research for a book entitled *Part of Our Lives: A People's History of the American Public Library* (2015), which Wayne also used to screen huge newspaper databases at the Library of Congress for valuable information used in *The Desegregation of Public Libraries in the Jim Crow South.*

THE DESEGREGATION OF PUBLIC LIBRARIES
IN THE JIM CROW SOUTH

INTRODUCTION

When did the civil rights movement begin? Upon being asked that question in the 1980s, native Mississippian and white Baptist minister Will B. Campbell, who had bravely escorted terrified black students through hostile crowds into the previously segregated Little Rock (Ark.) Central High School in 1957, showed no hesitation. For black people, he said, it began the first day an African slave was forcefully brought to North American shores. For southern whites, however, he insisted it was the Montgomery, Alabama, bus boycott in 1955. In the minds of white people, Campbell said, "harmonious race relations" persisted only when they "had their foot on black people's necks and the blacks weren't struggling to get up." Although the Supreme Court had issued its *Brown v. Board of Education* decision declaring "separate but equal" public schools unconstitutional in 1954, "not many people" in the South "took the decision seriously." But the bus boycott "was a different thing. I would say the Movement as white people experienced it began with Rosa Parks and ended on the balcony of the Lorraine Motel" when Martin Luther King Jr. was assassinated on April 4, 1968.[1] Civil rights historians often refer to the years 1954–68 as the "Second Reconstruction."

THE FIRST RECONSTRUCTION AND ITS AFTERMATH

The first Reconstruction period occurred immediately after the Civil War and involved federal legislation designed to eradicate all vestiges of the previous 250 years of the enslavement of black people in America. During the ten years after the Civil War ended in 1865, the United States adopted three constitutional amendments. The Thirteenth Amendment abolished slavery: "Neither slavery nor involuntary servitude . . . shall exist within the United States, or any place subject to their jurisdiction." The Fourteenth Amendment granted black Americans full citizenship: "All persons born or naturalized in the United States . . . are citizens of the United States and of the state wherein they reside. No state shall make or enforce any law which shall abridge the privileges or immunities of citizens of the United States; *nor shall any state deprive any person of life, liberty, or property, without due process of law; nor deny to any person within its jurisdiction the equal protection of the laws*" (emphasis added). The Fifteenth Amendment eliminated voting restrictions for black males: "The right of citizens of the United States to vote shall not be denied or abridged by the United States or by any state on account of race, color, or previous condition of servitude."[2]

In addition, Congress passed five civil rights statutes during this ten-year period, all designed to protect former slaves from discriminatory treatment, especially in the South. Although the Thirteenth Amendment abolished slavery, many states had enacted "Black Codes" designed to keep former slaves in a position of servitude. The Civil Rights Act of 1866 guaranteed a number of rights to all citizens: the right to make and enforce contracts; to buy, sell, and own real estate; to sue and serve as trial witnesses; and, perhaps most important, the right to the full and equal benefit of all laws. The law could be enforced against both state and private individual actions, and any person who "under color of law" denied any of these rights would be guilty of a federal crime.

After passage of the Fourteenth and Fifteenth Amendments, Congress enacted a new Civil Rights Act in 1870, reinforcing the guarantees in the earlier act, and the following year passed the Ku Klux Klan Act, making it a crime to "conspire together, or go in disguise upon the public highway or upon the premises of another for the purpose . . . of depriving any person . . . the equal protection of the laws." In 1875 Congress passed the Public Accommodations Act, which required all hotels, theaters, "and other places of public amusement" to admit all persons "of every race and color, regardless of any previous condition of servitude." Together, these legislative acts altered "substantially the balance between state and federal power," legal historian Eugene Gressman asserts, and "effectively nationalized the civil rights of all inhabitants of the United States, white or colored." Unfortunately, however, these early efforts to build a firm structure of civil rights for black Americans did not produce long-lasting results. Even before 1875, "corrosive elements were fast at work, elements which were eventually to leave the structure in ruins," notes Gressman.[3]

Beginning in 1873 and continuing for the next ten years, the United States Supreme Court interpreted both constitutional and statutory law in such a narrow fashion that private individual actions were immunized from enforcement. Individuals and private actors were free to discriminate at will.[4] Then, in 1883, the Court declared unconstitutional the 1875 Public Accommodations Act, in essence holding that individual proprietors could discriminate so long as their actions were private and not state sanctioned.[5] "The inevitable effect of these decisions," says Gressman, "was to transfer back to the states the prime responsibility for the protection of basic civil rights."[6]

Nevertheless, state regulations—conduct undertaken by the state or by its subdivisions (cities, counties, agencies)—were actionable under the law. The Fourteenth Amendment in particular provided that a state could not "deny to any person within its jurisdiction the equal protection of the laws." Southern states controlled by whites interpreted this provision as permitting segregated facilities. Segregation to them did not equal discrimination. Beginning in the 1880s, they passed a series of laws that permitted, even required, separation of the races. These were often termed "Jim Crow" laws after an early-nineteenth-century minstrel song, "Jump Jim Crow," popularized by a white comedian in blackface. In the postbellum South, "Jim Crow" became a racial epithet. Jim Crow laws helped support a series of oppressive social practices that had no basis in law and, like the laws, were intended to humiliate and control black Americans.

Some black Americans resisted, however. On June 7, 1892, for example, thirty-year-old Louisiana resident Homer Adolph Plessy took a seat in the all-white passenger car on a Louisiana railway. Although he appeared to be white, he was in fact one-eighth black. When confronted by a railroad employee, he refused to move to the car set aside "for persons not of the white race." He was then forcibly removed, arrested, and placed in a New Orleans jail for violating a state law that mandated "equal but separate accommodations for the white and colored races." He challenged the law as a violation of his constitutional rights and in 1896 ended up in the U.S. Supreme Court, where he lost. "Laws permitting, and even requiring, [racial] separation in places where they are liable to be brought into contact do not necessarily imply the inferiority of either race to the other," the Court reasoned: "We think the enforced separation of the races . . . neither abridges the privileges or immunities of the colored man, deprives him of his property without due process of law, nor denies him the equal protection of the laws, within the meaning of the Fourteenth Amendment." "We are unable to see how this statute deprives him of, or in any way affects his right to, such property," the Court declared. "If he be a white man and assigned to a colored coach, he may have his action for damages against the company for being deprived of his so-called property. Upon the other hand, if he be a colored man and be so assigned, he has been deprived of no property, since he is not lawfully entitled to the reputation of being a white man." It concluded: "If the two races are to meet upon terms of social equality, it must be the result of natural affinities, a mutual appreciation of each other's merits and a voluntary consent of individuals."[7]

The Court's approval of segregated facilities empowered the southern states. By 1900, notes legal historian Joseph William Singer, "every state in the former Confederacy . . . had adopted new statutes instituting the Jim Crow policy of forced racial segregation in public accommodations."[8] For the next half-century, the federal government seemed unwilling to offer even the barest protection to black people living in the South. In her award-winning historical study *The Warmth of Other Suns: The Epic Story of America's Great Migration* (2010), Isabel Wilkerson identifies the "facts" of life for southern blacks before midcentury:

> There were days when whites could go to the amusement park and a day when blacks could go, if they were permitted at all. There were white elevators and colored elevators (meaning freight elevators in back); white train platforms and colored train platforms. There were white ambulances to ferry the sick, and white hearses and colored hearses for those who didn't survive whatever was wrong with them. . . . There were white waiting rooms and colored waiting rooms in any conceivable place where a person might have to wait for something, from the bus depot to the doctor's office. A total of four restrooms had to be constructed and maintained at significant expense in any public establishment that bothered to provide any for colored people: one for white men, one for white women, one for colored men, and one for colored women. In 1958 a new bus station went up in Jacksonville, Florida, with two of everything, including two segregated cocktail lounges, "lest the races brush elbows over a martini," *The Wall Street Journal* reported.[9]

But change did come. Ira Berlin argues that a "new politics" emerged from the Great Depression and World War II experiences of blacks, and they were "quick to seize the celebratory rhetoric of American democracy and turn it against the American apartheid system."[10] Black resistance to Jim Crow laws and practices took a variety of forms over the years, gaining momentum during World War II, when A. Philip Randolph, founder of the Brotherhood of Sleeping Car Porters, threatened a march on Washington that President Franklin Roosevelt worried would damage the nation's war effort. In response, Roosevelt issued an executive order banning racial discrimination in war industrial plants.

In 1945, black Pulitzer Prize–winning novelist Richard Wright pored over a series of letters that the New York Public Library's Schomburg Research Center was collecting from blacks serving in the armed services. Reading them "was horrible," he later recalled, "a sea of despair to swim in." One man wrote, "I feel deeply and sincerely that the most important roles Negroes are playing in this war are that of hostages to prevent Hitler, Goebbels and company from using our omission from the war effort as propaganda." Another complained about being exploited: "I'm not afraid to fight when I find something worth fighting for," but after the war he wondered, "How willing is America to give full measure of democracy to the millions of poor people, white and black, in this country?" A third young man had been raised in the North but posted in the South. "I don't like it," he wrote his mother. He met Jim Crow humiliations at the local theater, the local cafeteria, and the main post exchange. "I think I'd just as soon be overseas, or dead, than to stay down here."[11] When black World War II veterans returned home, many were ready to challenge Jim Crow.

By the middle of the twentieth century, other outside pressures were cumulating against segregationist practices. On April 9, 1947, young civil rights activist Bayard Rustin led a group of sixteen black and white members of the Congress of Racial Equality (CORE), a Chicago-based interracial group of pacifist students founded in 1942 and dedicated to nonviolence, on a two-week "Journey of Reconciliation" through Virginia, North Carolina, Tennessee, and Kentucky. They hoped to test a 1946 Supreme Court decision prohibiting segregation in interstate travel. Less than a week later, Jackie Robinson broke the color barrier in major league baseball when he took the field for the Brooklyn Dodgers. That same year, a Committee on Civil Rights that President Harry S. Truman appointed recommended states pass laws that guaranteed all citizens equal and free access to public accommodations such as transportation, movie theaters, public parks, and hotels and motels. Some states north of the Mason-Dixon line followed the committee's recommendation in the early 1950s; southern states did not.

In June 1948 Truman also issued an executive order banishing "separate but equal" practices in all military training and facilities—which had never, in fact, been separate but equal. But reaction from the white establishment was quick. At the Democratic convention in August, southern Democrats angry at the civil rights positions taken by their party platform walked out to form the segregationist Dixiecrat Party and, with Strom Thurmond as its presidential candidate, carried Alabama, Louisiana, Mississippi, and South Carolina. Although Truman won the presidency, civil rights had nonetheless evolved into an issue tearing the Democratic Party apart.

More than Roosevelt's and Truman's actions, however, the strongest outside catalyst for challenging the Jim Crow South and initiating the Second Reconstruction was *Brown v. Board of Education*. After returning home from serving his country in World War II, McKinley Burnett, a Topeka, Kansas, black father, began challenging Topeka's segregated school system. He showed up at school board meetings armed with signed petitions but met little success. Eventually he contacted local attorneys considering legal action against the board, and together they searched for others in the neighborhood to join in a class action suit. Oliver Brown agreed. In 1950 Brown lived with his wife and children in an integrated Topeka neighborhood. He was a welder for the Santa Fe Railroad and served as an assistant pastor at a local church. Each morning, his children and other black neighborhood kids headed off to school in one direction, the white kids in another.

One day, however, Oliver took his daughter Linda to enroll her at the white school. "I remember going inside and my dad spoke with someone and then he went into the inner office with the principal, and they left me to sit outside with the secretary," his daughter later recalled. "And while he was in the inner office, I could hear voices and hear his voice raised as the conversation went on. And then he immediately came out of the office, took me by the hand, and we walked home from the school, and I just couldn't understand what was happening . . . because I was so sure that I was going to get to go to school with Mona, Guinevere, Wanda, and all of my [white] playmates."[12] Days later, Oliver Brown and twelve other parents filed a lawsuit against the Topeka Board of Education, challenging school segregation in the state.

In the 1954 *Brown* decision, the U.S. Supreme Court overturned *Plessy v. Ferguson* in no uncertain terms: "We conclude that in the field of public education the doctrine of 'separate but equal' has no place. Separate educational facilities are inherently unequal."[13] "I was home doing the family ironing that day . . . , all the kids were in school, my husband had gone to work," Brown's wife, Leola, later recalled. "And when it came over and they said . . . segregation had been defeated, was outlawed, oh, boy, I think I was doing the dance there at home by myself. (Laughs.) I was so elated. I could hardly wait until my kids and my husband got home to relate to them."[14] In a decision often referred to as *Brown II* a year later, the Court decreed that school systems desegregate with "all deliberate speed."

Brown I and *II* increased racial tension throughout the South. Virginia's Senator Harry F. Byrd Sr. quickly issued a "Southern Manifesto" opposing integrated schools; by 1956 it had been signed by over a hundred southern congressmen. Byrd also promoted passage of a group of laws prohibiting desegregation that became known as the "Massive Resistance" movement, and central to its agenda were eliminating state funding for any school that integrated and then closing it. Elsewhere, White Citizens' Councils formed throughout the South, while membership in the Ku Klux Klan greatly expanded.

And while Byrd was leading the movement to resist *Brown* in the South, on August 28, 1955, Emmett Till, a fourteen-year-old from Chicago who was visiting his mother's family in Mississippi, was beaten and lynched for ostensibly whistling at a white woman. Once his body was recovered, his mother chose to have an open-casket funeral in Chicago so that people could see what white racists had done to him. National media noticed. The next month, an all-white jury acquitted two white men responsible for Till's murder, both of whom later bragged about their act in a *Look* magazine interview.[15]

Then, on December 1, NAACP civil rights activist Rosa Parks refused to give up her seat to a white man on a Montgomery, Alabama, bus and was arrested. Days later, Montgomery's black community began a thirteen-month boycott of city buses that again drew national media attention. The boycott did not end until a year later, when the city agreed to honor a November 1956 Supreme Court ruling that segregation on buses was illegal. In the interim, racists had bombed the home of boycott leader Martin Luther King Jr., whose Gandhian strategy of nonviolent resistance to Jim Crow had guided the boycott.

On September 9, 1957, under the leadership of Texas senator Lyndon Johnson (who had not signed the Southern Manifesto), Congress passed the first civil rights legislation since Reconstruction. President Dwight Eisenhower—no friend of integration—signed it reluctantly. Although the law created a national Commission on Civil Rights, addressed voting rights, and gave the Justice Department greater powers to pursue civil rights violations, it did little to weaken Jim Crow customs and laws. And less than two weeks after the law passed, the nation's attention shifted to Little Rock, Arkansas, where efforts to desegregate the all-white Central High School had led to violence following the governor's order to block nine black students from entering the building. Eisenhower was forced to send federal troops to uphold the law and protect black students while they attended classes.

National Association for the Advancement of Colored People (NAACP) lawyers who had brought the *Brown* suit to the Supreme Court had assumed efforts to enforce the law would be aimed primarily at desegregating public schools, where attendance was compulsory and students closely interacted on a regular basis. Founded in 1909 to pursue justice for African Americans largely through the courts, the NAACP represented the oldest black organization involved with African American civil rights. But would this ruling also apply to other public spaces where attendance was voluntary, such as city buses? At the NAACP convention in Dallas shortly after the *Brown* decision, Legal Defense and Education Fund, Inc. (often referred to in NAACP circles simply as "Ink") lawyers met to plot strategy. As black New York attorney Constance Baker Motley later recalled, most thought they should directly attack school segregation, first from Mason-Dixon line states, then "work down." Oliver Hill from Richmond, Virginia, disagreed, however. Almost as if he anticipated Montgomery, he said: "I think what we ought to do is bring suits to desegregate the buses. Because that's something which black people meet every day, and it just riles them to think that they have to pay money and get on the bus and then stand while some white person sits." Motley later recalled their negative reaction to Hill's suggestion. "We felt that we had a purpose, a mission, and that was to desegregate the schools. . . . We thought we had to devote what resources we did have, and the staff, to trying to implement *Brown*." But that's not what happened, Motley noted. Because "we couldn't control" it, "the revolution got out of hand, so to speak, as far as we were concerned, and went off in many different directions. Southern blacks like Oliver Hill had perceived what it was that really got black people upset."[16]

That Hill was right was obvious. During the Second Reconstruction, *Brown* functioned as an open invitation to southern blacks to serve as plaintiffs in a series of lawsuits to desegregate public facilities across the South, not only in public transportation but also in restaurants, hotels, public parks, public beaches—and public libraries. Just like other public facilities, during the civil rights movement of the 1950s and 1960s public libraries frequently became sites for trial-and-error desegregation efforts to see what worked and what didn't. Protests against Jim Crow humiliations subsequent to the 1954 *Brown* decision found many other venues, just as Oliver Hill had predicted.

On February 1, 1960, for example, four students from the historically black North Carolina A&T College in Greensboro took seats at a segregated Woolworth's lunch counter and were denied service. They refused to leave and remained until closing. The next day they returned with fifteen more students. By the third day, three hundred had joined them, and soon one thousand. Their efforts received wide publicity and subsequently sparked lunch-counter sit-ins in more than a hundred other southern cities. "What demonstrators were saying, and meaning with all impatience and assumed immortality of youth, was 'Freedom now!' with the emphasis on the second word," notes civil rights journalist Fred Powledge. "And suddenly no other option seemed even worth considering."[17]

These protests also prompted the founding of the Student Nonviolent Coordinating Committee (SNCC) at the historically black Shaw University in Raleigh, North Carolina, in April 1960. SNCC's style of protest was much more confrontational than that of the NAACP and found substantial support especially among southern black college and high school students. Its members were eager to challenge Jim Crow laws by directly confronting white officials, who predictably often reacted violently to their demonstrations.

Tension increased throughout the South as civil rights activists kept up the pressure to kill Jim Crow. On December 5, 1960, the U.S. Supreme Court ruled in *Boynton v. Virginia* that segregating people by race on vehicles traveling between states violated the Interstate Commerce Act. The following summer, CORE organized a series of "Freedom Rides" consisting of black and white activists willing to test *Boynton* on interstate buses traveling through the South. Fourteen left the nation's capital on May 4. Days later, they divided into two groups, each of which met violent resistance in Anniston and Birmingham, Alabama. In Anniston, white supremacists tossed a firebomb into the bus and beat passengers as they fled the flames. Before intervening in Birmingham, police let Ku Klux Klan members beat Freedom Riders for fifteen minutes after the activists left the buses. Photos of the firebombed bus in Anniston and beaten students there and in Birmingham appeared the next day on the front pages of newspapers across the nation. But the Freedom Riders persisted.

For the remainder of the summer, over one thousand Freedom Riders, black and white, continued to test *Boynton*. Their actions deeply shook white establishments and segregationists across the South, as the prospect of hundreds of protesters from across the nation invading their Jim Crow states and testing local customs by citing federal laws threatened to flood local jails and overload the local judicial systems. In subsequent months, notes civil rights historian Raymond Arsenault, "the nation's first mobile nonviolent army expanded the realm of the possible in American political and social insurgency, redefining the limits of dissent and setting the stage for the escalating demands and rising expectations of the mid- and late 1960s." Their efforts, according to sociologist James Laue, "broke the charade of silence and with it the monolithic hold of the racist ethos of many Deep South communities." Freedom Rider Diane McWhorter summarized the rides differently, describing them as "one of history's rare alchemical phenomena, altering the structural makeup of everything they touched." At the same time, however, Freedom Rider activities often frightened local black leaders, who considered their actions dangerous and counterproductive.[18]

When CORE suspended the rides because of the violence, SNCC objected. The group's reaction sparked other Freedom Ride efforts and ultimately dragged a reluctant President John F. Kennedy into this mix of forces. Through his brother, Attorney General Robert F. Kennedy, the administration had a responsibility to guarantee safe passage for the Freedom Riders, although the federal government failed to protect civil rights activists once they were arrested and thrown into jails, where they were regularly harassed, treated poorly, and often beaten.

For a period of time in 1962, national attention focused on Albany, Georgia, where Martin Luther King's Southern Christian Leadership Council (SCLC, formed in 1957 after the Montgomery bus boycott) attempted to flood the jails with activists protesting the Jim Crow practices of local institutions, including the public library. Yet what became known as the "Albany Movement" also witnessed squabbles between the SCLC and local activists, many of whom were also SNCC leaders. The movement also sputtered because local city officials responded to protests relatively peacefully, unlike many other southern cities, such as Oxford, Mississippi, where black activist James Meredith attempted that fall to enroll at the University of Mississippi. When Oxford quickly erupted in violence, the Kennedy administration had to step in with federal troops to restore peace.

The year 1963 proved a turning point in the civil rights movement. On May 2 in Birmingham, Alabama, more than a thousand young people skipped school and met at the Sixteenth Street Baptist Church, where SCLC leaders helped them organize into groups. From the church they marched to downtown, on the way singing hymns and freedom songs, including "We Shall Overcome." They promised to return the next day and each day thereafter until Birmingham integrated all public accommodations and civic institutions. On May 3, however, Birmingham commissioner of public safety Eugene "Bull" Connor was ready. With a police force of scores of officers armed with clubs, attack dogs, and high-pressure fire hoses strong enough to knock people over and rip the clothes off their bodies, he and his subordinates attacked. News organizations from across the country captured the melee in photos and videos, which then showed up on the front pages of national newspapers and periodicals, and on evening television news broadcasts. The nation was shocked and the city paralyzed. On May 10, Birmingham officials and business owners eager to bring peace to their city negotiated a "Birmingham Truce Agreement" with local civil rights activists that promised to desegregate public water fountains, department store fitting rooms, and local lunch counters. Martin Luther King Jr. called it a "great victory"; Bull Connor hinted that his office might ignore the agreement. If the agreement raised hopes among civil rights activists, however, they were quickly dashed the next evening when, following a mass Ku Klux Klan rally in nearby Bessemer, bombs went off on King's front porch (he was out of town) and at a black-owned motel that had housed members of the Alabama Christian Movement for Human Rights. Across the nation, Americans began calling the city "Bombingham."

That other Alabama officials agreed with Connor's position on segregation was obvious. On June 11, Alabama governor George Wallace, who had campaigned for the office on a platform of "segregation now, segregation tomorrow, segregation forever," stood in front of the University of Alabama's Foster Auditorium to block entry by two black students seeking admission. There he was met by United States deputy attorney general Nicholas Katzenbach, federal marshals, and members of the Alabama National Guard, which President Kennedy had federalized, and told to step aside. Although he eventually did, the incident made Wallace into a national figure.

The very next day, NAACP Mississippi field secretary Medgar Evers was murdered in his Jackson, Mississippi, driveway. On June 20, his assassination became a subject of discussion in the Oval Office, where President Kennedy met with civil rights leaders (including Martin Luther King Jr.) in an attempt to call off the March on Washington being planned for late August. Kennedy failed. On August 28, more than a quarter-million people gathered on the National Mall to hear King deliver his famous "I Have a Dream" speech, which, notes Fred Powledge, "certified" King as the movement's "single most important leader." Americans— both white advocates of the Jim Crow system and also black people who had never publicly protested against segregation—now viewed King as *the* civil rights leader, someone who could be counted on to explain "what Negroes want."

Then, three weeks after the March on Washington, four black girls attending Sunday school classes lost their lives in the bombing of Birmingham's Sixteenth Street Baptist Church. Again the nation mourned. At the end of 1963, the Southern Regional Council, an Atlanta-based organization that since 1919 had advocated for racial equality (and for nearly one hundred years has produced influential reports on racial conditions in the South), counted 930 protests in eleven southern states that led to twenty thousand arrests, thirty-five bombings, and ten deaths. The violence on public display in the South that summer horrified Americans across the country and led Kennedy not only to condemn the violence publicly but also to propose significant legislation to address Jim Crow laws and customs.[19]

Kennedy's assassination on November 22, 1963, had a profound effect on civil rights legislation as it elevated Lyndon Johnson to the presidency. "No memorial or eulogy could more eloquently honor President Kennedy's memory," Johnson told a joint session of Congress four days after the assassination, "than the earliest possible passage of the civil rights bill for which he fought so long. We have talked long enough in this country about civil rights. We have talked for one hundred years or more. It is now time to write the next chapter, and write it in a book of law."[20] On July 2, 1964, Congress passed the Civil Rights Act, a wide-ranging law that prohibits discrimination on the basis of race, color, religion, sex, or national origin and authorizes punishments and financial penalties for violations. It also bars unequal application of voter registration requirements and outlaws discrimination in employment. Title II prohibits "discrimination or segregation" in "any place of public accommodation," which by definition includes hotels, restaurants, gas stations, places of entertainment, and public libraries (although they were not listed in the act).[21]

"In hammering out their legislation, Congress and the president were not aiming for a one-size-fits-all solution," notes legal historian Bruce Ackerman. "They followed [Chief Justice Earl] Warren's path. Step by step, they identified additional spheres of social life that were strategic sites for constitutional intervention; public accommodations, private employment, and fair housing." Federal officials then "set about achieving real-world equality in ways that were tailored to each sphere's prevailing practices and means—sometimes successfully, sometimes less so."[22] "From Charleston to Dallas, from Memphis to Tallahassee," *Time* magazine reported, "segregation walls that had stood for several generations began to tumble in the first week under the new civil rights law."[23] According to an October 1964 survey of fifty-three cities in nineteen states, desegregation had been accomplished in more than two-thirds of the hotels, motels, chain restaurants, theaters, and sports facilities as well as public bars and public libraries.[24]

Although both the legislative and judicial branches were clear in their commitment to civil rights by 1964, the period of adjustment between the *Brown* decision and passage of the Civil Rights Act did not go smoothly. In many areas, southern state and local governments had to be brought kicking and screaming into this new era. Some foresaw the inevitable and quietly changed their policies and practices. Others resisted as long as they were able, giving in only when ordered to do so and then not graciously. Some reacted violently, causing bloodshed and loss of life. A 1964 Freedom Summer campaign organized by CORE that brought hundreds of college students and other volunteers to Mississippi to register voters showed an extent of resistance made most obvious when Freedom Summer civil rights activists James Chaney, Andrew Goodman, and Michael "Mickey" Schwerner were murdered in the small town of Philadelphia on June 21 (Chaney was black, Goodman and Schwerner white). Their bodies were not discovered until forty-four days later.

PUBLIC LIBRARIES IN THE SOUTH

It was in this mix of forces and organizations that southern blacks forced the desegregation of American public libraries in the South. And like other efforts to integrate civic institutions, it was what historian Stephen Tuck calls "the persistence of local activism" that won the battle to integrate these institutions and genuinely make them "free to all."[25] In many respects the movement to desegregate public libraries was a local contest over public space. Many whites chose not to share space with blacks because they believed them dirty, uneducated, and promiscuous (any public space that allowed black men and white women to mix was particularly worrisome to the white establishment). Blacks naturally resented these attitudes, and their decision to contest this particular public space was as much about power and possession, as much about challenging racial hierarchies, as it was about changing white beliefs. Taken together, these local-level stories frame a narrative that demonstrates similarities and differences as individual communities negotiated—mostly peacefully, sometimes violently—the integration of the local public library as a place.[26]

But the black people who achieved the desegregation of public libraries were also demographically unique. The integration of southern public libraries was almost exclusively the result of "direct action" (a common term civil rights activists used in the 1960s to describe their protests and sit-ins) by a restless generation of very young southern blacks. By refusing to be pushed around, by brazenly defying segregationist practices, risking their lives, and daring local officials to arrest them, they forced local whites to confront questions of freedom, justice, and the democratic ideals the American public library claimed to embody. While the American Library Association, the profession's national voice, remained mute, a variety of civil rights organizations—including the NAACP, CORE, SCLC, and SNCC (though often disagreeing about strategies and competing for funds, members, and publicity)—stepped forward to lead efforts to desegregate southern public libraries. And though these groups offered support and direction, it was primarily because of the energy, courage, and determination of young blacks that these organizations achieved their goals. Black youths were the essential soldiers on the front lines of civil rights battles in segregated public libraries across the South. *The Desegregation of Public Libraries in the Jim Crow South* seeks to document their activities and, by bringing to the present generation the largely untold story of their courage and resolve, finally give them the historical credit they deserve.

The exhilaration this generation of black Americans felt for the battle against segregation in all public places is manifest in the recollections of Charles Jones. On February 2, 1960, he was on his way back to Charlotte, North Carolina, where he was a twenty-two-year-old student at historically black Johnson C. Smith University. He had just finishing testifying as a friendly witness before the House Committee on Un-American Activities in Washington, D.C., about his experiences the previous summer as a delegate to the Seventh World Youth Festival in Vienna, where he had initiated a "rather lively exchange" with leftist European students sympathetic to communism by praising the United States for progress in its fight against segregation, specifically citing the 1954 *Brown* decision and the 1955 Montgomery bus boycott. "I was feeling pretty strongly about being black," he later recalled. On August 6, 1959, the *Charlotte Observer* had even headlined a story about Jones, "Charlotte Negro Shows World American Way of Life," and started the process that got him invited to Washington.

The hearings had gone well for Jones; although he refused to condone any form of segregation, he acknowledged to committee members that democracy was better than communism. As he drove on rural highways that night, however, he had the car radio on to help him stay awake. Then, about 2:00 a.m., he heard first reports of the February 1 Greensboro lunch counter sit-ins. A rush of feelings came over him. "It was like the feelings I had when I first heard about Dr. [Martin Luther] King [Jr.]," he later recalled, "the feelings that I had when I heard about the 1954 [*Brown*] school desegregation ruling. All of a sudden there was a handle to getting this stuff," and speaking for his entire generation of young black Americans, he came to a sudden realization: "I knew—intuitively I knew this was our time."[27]

Although civil rights historians have evolved a rich literature that addresses the politics of racial discrimination in education, public accommodations, housing, and labor across the country, they have a shallow understanding of racial discrimination in public libraries. A glance at the indexes of most books broadly covering civil rights just in the South between the 1954 *Brown* decision and passage of the Voting Rights Act of 1965 shows few references to the painful history of the integration of southern public libraries that this book addresses. That public libraries are noncompulsory institutions that people of any color do not have to use may explain why historians of the Second Reconstruction have largely over-looked them.[28] Nonetheless, courts eventually included them as part of public accommodations (Title II) law.[29]

In the North, this discrimination in public library history was forced by real estate redlining supported by local politicians. These efforts isolated urban pub-lic library branches serving black populations in the ghettos to which they were effectively confined. In the South, this discrimination was the result of Jim Crow customs and practices. That this book addresses only the desegregation of public libraries in the South should not be taken as supporting the concept of southern exceptionalism against a national civil rights narrative. We are convinced that a historical analysis of segregation in northern public libraries will yield a number of stories (such as we found for the South) that are now "hidden in plain sight."[30]

And with rare exceptions, library history literature lacks attention to the real-ity of racial discrimination in public libraries across the nation in general and to the reality of white violence and black exclusion that many in the South's public li-brary community supported well into the 1960s in particular. Although American public libraries annually "celebrate" Black History Month with a series of events, almost never have they paid attention to their own participation in the struggles against racial discrimination that occurred between 1954 and 1965. Patterson Toby Graham's *A Right to Read: Segregation and Civil Rights in Alabama's Public Libraries, 1900–1965* is the best work on the civil rights protests in public libraries, but it covers only one state.[31] Cheryl Knott's *Not Free, Not for All: Public Libraries in the Age of Jim Crow* is the definitive history of public library Jim Crow practices before *Brown* but gives little attention to the sit-ins and violence we cover in depth.[32]

Another reason for not including these unpleasant events in the history of public libraries may reside in the public history that civic culture has crafted over the years to commemorate the era. Much of this history focuses on high-profile personalities such as Martin Luther King Jr. and Rosa Parks, leaders who seldom participated in demonstrations or sit-ins involving the desegregation of public libraries. Thus, young blacks who forced library integration seldom received na-tional media attention.

And yet there is an irony here. By the first decade of the twenty-first cen-tury, economic historian Gavin Wright concludes, the civil rights revolution of the 1960s had become "firmly embedded in American civic culture. Accounts and pic-tures of the Montgomery bus boycott, the Greensboro sit-ins, the Freedom Rides, and Martin Luther King, Jr.'s soaring speech at the Lincoln Memorial feature in textbooks and classrooms throughout the nation, including those in the southern states, where most of these famous events occurred." And four decades after these events, he notes, "civil rights heritage sites in Atlanta, Birmingham, Memphis, and other cities attract more than a million tourists each year, who come to see and hear tales of the epic struggle and to absorb lessons in what one historian calls 'the new regional civic ideology of tolerance.'"[33] Unlike public accommodation sites such as public pools, amusement parks, and skating rinks that closed rather than integrate, however, no public library in the South remained closed against integration for long, and many of the civil rights heritage sites putting their civic ideology of tolerance on public display are now located in the very public library systems that denied black Americans access until the 1960s.

In our coverage of the desegregation of public libraries in the American South after 1950, we focus on local stories to identify broader patterns of struggle. We admit to being drawn to stories that primary source documentation could support that also generated headlines (national, state, and local) and contained colorful (and some now famous) personalities. We follow the primary sources, including records for lawsuits filed in federal courts, local white newspapers (many on microfilm at state libraries), and regional and local black newspapers (many now digitized in an easily searchable ProQuest Historical Black Newspapers database). By focusing on the desegregation of public libraries in specific locations such as Memphis, Tennessee; Greenville, South Carolina; Petersburg and Danville, Virginia; and the states of Alabama, Georgia, Mississippi, and Louisiana, we recognize that we are telling only part of a much larger story. We hope our efforts here will encourage others to follow the example of Toby Graham's *Right to Read* and investigate the history of public library integration in other states and localities that will enable future civil rights or library historians to weave the story of racial discrimination in public libraries into a national narrative.

In chapter 1, we address Jim Crow libraries before *Brown*—a time when, historian Catherine Barnes notes, "southern blacks attempted only to equalize accommodations, not undo segregation"[34]—and show how African Americans crafted particular kinds of public library services and places that were safe and welcoming but still within the confines of the Jim Crow laws and practices surrounding them.

In chapter 2, we focus on protests before 1960, some successful, some not. We describe the first public library sit-in in Alexandria, Virginia, in 1939 and cover peaceful public library integration stories in Nashville, Tennessee; Richmond, Virginia; and Louisville, Kentucky, in the early 1950s, all of which preceded the desegregation of other public accommodations. We also discuss several lawsuits blacks filed in the Virginia towns of Newport News (1952), Purcellville (1957), and Portsmouth (1959) to force the integration of local public library services.

The public library desegregation attempts covered in chapters 3 through 8 largely occurred between 1960 and 1965. Chapters 3 and 4 concentrate on four cities: Memphis, Tennessee; Greenville, South Carolina (where Jesse Jackson, now a nationally known civil rights leader, participated in his first sit-in); and Petersburg and Danville, Virginia. At each locale protests were particularly vehement, in large part because they were driven by the "this was our time" feelings the February 1960 Greensboro lunch counter sit-ins generated. Chapter 5 focuses on public library integration activities in Alabama (particularly Mobile, Birmingham, and Montgomery); chapter 6 on Georgia (especially Albany and the "Albany Movement"); chapter 7 on Mississippi (including the "Tougaloo [College] Nine," and events they forced at the Jackson Public Library that involved Medgar Evers, and the Freedom School students' 1964 effort to desegregate the Hattiesburg Public Library); and chapter 8 on rural Louisiana, where sit-ins largely escaped national media attention.

In chapter 9, we discuss the limited role library associations played in all these events, particularly the role of the American Library Association, which was largely absent and mostly silent about Jim Crow public libraries until well into the 1960s. An epilogue summarizes our findings, including proof that over time many of the public libraries that practiced Jim Crow services before 1965 eventually became sites of racial reconciliation.

1

JIM CROW PUBLIC LIBRARIES BEFORE 1954

"America was founded on white supremacy and the notion of black inferiority and black unfreedom," writes Leon F. Litwack in his seminal *Trouble in Mind: Black Southerners in the Age of Jim Crow*.[1] This legacy, which some have argued constitutes America's original sin, has been evident—albeit seldom acknowledged—in American library history until well into the twentieth century. As slaves in the antebellum South, blacks were denied access to libraries of any sort. Their free brothers and sisters in the North, however, managed to create some library opportunities for themselves. Because most white literary societies would not admit them, early-nineteenth-century blacks in Massachusetts, New York, and Pennsylvania organized nearly fifty literary societies that sponsored debates and reading rooms with small circulating book collections. Many were run by women; most did not survive more than a decade.

Although teaching "the Negro how to use his leisure time to advantage" formed one objective, the New York Garrison Literary Association's 1834 charter noted, its circulating library "made available to many readers anti-slavery and colonization publications" and "books relating to the Negro and to slavery." These information resources guided the society's discourse. "The subjects of discussion generally relate to their own rights and interests and frequently result in decisions from which the prejudiced mind of the white man would startle and shrink with apprehension," reported one observer of a Philadelphia Library Company of Colored Persons early-nineteenth-century meeting. These kinds of societies, he continued, were "numerous, united and bitterly conscious of their degradation and their power."[2]

As education became compulsory, as literacy increased, and as improved technologies reduced the cost of printed materials in the first half of the nineteenth century, a new type of library appeared. In 1854 Boston opened a "public library" funded by local tax dollars. Its founders argued that democracy required an informed citizenry and that providing the public with good books containing practical information was a civic responsibility. Other communities followed Boston's lead.

As northern public libraries grew in number after the Civil War, black experiences in some of them were positive. When, for example, Cincinnati built its new public library in 1868, the city's "Colored School Board" petitioned trustees to admit black children. The building opened two years later, and residents over age fourteen (including "colored children") could draw books as long as a "responsible citizen" vouched for them.[3] And in the late 1890s a black Pullman railroad car porter specifically arranged his work schedule so that he would be in Boston every Sunday to use the Boston Public Library. "As far as the library is concerned," he told an attendant, "one man has as good a chance as another."[4]

In the South, postbellum Jim Crow practices affecting what minimal public library services existed in the late nineteenth century mirrored the kind of humiliating experiences other civic institutions exercised on black people. When the Colored National Liberal Convention met in the Louisville, Kentucky, Public Library auditorium in 1872, for example, none of the delegates were welcome in the library proper.[5] And when a black man tried to buy a "first-class ticket" to a public library auditorium event three years later, the manager refused, saying: "I will allow no white person to occupy a seat in the balcony, nor is it fair to suppose that I will permit a black person to occupy a seat in the dress-circle or parquet. To preserve the dignity and character of the hall, I must have a separation of the races."[6]

Why couldn't blacks check out books in public libraries? a northern magazine columnist asked a southern librarian in 1891. "Southern people do not believe in 'social equality,'" she responded. "The libraries in the Southern States are closed to the low down negro eyes," one Florida white wrote in 1911. "All the mean crimes that are done are committed by some educated negro." Under circumstances that in white people's eyes confirmed black inferiority and baseness and through social practices effected what Litwack calls "ritualized and institutionalized subordination,"[7] the few black libraries that did take root in the South often also functioned as subtle acts of defiance against prevailing Jim Crow norms.

ON THEIR OWN

As late-nineteenth-century Jim Crow practices spreading across the South choked their economic opportunities and limited their access to education, blacks turned inward to craft their own institutions, all providing some shelter from the often violent and constant indignities racism brought, all enabling a degree of social authority and acknowledging intelligence and independence they could not enjoy in larger southern society. In 1898 James A. Atkins, a Knoxville College black student forced to live at home because he could not afford dormitories near the college library, longed for a public library "in East Knoxville where I might run down a lot of additional information to various prescribed readings in our lesson texts. . . . A hidden intellectual hunger gripped me, with no chance to satisfy it."[8] It was this kind of hunger that led some southern blacks to establish lyceums, literary societies, and libraries in the late nineteenth century. Some people—black and white—who lamented the lack of public library services to blacks took matters into their own hands.

Because only whites could use the new Macon, Georgia, Public Library, for example, in 1881 blacks accessed a one thousand–volume subscription library that a local clergyman operated out of his house.[9] Two years later, Memphis blacks established the Memphis Lyceum, where Ida B. Wells not only made friends, participated in readings, and listened to poetry, recitations, and music, but also honed the oratorical skills she successfully harnessed in later life as a leading civil rights activist and founding member of the NAACP.[10] In a borrowed room of the White Rock Baptist Church in Durham, North Carolina, blacks organized a library of eight hundred books in 1913. Three years later, it moved into the Durham Colored Library built with $2,400 in contributions.[11]

In Alabama in 1940, the Savery Library at the historically black Talladega College established a "Community Library" service that included not only a children's corner and teenage section in the library; it also sponsored a bookmobile service to black people in the city and county. Beginning in 1941, a bright blue bookmobile bearing the words "Free Library Service" in red letters visited city and rural schools, library stations, and preschools. "The reports of many phases of the extension work are filled with heart-warming stories of reading materials going into bookless homes," noted a 1950s Savery Library flyer, "and of both city and rural persons drawing out their first book from a 'public library.'"[12]

In 1950 the Delta Sigma Theta sorority, founded at historically black Howard University in 1913, raised enough money to purchase a bookmobile for blacks in northwest rural Georgia, the culmination of a five-year program to furnish books and reading material to the South's underprivileged areas. The Georgia State Department of Education and the Georgia Library Commission expressed gratitude for the gift and accepted the bookmobile into its regular public services. Events celebrating the donation, however, took place not in Georgia but in New York City— headquarters for the Deltas. There an eleven-year-old girl cut the ribbon. "I am happy to launch the Bookmobile for the children, farmers, housewives and business people of Georgia," she said, "and send you on your way with Godspeed." Deltas promised that the bookmobile "would be available for the use of all the rural people," not just blacks.[13]

WITH SOME WHITE ASSISTANCE

In 1909 James J. H. Gregory of Marblehead, Massachusetts, who as a white Civil War Union soldier had seen the plight of southern blacks and recognized how they were being left behind in the turn-of-the-century public library movement, arranged with historically black Atlanta University to disseminate fifty libraries of thirty to fifty books each to southern sites (particularly educational institutions) located in communities where blacks were denied access to public libraries.[14] In the 1930s, at twenty South Carolina locations, blacks had access to collections donated by a white clergyman befriended in his youth by a black schoolteacher. Because these libraries had been "founded on faith," they were called "Faith Cabin Libraries."[15]

By the beginning of the twentieth century, steel magnate Andrew Carnegie had begun issuing building grants to communities with inadequate libraries and library services. Between 1890 and 1919 he contributed $45 million to construct 1,689 public library buildings, a number of them in southern cities. To qualify, communities had to promise annual support of 10 percent of the construction grant and provide an adequate site. Even though many of them sported the title "Free Public Library," Carnegie made no demands about racial restrictions.

Although Jackson, Mississippi, received its first public library—a Carnegie building—in 1914, it was available to Jackson's white citizens only. In 1938 several black community leaders petitioned the Jackson city commission to take over a small library they had started; it held 784 books, all donated by blacks.[16] The petition failed. But in 1944 Pearl Sneed became head of the Jackson Public Library and began lobbying for part of a new municipal auditorium for blacks to include a room for a library. In the meantime, she "on numerous occasions permitted Negroes, who needed to make use of library resources, to use them in her office."[17]

In the late 1940s, members of the white Jackson Junior League began a campaign to open a public library for blacks. With some assistance from the white public library board, the George Washington Carver Branch opened its doors in 1950. For twenty-one months the Junior League financed and operated the branch, but in late 1951 the board assumed responsibility. The following year a second library for blacks—the College Park Branch Library—opened, and in 1956 the Carver branch library moved into a new and modern structure. Blacks, who made up nearly 40 percent of Jackson's population, could receive other materials from white libraries only through interlibrary loan.[18]

Sneed's action mirrored those of a few other white, mostly female, librarians. To provide blacks access to collections without threatening the Jim Crow culture in which she operated, in the century's second decade Gadsden, Alabama, public librarian Lena Martin evolved a practice later adopted by several public libraries in southern cities unable to afford a separate "colored" branch. Black teachers and students could use collections by directly contacting either her or Ruby Prater, a black maid who cleaned the library. By midcentury the library allowed blacks in the building (rather than serving them through the back door) but only at reference tables marked "Colored Only."[19]

Although southern whites occasionally supported library services to southern blacks, that support was heavily circumscribed by local conditions. When Birmingham opened a public library in 1891, African Americans at first were allowed to use it. Seven years later, after black people raised funds for a library in the local high school, town officials formally denied them use of the main library. For years, black school principals pressed the white library board to extend public library service to black communities, but the city responded only after the principals raised over $4,000 and offered it to the board to jump-start library services if the city agreed to support the facility and pay for a librarian. What became the Booker T. Washington Branch Library opened in a vacant store in 1918. Washington, a leading civil rights activist and founder of Tuskegee University, had advocated for such a branch when he visited Birmingham in 1913.

Like most black branches, collections included periodicals and newspapers issued "by and for the colored people." Like many black branches, its collections could not mix with other books in the system. (Not all library systems followed this model, however. In many, blacks and whites could share use of any books the system owned, although system spaces in which they handled books were separated by race.) "Books for the colored branch are to be held entirely separate and distinct," a rule stated. And while the city paid the rent and librarian's salary, it refused appropriations for acquisitions. To compensate, blacks raised money through local black schools, but when through their branch they requested books that were available only in the white library, the board created a new rule. If "the need of a loan is urgent the copy from the Central Library may be *given* to the Branch," the rule read, "and a new one bought from the colored library book fund to replace it." Thus, Birmingham's blacks could handle books whites had touched; whites would not handle books blacks touched.

When the Washington branch librarian allowed one white to use the library in 1919, he was soundly scolded. "Do not permit a white person in the future to register at the Washington Branch," the system vice director wrote him. "Colored members are not enrolled" in the main library, "nor should white ones join the Washington Branch." Officials routinely underfunded the black branch, for years the only one of its kind in the state. And although "the black community provided the stimulus for the creation of the branch, whites took most of the credit," library historian Toby Graham observes. "Their reports applauded their own enlightened behavior. . . . The spirit of reform that animated board members and administrators presumed a belief in white supremacy and an obligation to uphold southern mores."[20] In the 1930s the main library was still open only to whites, but library officials did hire a black librarian, located her in a back room, and through a back door she retrieved books requested by blacks who knocked and made requests. It is unknown if white patrons knew about this breach of Jim Crow library practice.[21]

In the early 1920s, in Georgia, ten-year-old African American Annie Watters climbed the two flights of steps necessary to enter the Rome Public Library. "As I was about to enter," she later recalled, the librarian arose from her chair, adjusted her glasses, and said, "Go back; you cannot come in here." Stunned, Watters stood still. "Finally, as I turned to go and with tears in my eyes and a heart full of hurt . . . [I] said, 'I'm leaving now, but I promise that one of these days I'll be back and won't have to leave.'" So taken was Annie's mother at her daughter's rejection that she organized a group to petition the white library board for a "colored branch." After several years the board agreed to open one in the basement of a black Presbyterian church.[22] Young Annie would ultimately become a librarian herself and a strong civil rights activist, providing library services to segregated communities in Greenville, South Carolina, and later throughout the Atlanta area.

As the public library movement that Carnegie grants accelerated in the North after 1890 took root in the turn-of-the-century South, several urban southern public library systems agreed to open separate branches for blacks. Experiences were mixed. Ten years after Memphis's Cossitt Free Library opened in 1893, for example, the city started a black branch as a joint endeavor with LeMoyne College, a black school founded in 1870.[23] In 1903 the city of Charlotte, North Carolina, authorized a Charlotte Public Library for Colored People separate from an equally new white public library. It opened in 1906 with six hundred donated volumes.[24] By the summer of 1916, the San Antonio Public Library weakly supported four library stations in black schools.[25] In Beaumont, Texas, the public library opened a branch in 1929 for black people in a local black high school.[26]

Because it would "place Mobile [Ala.] before the world as the most liberal and fair-minded Southern City in America," members of Mobile's black middle class reasoned, they requested public library service in 1928. At first they wanted a room in the main library, but white citizens protested. "The question of the negro library is becoming acute," the board chairman wrote white consultants Arthur E. Bostwick, St. Louis Public Library director and former American Library Association (ALA) president, and Carl Milam, one-time director of the Birmingham Public Library and the current ALA executive director. "The negroes themselves are very anxious to have it in . . . the rear of the main library and as nearly a part thereof as possible." After Milam identified potential trouble between the races "in their going and coming" and Bostwick argued that black patrons would more readily see inequities in services leading to a "dissatisfaction with the whole arrangement" that a separate black facility would mask, the board decided on a separate "colored branch." Mobile opened its Davis Avenue Branch on July 14, 1931, but three months later the branch lost all funds because of the Great Depression economy. To keep their library open, black people solicited donations, hosted fundraisers, and charged patrons a dollar a year for use. In 1932 the librarian also wrote the *New York Times* to ask its readers for donations of books and money. The branch survived until 1961, when Mobile desegregated its public library system.[27]

Blacks opened the Richard B. Harrison Public Library in Raleigh, North Carolina, in 1935 with funds from the city, county, and local black people, who raised $500 by giving a play and soliciting donations. Within a year they had two thousand books and a circulation of eight thousand.[28] After World War II, the branch started a bookmobile service to Raleigh's rural environs. Without mentioning race or segregation of public library services in the state, bookmobile librarian Anne Robinson described several visits to black rural churches in a 1953 *Bulletin of the American Library Association*. At a bookmobile stop in a rural area, an elderly gentleman approached. Asked if he needed help, he replied: "Not today, Ma'am. I can't read much, but I've heard so much about this here bookwagon, just thought I would come and see for myself." Would he like to learn to read? "Yep, lady, I sho' would," he responded. He then joined a group of seventeen who met weekly at a local black Baptist church.[29]

Shortly after World War II, the Carroll-Heard Regional Library opened a "colored branch" in Carrollton, Georgia. Its origins demonstrate the limits Jim Crow communities placed on their citizens—white and black. White library director

Edith Foster realized the only way she could serve blacks, who made up 20 percent of her service area, was to establish a separate branch. "I recognized that in setting up a dual library system I would be making my assignment painfully difficult as a few white citizens would be wary of what I was doing and some Black leaders outside the area might attempt to use the program to 'stir folks up.'" She sought out local black leaders, promised "to buy only brand new books and not to put old and used books off on the Blacks," won their approval, and then approached her all-white board, which also approved the initiative. But how to keep costs down? One board member suggested they get a war surplus building from nearby Fort Oglethorpe. Ultimately, the library acquired the fort's telephone exchange building, which it dismantled and trucked to Carrollton. Local blacks raised $4,000 to complete the work, Delta Sigma Theta's Iota Chapter threw in $450, and in 1948 the King Street Library opened.

In advance of opening, however, Foster recognized "the possibility of an ugly problem that might raise its head." Someone, she predicted, would ask, "Edith, are you mixing the books?" To prevent this, she had a "neat triangle" imprinted on the spine of every King Street Library book. As anticipated, at the library opening one white attending the ceremony asked if the system mixed the books. "I pointed to the books in front of us—all new, neatly processed and arranged. 'See that triangle? That assures the Negroes that their books are *theirs*.'" Days later, a black post office janitor approached Foster outside the library one night, just as a streetlight came on over their heads. "You know what you are to my people?" he asked. "You are that light."[30]

Public libraries in Mason-Dixon borderline cities often had different practices. From its 1886 opening, Baltimore's Enoch Pratt Free Library allowed black people to access collections and services but not without some white protest. In 1910 a white woman complained to the *Baltimore Sun* of having to share reading space with ragged, dirty, and semiliterate black children. Weeks later, another white citizen suggested separate reading rooms. Library officials ignored their comments. In 1934, however, the Pratt established "Colored Men" and "Colored Women" washrooms because whites complained that they did not want to share the same facilities. "Pratt Library Stoops to Jim Crow," headlined an article in Baltimore's weekly black newspaper, the *Afro-American*. Except for the Pratt, the *Afro-American* reported in 1936, "there is not a single public library, not a swimming pool or public park in [Maryland], open to colored."[31]

From its beginnings in 1898, the District of Columbia Public Library (DCPL) was open to black people. But segregated services were not out of sight. Of the eighteen "home libraries" the DCPL sponsored in 1910, seven were in the homes of "colored" people. "It is interesting to note that the best circulation figures were received from one of these groups," the library reported in 1911.[32] On the other hand, when the DCPL proposed to locate public library branches in local schools after World War I, the board of education—worried about potential race conflict—attempted to segregate them based on whether they were white or black schools. Blacks protested so vehemently that the board backed down. "If patrons go into the [central] public library to receive books without regard to color, why should the Board assume there would be any friction or conflict in receiving similar service at a branch library?" queried the attorney representing eighteen black civic organizations. "There is not and has never been any friction attendant upon children of the two races standing at the counter of the central library to receive books."[33]

THE IMPACT OF CARNEGIE

At the turn of the century, Atlanta obtained a Carnegie grant to build a public library. When the new building opened in 1902, Atlanta University professor W. E. B. Du Bois—in later life one of America's leading black intellectuals but at the time working on his seminal *The Souls of Black Folk,* in which he rejected the accommodationism Booker T. Washington advocated—led several colleagues to a meeting with trustees to ask why "black folk" were not allowed to use a "free public library" serving a city of 53,905 white and 35,912 black people. "It was not pleasant going in," he reported later to the nationally circulated *Independent* magazine, and although trustees were "polite," people "stared and wondered what business we had there." "Do justice to the black people of Atlanta by giving them the same free library privileges that you propose giving the whites," he pleaded. It was illegal to tax blacks for services they could not use, he argued. "The spirit of this great gift to the city was not the spirit of caste or exclusion, but rather the catholic spirit which recognizes no artificial differences of rank or birth or race, but seeks to give all men equal opportunity to make the most of themselves."

The board chairman responded, "Do you not think that allowing whites and negroes to use this library would be fatal to its usefulness?" Du Bois was puzzled. "The answer seemed to me so distressingly obvious," he told the *Independent,* "that I said simply, 'I will express no opinion on that point.'" One of Du Bois's colleagues, recognizing the futility of their request, then asked if Atlanta's black population would get separate public library services. The chairman said the city council would be solicited for sums "proportionate to the amount of taxes paid by negroes of the city" and that "Northern philanthropists" would be solicited to fund a library building. "Then he bade us adieu politely and we walked home wondering."[34] Du Bois later complained to the *Waterbury (Conn.) American* newspaper: "I am taxed for the Carnegie Public Library of Atlanta, where I cannot enter to draw my own books." The *American* commented: "Is it possible to conceive a greater absurdity from the American point of view?"[35] But Atlanta blacks responded differently. In 1904 Atlanta's Sojourner Truth Club opened a Free Reading-Room and Library supported by contributions and "entertainments . . . at all times uplifting and elevating." Speakers included Du Bois, whose *Souls of Black Folk* had been published the previous year; black suffragist and first president of the National Association of Colored Women, Mary Church Terrell; and Booker T. Washington, who himself had established a reading room and debating society for emancipated slaves in his hometown of Malden, West Virginia, in 1875.[36]

Not until 1920 did white Atlanta Public Library director Tommie Dora Barker press her board to build a branch for Atlanta's black citizens with a $25,000 grant from the Carnegie Corporation. A year later, Atlanta opened one in a black neighborhood known as "Sweet Auburn." Besides the $25,000 Carnegie grant, the building fund received $10,000 from the city, $10,000 from the county, and $5,000 from the "white citizens of Atlanta," the latter sum "raised entirely by letter" in "two days' time." The board expected to make the branch "a center for many activities among the colored people" and "the building itself a thing of beauty in their community," Barker noted. "The yard will be planted with shrubbery and flowers, and we want the whole appearance of the building and its surroundings to set a standard for their homes." As librarian, she selected Alice Cary, activist for black kindergartens in Atlanta and recently retired Morris Brown College instructor; Cary quickly hired two black assistants. By mid-decade, the branch was functioning as a community center in the neighborhood.[37]

Carnegie money enabled a number of public library systems in the urban South to provide services to black people. Some incorporated services to blacks within Carnegie buildings. In 1905 the Jacksonville, Florida, Public Library opened its doors in a new Carnegie building and designated a room on the second floor the "colored" reading room.[38] In 1908 the Oklahoma legislature considered whether to amend Jim Crow laws to include public libraries. In Oklahoma City, for example, "the negroes take their seats at the reading tables and have all the same privileges as the whites," and "many whites have made complaints." Some worried that if the law passed, Carnegie would stop donating libraries in Oklahoma. A month later, the *Daily Oklahoman* noted: "The better element of negroes in the city are urging separate accommodations at the public library. They are asking it in an excellent spirit and the request should be promptly heeded."[39] On the one hand, the statement dripped with a patronization masking the racism the Jim Crow South rationalized. On the other, it reflected the limited options southern blacks had available to obtain public library services. And even minimal services were always at risk. In the Tulsa race riot of 1921, whites burned one thousand black homes, five hotels, thirty-one restaurants, twenty-four grocery stores, one school, and Tulsa's black library branch.[40]

Other cities also used Carnegie grants to open separate black branches. "We do not allow negroes to draw books from or to read in either branches or central library," the New Orleans Public Library director wrote a colleague in 1909. "We have been very fortunate in the enforcement of this regulation; comparatively few negroes have applied for library privileges and these have been very politely told that we regret we have no arrangements that permit negroes to borrow from the library."[41] In 1912, however, Carnegie donated $50,000 to New Orleans, half for a main library addition, the other half for a "colored branch": "Our board fully realizes the need of this provision," wrote the board president, "just as . . . other southern cities have had similar need."[42] By the early 1940s some blacks were permitted to use the main library but only in the librarian's office—and away from white patrons—while he watched; they were not permitted to use the card catalog. After World War II, library officials did allow "adult colored persons" to use one table in the main reading room—not without grousing, however. "The negroes in this community are receiving too much rather than too little," complained one white patron, "and to a sizeable extent they are not taking care of what they receive."[43]

In Savannah, Georgia, a Free Public Library for Negroes opened in 1906, funded by city money and subscription fees. Within a year it had twelve hundred volumes, many donated by whites. By 1910 Carnegie had approved an application by Savannah's black community leaders for a $12,000 grant, and the city agreed to provide the necessary $1,200 per year to support it. Locals only had to come up with a site. The quest to purchase a library site took four years, however. For several months, officials sold buttons reading, "Let's Have the Colored Public Library" and encouraged people to wear them on the streets as evidence they had contributed. Regularly, the black weekly *Savannah Tribune* carried announcements of concerts, plays, and direct appeals for funds, at the same time reporting contributions as small as twenty-five and fifty cents; many whites also contributed money and books. The building finally opened in 1914.[44] Over the years, the library provided a welcoming and safe environment for Savannah's blacks. "I loved the Colored Branch of the Carnegie Public Library," Pulitzer Prize–winning author James Alan McPherson later wrote about his childhood experiences there in the early 1950s.[45] So did future U.S. Supreme Court justice Clarence Thomas. As a grade school student, he regularly visited the library in the late 1950s. "I was never prouder than when I got my first library card, though the day when I'd checked out enough books to fill it up came close."[46]

In 1914 the Gainesville, Texas, Public Library opened, designating a reading room "on the lower level . . . with separate entrance" for Gainesville's blacks, who were expected to raise money for the books to be housed there. The room was never used for that purpose, however; instead, ten years later, local officials authorized a branch in the Gainesville Negro School.[47] "A beginning has been made," the white librarian wrote in her diary. "We will give these Negroes something worthwhile yet."[48] With a Carnegie grant, Nashville opened the Nashville Negro Public Library in 1916.[49] At about the same time, Carnegie donated $15,000 for a public library for Houston's "colored residents." Local blacks raised funds to buy the lot and furniture and build the sidewalks.[50] In 1920 Dallas opened its first black branch.[51]

Yet not all Carnegie building grants for black branch libraries were successful. To Mound Bayou, Mississippi—a "widely known negro town" of a thousand founded in 1887—Andrew Carnegie donated $4,000 to erect a brick public library in 1909, the *Savannah Tribune* proudly reported. What the *Tribune* did not mention, however, was that Charles Banks—friend of Booker T. Washington (who had recommended the grant to Carnegie), director of the local bank, and a local political "boss"—failed to fulfill Mound Bayou's obligation to allocate 10 percent of the gift for acquisitions annually. In 1916 Banks's political rivals complained to Carnegie that after the building opened in 1910, it was rented for four years to the local Masonic Benefit Association (Banks was the association's secretary-treasurer). It also hosted a few public meetings and a local school but, as late as 1917, had no bookshelves and no books, except for a small collection the school supported. When queried, Banks attributed the problem to Mound Bayou's "financial difficulties and embarrassments by reason of the advent of the boll weevil as far back as 1912, and then in 1914 the War breaking out paralyzed the entire cotton section." Eight years after Mississippi's governor removed and replaced all Mound Bayou officers (including Banks) for failing to hold local elections, the City Federation of Women's Clubs petitioned to reopen the building as a public library and promised to run it.[52]

When construction of a Carnegie-funded building in Little Rock, Arkansas, was well under way in 1909, black leaders approached trustees to open "a Negro Library" in the black community. Trustees balked. According to board member Samuel W. Reyburn, son of slave owners, he and Carnegie's secretary argued about whether blacks should be admitted to a building that Carnegie funded. To resolve the problem, they agreed to wait until Booker T. Washington met with Carnegie in New York. At the meeting Washington apparently recommended separate libraries, probably because he recognized that if they were not separate, Little Rock blacks would likely have access to no library services at all. Feeling victorious, Reyburn put his own spin on the agreement: "Carnegie aid for the [Little Rock] library for whites alone we owe to Booker T. Washington." Not until 1917 did Little Rock's black community get a separate branch (not funded by the Carnegie grant a decade earlier), but the central library regarded it as little more than a deposit station for books and tended to ignore it.[53]

THE LOUISVILLE MODEL

"Through a veil I could perceive the forbidden city, the Louisville where white folks lived," wrote Blyden Jackson—the first black professor the University of North Carolina tenured—of his childhood experiences there in the twentieth century's second decade. "It was the Louisville of the downtown hotels, the lower floor of big movie houses, the high schools I read about in the daily newspapers, the restricted haunts I sometimes passed, like the white restaurants and country clubs, the other side of windows in the banks, and, of course, the inner sanctums of offices where I could go only as a humble client or a menial custodian."[54] Among the very few institutions within the "forbidden city" that welcomed black people, however, were "colored branches" of the Louisville public library system. "I have just come from Louisville," Booker T. Washington wrote Carnegie's secretary in 1909, "where I had the opportunity of inspecting the Branch library provided for the colored people in that city from Mr. Carnegie's gift. It is a model in many respects."[55]

Initially, however, the model was not universally accepted by Louisville's black community. "When we first opened a colored branch [in 1905], there were some of our race seriously opposed to the project," recalled an assistant librarian. "The segregation idea was repulsive, and they did not give the work their support." On the other hand, she argued, "those of another race cannot know our wants, our habits, our likes and dislikes as we do. . . . It would be impossible for them to give us the service that one of our race can give in an atmosphere where welcome and freedom are the predominant elements, and this is surely the condition in the colored branch libraries in Louisville."[56]

Like whites across the country, blacks perceived public libraries as important civic institutions that helped create an informed citizenry and offered myriad opportunities for self-improvement, and they eagerly wanted to benefit from the public library movement. Equally as important to black people as books and periodicals, however, was the library as a place in a Jim Crow South where in "public" parks they often found signs reading "No Dogs and Niggers Allowed." For black and most diaspora people, "place" had special meaning. Places they could access easily and safely constituted "points of sociability where bonds of trust and collaboration were established and maintained," notes historian Ira Berlin. "More than an attachment to . . . [a specific geographical site], the concept of *place* spoke to relationships, often deeply personal. . . . In such places, men and women knew one another and knew one another's kin and near kin. . . . Intimacy made for belonging."[57] Like black churches, black branch libraries became safe and welcoming places.

Thomas Fountain Blue, branch library director and himself the son of slaves, recognized this need quickly. In his 1906 annual report he noted, "One of the features of the [black] library is the attractiveness of the quarters." He particularly addressed "the front yard with its well kept lawn and flower bed. . . . It is not only supplying the intellectual wants of the people but it serves as a permanent object lesson in cleanliness and order." The branch also hosted a boys' reading club, "to acquaint the boys with some of the best authors and to create a taste for wholesome literature," and a children's story hour, at which "new ideas are formed and unconsciously a taste for reading is acquired."[58]

In addition, Blue instituted a training class for black librarians where apprentice students learned the essential skills of librarianship, such as cataloging, classification, and the development of collections. Like the broader world of American librarianship, black women more than men sought to become librarians, in part because it was one of the few emerging professions that welcomed them, and they would work for less than men. Unlike white library school students, however, Blue's students directly observed the benefits of "library as place" for black society and, after they completed his training program, took his ideas about librarianship to positions in Carnegie-funded "colored branches" opening up across the South in the early twentieth century.[59]

That Blue's branch library had quickly become a community social center was obvious. Not including the wildly popular story hour, in 1910 the library hosted 657 meetings, "an increase of 313 percent over last year in this phase of activity."[60]

So successful was this branch that the library system used Carnegie money to open a second in 1914. For the dedication ceremony, local poet Joseph S. Cotter Sr. read a poem he had written for the fifth anniversary of the first black branch:

The Story Hour

Ef you want to play at livin'
So's to keep you spry an' sweet,
Ef you'd ketch de gist o' wisdom
As it sparkles in defeat;
Ef you'd have a tip in pleasure
Whar de worth outstrips de bids,
Heah de lady tell de stories
To de kids.

Some is settin' on dey haunches,
Some is leanin' on dey hands,
Not a single one gits tired
Kase dey roams in fairy lands.
Dey plays hide-an'-seek wid nations,
Deys de 'arth an' heaven's hybrids
As de lady tells de stories
To de kids.

Now you needn't talk like big folks,
An' you needn't spruce so fine,
An' you needn't long for rubies,
An' you needn't pause to dine,
For all dis will come by dreamin',
Whilst yo' eyes one wakeful lids,
Whar de lady tells de stories
To de kids.

An' you think you rule in China,
An' you dream you own Japan,
An' you bow befo' de cradle
In de blessed Holy Lan',

An' you see de Grecian temples,
An' you climb de pyramids
When de lady tells de stories
To de kids.[61]

The new building had three classrooms and an auditorium for 350. Like the "Eastern Colored Branch," the "Western Colored Branch" quickly developed into a social center. "During a single month," a 1914 pamphlet announced, "as many as 93 meetings have been held" in the two branches, including a baby clinic, Sunday school teachers' training classes, story hours, and meetings of the Ministers' Alliance, Boy Scouts, Boys' Basketball Club, Community Chest Committee, Inter-Racial Committee, Bannecker Reading Circle, Dunbar Literary Club, Douglass Debating Club, Wilberforce Club, Manhattan Athletic Club, Orphan Home Board, Parent Teachers Association, Girls' Library Club, and the Urban League. "The citizens are made to feel that the buildings belong to them, and that they may use them for anything that makes for their welfare."[62] "Our white friends could do us no greater service than build us a library," said one black community leader. Said another: "There are more colored people reading in Louisville now than in any time since the days of freedom. This opportunity has been given them by the Public Library." By 1915, locals called the library "the greatest social center for the colored people of that end of the city."[63]

The "library as community center" that Blue crafted in Louisville not only became an institutional imperative linking "colored branches" across the nation; it also served as a model for all public libraries. Little wonder, then, that when he became the first black to speak at an American Library Association conference in 1927 (more than a half-century after ALA organized), he chose as his topic "The Library as a Community Center":

The library community center . . . has contributed to the public peace by providing a public meeting place, free from political and partisan influences, . . . has contributed to the public welfare by providing for social workers, representing different denominations, a suitable meeting place free from sectarian bias, . . . by providing for our boys and girls a suitable place for amusement and recreation, without which many would be denied this privilege. . . . It has contributed to the educational, professional, business, and social uplift of the community in that it has provided for teachers, doctors, and businessmen and women an acceptable meeting place, where they can hold their conferences and discuss problems under pleasant and cultural surroundings. . . . It has been a means of reaching other groups and making new readers. Frequently strangers who come to attend a meeting remain to join the library.[64]

Southern Workman, organ of Virginia's historically black Hampton Institute, agreed. "These branches have become the centers of much of the educational and civic life of the colored people of Louisville, the chief source of inspiration to tens of thousands of Negro boys and girls," and "an outstanding illustration of interracial cooperation in a public utility which provides equal service and gives general satisfaction to all concerned."[65] When the editor of the *Philadelphia Tribune,* a black weekly newspaper, visited both branches in 1928, he found "a host of young people poring over books" and "Negro literature and Negro art well represented."[66]

These kinds of library-as-place experiences were replicated elsewhere. Although black leaders in Greensboro, North Carolina, obtained a $10,000 Carnegie commitment in 1904, squabbles over where to locate the building delayed its construction until 1924. Once erected, however, the library quickly became a community gathering place. As the "only Carnegie Library for Negroes in North Carolina," a 1928 *Greensboro Daily Record* article concluded, the community need it filled "is shown by the manner in which they throng the building. Oftentimes, the building is filled to overflowing with all chairs occupied, and those who cannot find another place sit on the steps." Elementary and high school students used its collections after school and especially on Saturdays. Adults attended book review, world affairs, and film forums during the week. At various times in its history the library also served as headquarters of the Greensboro Art Center, monitored a teen corner, sponsored a lecture series, and hosted three nursery school groups every week and an afternoon story hour for grade school children. A Heritage Club met monthly to discuss community issues and black history. Several black newspapers informed them. One patron later recalled reading there the weekly *Norfolk Journal and Guide,* "one of those papers" that kept her informed about "what was going on" in southern black communities. "The real value of any library to its community," noted the librarian in 1956, "lies in activities which do not readily lend themselves to quantitative reporting."[67]

And in 1936 the husband of a recently deceased white teacher of black children in Winter Park, Florida, asked friends and families to help start a library for these children to commemorate his wife. The response was generous, including a city promise of $360 annually. When the "Hannibal Square Library" (the name was taken from the section of town where blacks lived) opened in 1937 with fourteen hundred books, it quickly became a community center, where children called the librarian "Mother" and played board games, Boy Scouts met weekly, and the local Benevolent Society, Sewing Society, and Colored Woman's Club all organized. "While these are not library activities," reported one library periodical in 1952, echoing a professional orthodoxy that undervalued library as place, "who can doubt that these gatherings sponsored by the library have been fruitful influences in these manifestations of community spirit?" The article included two photographs of children using the library but failed to mention that Winter Park also supported a public library to which its black citizens had no access.[68]

THE GREAT DEPRESSION

While two-thirds of inhabitants of thirteen southern states had no local library service in 1932 (three-fourths in rural areas), services to black people were worse: 89 percent had none.[69] A 1935 federal survey showed that only 94 of the 509 public libraries in these states served local black people; half of them were in Kentucky, North Carolina, Texas, and West Virginia.[70] Alabama's 18 public libraries included two black branches, Arkansas's 19 had one, Florida's 44 had four, Georgia's 53 had five, Louisiana's 16 had three, Mississippi's 22 had two, South Carolina's 53 had four, Tennessee's 34 had five, and Virginia's 46 had eight.[71]

Yet during the Great Depression public library services to black southerners actually improved, partly because of philanthropy, partly because of federal government intervention. To expand public library services beyond "colored branches" in urban systems, the Julius Rosenwald Foundation built on earlier efforts to construct schools for southern black children. Rosenwald, president of Sears & Roebuck Department Store, established the foundation in 1917 "for the well being of mankind." He donated millions of dollars to a variety of causes but had a particular interest in improving the lives of black people. By 1932, when its school-building program ended, the Rosenwald Fund had spent over $28 million to open nearly five thousand new schools—fondly known as Rosenwald Schools—which subsequently served 663,615 students in 883 counties of fifteen southern states. Rosenwald-funded library services to black southerners grew out of this program in the form of demonstration projects. Between 1928 and 1935, these projects expanded public library services to 140,459 blacks. They also increased book circulation to rural blacks by 579 percent.[72] In Aberdeen, Mississippi, for example, one Rosenwald agent helped local black communities open a public library containing three hundred volumes in 1938. "The Rosenwald Fund, the local white Women's Club, and various colored groups and individuals have added to the collection," she reported.[73]

Between 1925 and 1930, the Louisiana Library Commission ran its Rosenwald library demonstration projects through black public schools. Headquarters for Webster Parish (over 50 percent black) was the town of Minden, which supported eight separate stations that in 1930 had 981 registered borrowers (460 were schoolchildren). "Students from the illiterate classes are coming into the library asking that their branch be continued through the summer so that they will be able to carry on their work and read when the schools open again next fall," reported the Rosenwald agent. "Negro preachers are using the library largely for sermon material and getting their congregations to read the books they tell about."[74]

In 1931 the Rosenwald Foundation offered officials in Charleston County, South Carolina, five years of funding, up to $20,000, for a library that would provide service to "white and colored with equal opportunities for both and with facilities adopted to the needs of each." As a result, the Charleston County Free Library opened its Dart Hall Branch with thirty-six hundred books, but because whites shunned it, the facility quickly became known as the "Colored Branch" and served blacks exclusively.[75] Rosenwald funding also supported a black branch and rural library stations in Walker County, Alabama, between 1931 and 1936. Although local officials used funds to support a bookmobile and driver to rural white populations, they denied similar funding to black communities, thus forcing the black librarian to use her personal car to carry books to rural black patrons. This service, argues library historian Toby Graham, represented Alabama's "first thorough and systematic attempt to provide library service to rural blacks." In 1936 one black Alabama high school principal noted that library services improved the "everyday intelligence" of library users. To prove it, he noted that before the service began, 46 percent of his graduates who subsequently attended college ranked in the "first and second division in their classes"; thereafter, the number jumped to 90 percent.[76]

Through New Deal programs such as the Works Progress Administration (WPA), the federal government also made funds available for library projects that reached southern black people. As early as 1934, librarians at the Durham Colored Library in North Carolina used these funds to transport books in their cars to the county's rural black residents. In 1941 federal funds enabled the library to purchase a half-ton Chevy "with revolving bookshelves."[77] Thomas County, Georgia, used WPA funds to inaugurate its first bookmobile service to rural blacks as a demonstration project.[78] In South Carolina, the WPA provided funds for staffing and two bookmobiles, one run out of Lancaster's black high school, the other out of the Phillis Wheatley Negro Branch of the Greenville Public Library.[79] Librarian Annie Watters McPheeters, who had been refused library service as a child, later recalled: "I have fond memories of those [bookmobile] stations, one in particular. It was under a large spreading oak tree near a country church. . . . I could see [people] coming down the road and across the field. The books they were returning were carefully wrapped in newspaper or in a brown paper bag for protection while they worked in the field or elsewhere. To watch them as they left with their selections from the bookmobile gave me an inner joy hard to explain."[80]

The WPA also conducted a library program, but because funded activities were run through local white communities, Jim Crow governed decisions about allocating resources. After efforts failed to interest WPA officials in establishing a black branch in Luverne, Alabama, Dalzie M. Powell complained to a WPA supervisor. Petition them again, she was advised. She did; 209 blacks registered their desire for service, she noted, and a local black school was ready to house a collection. Again officials ignored her. Tired of being "put off," she once again complained to the supervisor: "It is hard for a Colored person to get anything here." The county had three white public libraries but would not fund a small deposit station for blacks. Again the supervisor advised persistence, but Powell was never able to extract funds from WPA officials.[81]

Although the federal government established the Tennessee Valley Authority (TVA) in 1933 primarily to provide flood control and navigation on the Tennessee River, it also used funds to improve the lives of the valley's poor rural people. Establishing library services at dam sites under construction was a part of that effort, and in 1934 Mary Utopia Rothrock, a white librarian who had obtained a Carnegie grant in 1918 for a black branch for the Knoxville Public Library she directed, became TVA supervisor of library service. During the Depression, she opened twenty-six regional TVA public libraries. Consistently, however, she ran into local Jim Crow practices. Although eighteen blacks "made frequent use" of the otherwise all-white Wilson Dam Library, it was the exception. Of its seventeen deposit stations—most located in schools—only four served blacks.

After 1936, the TVA began contracting services through existing library agencies. When the Huntsville Public Library contracted with the TVA that year to provide service to people working at the Guntersville Dam site, the three affected north Alabama counties had two whites-only public libraries, one in Huntsville and the other in Scottsboro. Three years later, with TVA funding, the region hosted thirty-six library stations, six public libraries, and a bookmobile, all serving whites only. At the dam site, TVA established a "basic negro deposit" station intended "to serve the needs of the employees in the recreation, general adult education and job training programs" that it located in its "Negro Recreation Hall." Only with great effort did black people benefit in the three-county region, however. In 1937 a black minister employed by the WPA made sure TVA funds established a Jackson County–wide service that eventually boasted a thousand-volume collection housed in rented quarters in Scottsboro. From that center, volunteers delivered books to remote stations in rural black communities from their own cars.[82]

After the TVA withdrew funds for the Guntersville Dam site regional library service it ran through the Huntsville Public Library, the city abandoned service for black people. Dismayed, Dulcina DeBerry, a black, college-educated retired teacher and minister's wife who had recently moved to Huntsville to care for her aging parents—and to whom a white library assistant had sneaked books in defiance of Jim Crow rules—met with the library director. He said some WPA funds were still available for library service to blacks but was not sanguine about how long they would last. In May 1940 he walked her through the black Lakeside Methodist Church basement, told her WPA funds would pay her salary as long as they lasted, then gave her a key and said, "Make something of it, if you can." DeBerry immediately mobilized the local black community. In two weeks young men cleaned the room, a local girls' club donated flowers, a minister's wife donated a librarian's chair, citizens lent tables and chairs and gave them a fresh coat of paint, and DeBerry's nephew lined the walls with donated art posters. After the library opened in June with a small collection, a bookmobile service connecting it to the white main library supplemented its collections.

Following the "library as community place" model that Louisville's Thomas Fountain Blue had established decades earlier, DeBerry quickly turned the basement station into a community center for local black people. Her Vacation Reading Club and Children's Story Hour proved so successful that many in the black community called for a separate "Negro Library." DeBerry harnessed the enthusiasm to set up an unofficial board of prominent black citizens, who helped her move the library out of the poorly heated church basement into an unfurnished room in a local school in November. Still, she received no funding from the white-run Huntsville Public Library. In February 1941, her board hosted a "Negro Book Week Musical" (which later became an annual event) to raise funds that provided essential furniture built by black craftsmen in a local workshop. A Rosenwald grant a year later brought in more books, but when WPA funds dried up in the summer of 1943, the library was forced to close. The Huntsville board of education came to the library's rescue, however, hired DeBerry as a teacher at the school, and then absorbed the library as the black branch in Huntsville's public library system.

Like many other black branches, it became the major resource for reading materials at local black schools. Teachers came to the branch library for books and periodicals and set up "reading corners" in thirty school classrooms. Because segregation laws and practices prevented the main library from providing separate bookmobile service to blacks, the main library's director used the system's one bookmobile to establish a separate Negro section with books selected from the Negro Library, thereby providing black readers with "books from their own collection" and honoring Jim Crow's "no interracial touching" practices. In 1948 the library moved from its school quarters into a separate building, which it named the "Dulcina DeBerry Branch." In the 1940s and 1950s, the black "public library movement" in Alabama "was, at its core," Toby Graham argues, "an indigenous enterprise driven by the work of black civic and religious organizations, educators, clergy, business leaders, and librarians."[83] His observations about Alabama largely apply to black public library services across the rest of the South.

BLACK READING INTERESTS

Hand-me-down books that white main libraries across the South gave to black branches—often "greasy, torn," and "dog-eared," like textbooks transferred from white to black schools—generally carried in them a gospel of white superiority that sanitized the nation's racist history and, in what historian Leon Litwack calls a white "literature of nostalgia," crafted imagined historical myths that caricatured blacks as naturally inferior, docile, and happy and sought to teach them subservience rather than independence. In her 1973 study of blacks in children's fiction published between 1827 and 1967, Dorothy Broderick finds the overwhelming majority "condescendingly . . . racist."[84] Many black branch libraries worked to counter these mythical and racist narratives.

That many blacks hungered for black news was obvious. When Pullman porters smuggled copies of the *Chicago Defender* into southern states along north-south railroad lines, "negroes [would] grab the *Defender* like a hungry mule grabs fodder," one early-twentieth-century black male observed. It was one of the few information sources that covered southern white atrocities and celebrated black accomplishments. Yet even here, Litwack notes, the black press showed a bias toward Booker T. Washington's accommodationist creed, which advocated "economic uplift over agitation" and tempered "opposition to Jim Crow with appeals for racial harmony." That exposure to black history and literature had an impact was also obvious. As a black adolescent in rural turn-of-the-century South Carolina, one man later recalled: "In my high school days Booker T. Washington meant more to me than George Washington; Frederick Douglass was more of a hero than William Lloyd Garrison; [poet Paul Laurence] Dunbar inspired me more than Longfellow." Through them, he says, "I had identity."[85]

Black people who patronized the integrated District of Columbia Public Library showed different reading preferences than whites. "Contrary to what one might suppose," a *Washington Post* reporter noted in 1902, "the colored patrons take some very solid reading matter. . . . They have decided preferences for works from the pen of members of their own race," such as Dunbar and novelist Charles Chesnutt, "and more particularly Booker Washington's 'Up From Slavery,' which is in great demand." And they "never tired" of Harriet Beecher Stowe's *Uncle Tom's Cabin.*[86] When the Jacksonville, Florida, Public Library director analyzed the reading patterns of black patrons in 1906, he noticed they were mostly from the middle class and were predominantly young (he assumed the elderly could not read): "They are all anxious to read of what their own race is doing, what advances they are making, what conventions they are holding, especially if the accounts are by colored writers." Black magazines "are thoroughly read, more thoroughly than some of the best of the popular periodicals."[87]

From the day it opened under Thomas Fountain Blue's direction, Louisville's first black branch not only had open stacks; it also determined to collect black literature. The *Colored American,* for example, was the most popular periodical, *Up from Slavery* the first book withdrawn. Other popular authors included Chesnutt, Douglass, Dunbar, and Du Bois; patrons were particularly interested in Du Bois's *Souls of Black Folk,* which struck a decidedly different approach to race than Washington's accommodationist creed and probably sparked some lively debates in branch library meeting rooms.[88]

In 1920 a Biloxi, Mississippi, reporter noted that unlike the main library, "negro branch" patrons did not favor fiction. "The greatest demand is for books on handicraft," the librarian told him.[89] Similarly, in the late 1920s at the Minden black branch in Webster Parish, Louisiana, nonfiction out-circulated fiction five to four.[90] Ironically, most black branch libraries had nonfiction circulation rates much closer to an ideal the American Library Association propounded in its rhetoric than did white libraries, which consistently showed fiction circulation rates between 66 and 75 percent.

Uncle Tom's Cabin may have been a favorite in black public library branches in the South but not at white main libraries. In response to a 1903 Chicago Public Library patron survey that found *Uncle Tom's Cabin* a children's favorite, the *Dallas Morning News* responded, "There is no particular reason why the infants of Chicago should be urged to read" the book "unless the purpose is to begin to cultivate the sectional spirit at the cradle side."[91] "As long as 'Uncle Tom's Cabin' continues to be the primary volume in the family, school, and public libraries north of the Ohio and Potomac rivers," complained an *Atlanta Constitution* columnist in 1928, "sectional enmities between the southern and northern people will endure." Public libraries that stocked this "colossal libel upon the southern people" nurtured a "serpent of sectionalism."[92] When a student doing a thesis on Harriet Beecher Stowe asked for a copy at the main Savannah Public Library in 1931, a library attendant told her, "We have other works by Mrs. Stowe, but we have never had a copy of that one."[93] It is not known if a copy was in the system's black branch; perhaps the patron was white and not inclined to visit it.

Young people, journalist David Halberstam observes, found in the black branch history collections "for the first time the traces of an almost secret history of black life in America, a rich, conflicted, often suppressed, often ignored history of black men and women fighting white repression over this country's entire history." At Atlanta's "Sweet Auburn" branch, librarian Annie Watters started an African American collection in 1934 and solicited autographed donations from touring lecturers such as Langston Hughes.[94]

Watters's path to librarianship was not unlike that of most other female black librarians at the time. After graduating from Clark University in Atlanta in 1929, she took a job as teacher-librarian in a Rosenwald school in Simpsonville, South Carolina. From there she became director of the Phillis Wheatley Branch of the Greenville, South Carolina, Public Library system. After obtaining a degree in library science from Hampton Institute (when the Carnegie Corporation provided the institute with a grant in 1925 to start a black library school, the black Louisville training school gradually closed), she moved in 1934 to the Auburn Avenue branch of the Atlanta Public Library, where she spent the next three decades serving in various positions to improve library services to Atlanta's blacks and participating very directly in efforts to desegregate the entire system in 1959. In 1940 she changed her name when she married Alphonso McPheeters. After her death in 1994, the Atlanta Public Library named its Washington Park branch in her honor.

At Atlanta's Sweet Auburn branch in 1934, Watters secured a grant to fund several adult education programs, including discussion groups focused on Mahatma

Gandhi. To ground these discussions, Watters purchased a number of books. Among their most devoted readers was a young Martin Luther King Jr., who "came to the library many times during the week." She later recalled their interactions, which not only showed King's reading interests but also manifested the value of library as place to Atlanta's black community. "He would walk up to the desk and . . . look me straight in the eye." "Hello, Martin Luther," she would respond, always calling him by his first and middle names. "What's on your mind?" "Oh, nothing, particularly." For Watters that was the cue that King had learned a new "big word," and between them they then had a conversation in which King used the word repeatedly. Another game they played involved poetry. Again, King would stand by the desk, waiting. "What's on your mind, Martin Luther?" Watters would ask. "For I dipped into the future, far as the human eye could see," he responded. Watters immediately recognized the poem and finished the verse: "saw the vision of the world and all the wonder that would be." The Gandhi collection presented a problem, however, because King was too young to check out these adult books on his children's card. To solve it, Watters told him to ask his father to get a library card, "and I would check the books out . . . on his father's card. And that's how I made it possible for Martin Luther to read those books on Gandhi. . . . And he read every one of those books that we had."[95]

Ten years later, Annie Watters McPheeters noticed Maynard Jackson, a lad who regularly frequented the Sweet Auburn branch with a "big brown paper bag in his hand." He regularly circled the children's room, selected books he wanted to read, and put them on the table next to his bag. When, moments later, McPheeters heard paper rustling, she checked on Maynard, only to find him eating the lunch the bag contained. We do "not eat in the library," she told Maynard, and we certainly do "not eat when we are reading books." "Yes, Mrs. McPheeters," he would respond, and closed up the bag. "Later on," McPheeters recalled, "I would hear that bag opening again. . . . Maynard loved to eat while he was reading."[96] In 1974, Jackson was elected Atlanta's first black mayor.

No matter the successes of library services to blacks, the white establishment nonetheless tried as best it could to control what black people could read in the Jim Crow South. Turn-of-the-century Confederate veterans' groups, for example, carefully monitored school textbooks for what they perceived as negative accounts of the Civil War (which some called the "War between the States" and others the "War of Northern Aggression"). White southern librarians took note. When the American Association of Adult Education's Marion Humble toured the South in the Great Depression to study rural library services, she noted that in Louisiana "books that describe the emancipated Negro are sometimes excluded from the school-community libraries for Negroes." In Mississippi one librarian erroneously stated, "The circulation of books that portray social equality between Negroes and whites is illegal."[97] By the time of the *Brown v. Board of Education* decision, most history texts sold throughout the country reflected a tacit bargain between northeastern textbook publishers and southern textbook adoption committees that the Civil War be referred to as the "War between the States," that blacks be depicted in illustrations only in subordinate positions, and that black and white children never appear together in the same photo. "Blacks were systematically imagined out of the nation's story," concludes textbook historian Joseph Moreau. "You got any niggers in your book?" asked a member of the Louisiana textbook adoption committee in the early 1960s, when visited by a Silver Burdett textbook salesman. "No, sir," the salesman replied.[98]

Against tremendous opposition and with help from northern philanthropists such as Andrew Carnegie and Julius Rosenwald and Great Depression federal government programs such as the WPA—and only occasionally (and often reluctantly) with help from the southern white establishment and the library community that served it—black southerners struggled to establish the rudiments of public library services for themselves in the first half of the twentieth century. Although their accomplishments against Jim Crow opposition were significant, civil rights historians have largely overlooked them, and the American library community has largely forgotten the precedents they set. Because they were granted access to few public spaces, for example, black branch libraries evolved a concept of their public library as a social center in the first decade of the twentieth century that in the early twenty-first century librarians are now claiming as something new in contemporary public library practice.

As with traveling on public transit in the South before *Brown*—in which, historian Catherine Barnes notes, "southern blacks attempted only to equalize accommodations, not undo segregation"[99]—most African Americans who advocated expanded library services struggled to push the boundaries of the possible within the confines of Jim Crow public library practices. But ripples of protest did surface, and after *Brown v. Board of Education* they increased in number and intensity.

2

RUMBLES OF DISCONTENT
BEFORE 1960

In her pioneering 1939 study of public libraries and black people in thirteen southern states, Eliza Atkins Gleason reported that public library services to blacks had taken several forms. In some urban areas—such as Atlanta, Birmingham, Louisville, Memphis, and New Orleans—separate system branches also functioned as community centers for a variety of activities. Several communities supported library stations at black grade and high schools. In a few areas—Winter Park, Florida; Jackson, Mississippi; and Raleigh, North Carolina—blacks largely supported their own libraries. Services to blacks at main public libraries varied. Very few offered full privileges; Covington, Kentucky, and El Paso and Pecos, Texas, were exceptions. Some, such as those in Fort Worth and Port Arthur, Texas, allowed blacks to withdraw books but not use reading rooms. Petersburg, Virginia, housed its separate black branch in the basement of the main library, and several libraries—in Boydton, Virginia, and Charlotte, North Carolina—offered full borrowing privileges through segregated reading rooms with separate entrances. Gleason's findings showed that white attitudes toward blacks handling the same books they did were not uniform throughout the South.

Twelve percent of public libraries in the South provided some kind of services to blacks, who constituted 26 percent of the population. Whereas 44 percent of whites in southern states had access to some kind of public library services, only 21 percent of blacks did.[1] A survey conducted in 1954, the same year as the *Brown v. Board of Education* decision, showed some improvement from Gleason's study but not much. Fifty-nine cities and towns in the South provided local blacks free use of the main public library, twenty-four gave them limited services at those main public libraries, and another eleven served blacks in separate branches.[2]

"Usually Negroes are excluded as rigidly from the use of the library in one-library towns as if they had no rights at all," noted a black *Philadelphia Tribune* columnist in 1951. "Typically it is only when the locality is big enough for at least one branch library do Negroes have any access at all to the public library facilities. . . . It is also typical that the 'colored branch' is definitely inferior to the main library (whose services are not available to them), in number and quality of books, in plant and equipment, services and personnel."[3] Particularly disturbing, many of the donated books passed to black branches by white central libraries not only depicted a national culture largely constructed by European Americans; they also often carried ideological justifications for Jim Crow laws and practices that black patrons were forced to endure. "From Washington, D.C., to the Gulf of Mexico and from the Atlantic Ocean to the westernmost fringes of Texas and Oklahoma," noted black author L. D. Reddick in a 1954 magazine article, "the public places are few and far between where a Negro may sit down and read a book—even though his tax dollar has helped buy that book, erect the building which houses it and pay the salary of the librarian who may tell him curtly or apologetically: 'We do not serve Negroes.'"[4]

Southern small-town public libraries were particularly resistant to serving local black citizens. In interviews for a 1963 national survey of public library access, one white librarian noted about southern small towns: "The people are so close and know so much about each other that their feelings run high. The only thing people have left is a social standing which puts them a shade above the Negroes. It will be awfully hard for them to accept Negroes as equals." Said one small-town librarian who favored integration but refused to act: "We can't do anything about it. We don't care to be run out of the social structure." Said another: "People feel as strongly about the library as they do about the buses, the lunch counters, the parks and so on. The majority does not want *anything* desegregated."

A library board member said: "Regardless of what I may think, I work within the framework of the community leaders. . . . Our town is filled with a great many people still so provincial that they do not realize they are part of a very large world." A black respondent recalled a conversation he had with two local white businessmen aboard a plane. Confessed one: "I could not exist if I did not belong to the White Citizens' Council. It's the most dominant political force. Everybody must belong or be boycotted." That many white members of southern library communities were racist was also obvious. One library board member told an interviewer that racial tensions were caused by outsiders. "We've never had anything but pleasant relations with Negroes," she claimed, because her community had "done everything to keep them happy."

Blacks, of course, felt differently about segregated public library services in the South. "We play Uncle Tom on the outside and boil on the inside," one told an interviewer. Said another: "Most Negroes [in this town] are obligated and afraid of economic pressure. . . . There are no Negro doctors or dentists and very few businessmen. The intellectual faction among the Negroes is very low. The school teachers are afraid of losing their jobs."[5] Most also cringed at the kind of humiliation experienced in the 1950s by black seventeen-year-old James R. Wright of Fayette, Alabama, who, because he had exhausted his school library, turned to the county public library—"a lovely building" in which his small town "took great pride." He called and explained to the person who answered that he was a "Negro" and wanted to use the library. "This difficult and unusual question was immediately referred to the librarian," he later recalled. "I remember, as if it were yesterday, her reply, in a very soft and mild voice, 'I am sorry, we cannot allow Negroes to come here.'"[6]

Although library historians often celebrate the passage of the 1956 Library Services Act (LSA), the first federal legislation intended to fund some library services, they generally fail to acknowledge how it was used to reinforce midcentury segregated public library services. The act made it to President Dwight Eisenhower's desk mostly because state librarians from the South convinced their representatives and senators (many of whom held crucial committee chairs) that the act would not curtail states' rights because state library agencies would have authority to determine the distribution of funds. LSA funds gave state library agencies new power. Many bought bookmobiles to reach remote parts of their states with no library service; others issued grants directly to public libraries. In the South, however, service to blacks was a constant subtext in the allocation of resources, and in many cases southern state library agencies refused to tap this new federal funding to expand library services to blacks. As a teenager in the late 1950s, future novelist and National Book Award winner Alice Walker had read most of Shakespeare's works, not because she could get them at the segregated public library in her hometown of Eatonville, Georgia, or through any bookmobile the state of Georgia purchased with LSA dollars, but because her father had rescued a collection of the Bard's work from a trash heap at the white high school there.[7]

SUBVERTING JIM CROW PRACTICES

Long before presidential executive orders, *Brown v. Board of Education*, federal civil rights legislation, and LSA, however, black discontent with Jim Crow public libraries—and efforts to subvert their practices—surfaced frequently. In the late 1920s, for example, nineteen-year-old African American Richard Wright was trying to figure out how to access Memphis's public library collections. As a sixth grader in Jackson, Mississippi, he had marveled at articles in the *Chicago Defender* reporting that "Lake Michigan Negroes" could not only go into public libraries, but they could also take out any book they wanted. Like most southern libraries, however, at the Memphis library, "Negroes were not allowed to patronize its shelves any more than they were the parks and playgrounds of the city"—except "to get books for white men." Wright plotted.

One morning he approached a fellow worker. "I want to ask you a favor," Wright whispered. "What is it?" "I want to read. I can't get books from the library. I wonder if you'd let me use your card?" The white man balked. "You're not trying to get me in trouble, are you, boy?" When asked what he wanted to read, Wright replied: "Mencken." Eventually, the man agreed to the ploy but only after pledging Wright not to "mention this" to fellow workers. One day soon thereafter he gave Wright his wife's library card. "That afternoon I addressed myself to forging a note," Wright wrote in his autobiography. *"Dear Madam: Will you please let this nigger boy*—I used the word 'nigger' to make the librarian feel that I could not possibly be the author of the note—*have some books by H. L. Mencken?"* Wright then describes what happened next.

> I entered the library as I had always done when on errands for whites, but I felt that I would somehow slip up and betray myself. I doffed my hat, stood a respectful distance from the desk, looked as unbookish as possible, and waited for the white patrons to be taken care of. When the desk was clear of people, I still waited. The white librarian looked at me.
>
> "What do you want, boy?"
>
> As though I did not possess the power of speech, I stepped forward and simply handed her the forged note, not parting my lips.
>
> "What books by Mencken does she want?" she asked.
>
> "I don't know, ma'am," I said, avoiding her eyes.
>
> "You're not using these books, are you?" she asked pointedly.
>
> "Oh, no, ma'am. I can't read."

The ploy worked; the librarian delivered two Mencken books. Outside the library Wright wrapped them in a newspaper—in part to protect these treasures, in part because he knew white people might question his reading if they saw him with books by Mencken. Later, as an influential African American author, Wright recalled what this reading meant to him and in the process identified several reasons why Jim Crow whites so wanted to control black reading:

It had been my accidental reading of fiction and literary criticism that had
evoked in me vague glimpses of life's possibilities. Of course, I had never seen or
met the men who wrote the books I read, and the kind of world in which they lived
was as alien to me as the moon. But what enabled me to overcome my chronic dis-
trust was that these books—written by men like [Theodore] Dreiser, [Edgar Lee]
Masters, Mencken, [Sherwood] Anderson and [Sinclair] Lewis—seemed defen-
sively critical of the straitened American environment. These writers seemed to
feel that America could be shaped nearer to the hearts of those who lived it. And
it was out of these novels and stories and articles, out of the emotional impact of
imaginative constructions of heroic or tragic deeds, that I felt touching my face a
tinge of warmth from an unseen light; . . . I was groping toward that invisible light,
always trying to keep my face so set and turned that I would not lose the hope of
its faint promise, using it as my justification for action.[8]

That Wright's experiences in subverting Jim Crow public library practices
replicated others is evident from surveys and interviews with black people that
Charles S. Johnson conducted as part of Swedish social scientist Gunnar Myrdal's
research on black Americans in the 1930s. One informant from Marked Tree, Arkansas, told Johnson: "They have a city library here, but colored people can't take
any books out. They won't let colored people go there unless they was [sic] sent by
white people. I go up there to get books for the family I work for and to take back
books. I never got any for myself, but I read all I get for the boss's family." The wife
of a black South Carolina school principal reported: "Negroes can't borrow books
under any conditions. We get them but we get them through a white lady friend
who borrows them like she was borrowing them for herself and gives them to us."[9]
These kinds of experiences not only illustrate the cultural context in which public
library service to blacks existed in the early twentieth century; they also show the
lengths to which black people had to go to subvert the Jim Crow world they were
born into in order to obtain those services.

THE FIRST SIT-IN

Although many black people used separate public library services in the Jim Crow
South, some refused. In Virginia in the mid-1930s, every day on the way to his
office, African American lawyer Samuel W. Tucker passed the whites-only Alex-

andria Public Library, a building constructed in 1937 with federally funded labor. Although a native Alexandrian, he had been forced to attend high school across the Potomac because of his color. There he also graduated from Howard University and read for the bar at the Library of Congress and the District of Columbia Public Library, both open to him. In March 1939, however, he and retired army sergeant George Wilson decided to test Jim Crow. They walked into the Alexandria Public Library, where Wilson asked for a borrower's card. The librarian politely said no. The two men left. In May, on Wilson's behalf, Tucker filed a writ of mandamus to force the library to issue him a borrower's card. While waiting for a decision, he hatched a plot. That summer he recruited eleven young men and in secret meetings trained them for a nonviolent sit-in. On August 20 he told them to be prepared for action the next day.

Because five could not overcome their families' misgivings, only the remaining six showed up at the library the next morning, all dressed in their Sunday best. The first of the protesters entered the library and requested a library card application. When one of the assistant librarians refused him, he did not leave the library but went to the stacks, picked out a book, and sat down to read. The librarian was incredulous, but before she could react, another well-dressed young black male came in and asked for a borrower's card. Once denied, he too headed for the stacks, picked out a book, and sat down at a table. This happened three more times, and while the sixth protester lingered in the library doorway, an assistant librarian ran to library director Katharine Scoggin's office and shouted, "Oh mercy, Miss Scoggin, there's colored people all over the library!"

Scoggin emerged from her office and told the men to leave the library, but they refused to respond and—although obviously nervous—continued turning pages. She then telephoned the city manager and the chief of police, who dispatched two officers. When the police officers arrived, they repeated Scoggin's demand. None of the protesters budged, but nineteen-year-old Buddy Evans asked, "What would happen if we don't leave?" "I would have to arrest you," one officer replied. "We're staying," Evans unhesitatingly responded. True to his word, the police officer arrested the five young men and took them to jail, where they were charged with disorderly conduct. At that point, two to three hundred spectators and the local press had already gathered outside. The sixth young man, who had stayed outside the library, ran straight to Tucker's office to report what he saw.[10]

In a packed courtroom the following day, Tucker moved for dismissal of all charges, arguing no law had been broken. "Every one of the lads" charged with disorderly conduct, the black *Norfolk New Journal and Guide* weekly newspaper observed, "was neatly dressed, intelligent in appearance, and conducted themselves as gentlemen should." When Tucker pressed Scoggin in cross-examination, she admitted "she had had the young men removed because they were colored and not disorderly." After Tucker got the arresting officer to say the same thing, the judge concluded, "There seems to be no evidence of disorderly conduct here, but it is a matter of constitutional privileges."[11]

Yet the city still refused to open the library to black Alexandrians and instead began a series of delaying tactics. And because Wilson had not made a proper application, in mid-January the judge issued a ruling denying his writ of mandamus to force Scoggin to give him a library card. In the ruling, however, the judge noted, "There has not been introduced any evidence that the Alexandria Library Association has any regulation limiting the library's use and facilities to the white race." In this statement the black press found hope. "The decision, in all probability, means that all public libraries in the South, which now bar colored, can be forced to admit them," predicted the *Afro-American*, a black Baltimore weekly newspaper.[12]

But these hopes were quickly dashed. On January 30, 1940, Tucker and Wilson again went to the library circulation desk to request borrower's cards. This time Scoggin did issue cards, but they were valid only at the Colored Library, scheduled to open in March. Tucker was not swayed by the gesture or by the name: "I refuse and I will always refuse to accept a card—in lieu of a card to be used at the existing library." Although he threatened future legal action, he became ill shortly thereafter, during which time a group of black Alexandrians met with city and library officials and accepted their proposal of a segregated library. And ultimately, the judge in the demonstrators' case never ruled on the charges against the five youths.[13]

ACTION AND REACTION

In Bartlesville, Oklahoma, white librarian Ruth Brown—for thirty years the public library's director—was fired in 1950 for allegedly circulating "commie magazines and papers" such as the *Nation*, the *New Republic*, and *Soviet Today*, a library board chairman charged. But these charges were a ruse for the real reason she was dismissed: attempting to integrate the public library and the Bartlesville community by challenging local segregationist practices.[14] In Macon, Georgia, WMAZ radio announcer Sally Veatch reported on a 1952 city council hearing that denied a request by local blacks for public library service. "I am ashamed that such a meeting was necessary . . . where Negroes must plead and demand access to books," she wrote. "If I were a member of a group trying to get books to read, I think I would have broken down the doors of the city library a long time ago." Unlike Ruth Brown, however, Veatch preempted her employer. She resigned from her job immediately after airing her complaint.[15]

White opposition to proposed public library services to blacks found many rationales. When a group of Calvert County, Maryland, residents rose in opposition to county bookmobile services that would include rural blacks in 1952, the *Washington Post* decided to investigate. Leading the opposition was seventy-nine-year-old trial magistrate William W. Duke, who had helped found the local public library in 1912. "A Negro will never set foot in that library as long as I have anything to do with it," he told a *Post* reporter. But why resist bookmobile services to the rest of the county? he was asked. "The two angles to the question are that many of the Negroes in this county have a venereal disease, which can be spread by the exchange of books, and that a Negro is not above stealing a book from the library if he wants it bad enough." Another person threatened bookmobile advocates: "If you get the bookmobile, we'll burn it and all the books in it." A local white high school principal disagreed. "Colored people are employed hereabouts to clean homes, prepare meals, serve at tables, make up beds and launder clothes," he said. "I can't see how handling books would be more dangerous."[16]

In Montgomery, Alabama, white citizens had access to a public library as early as 1899, but its black citizens waited nearly a half-century for any kind of library service. In 1947 a faculty member at the Alabama State Teachers College for Negroes decided to challenge the white Montgomery Public Library. Shortly after he was denied service, sixty other Montgomery blacks requested similar service over a two-week period. Perceiving a troublesome campaign, the librarian argued to her board that because blacks pay taxes, they should have their own library branch. (Apparently, permitting them to use the white library was out of the question.) About the same time, the Montgomery Negro Ministerial Association began discussing a library for blacks. Initially the organization contacted the director of the Alabama Public Library Service Division, who offered to lend state library books if black Montgomerians started their own library.

When the Montgomery Public Library director heard of it, she promised "duplicate copies and similar material" from the main library collection, but when she also added that her board was unlikely to provide funds, association members resolved to create their own library and formed a Friends of the Library group to move the project along. The City Federation of Women's Clubs offered free space within their facility. The city then agreed to provide some financial support so long as the group was able to find a black librarian to administer the library. In August 1948 association leaders hired Bertha Pleasant, who, after being denied admission to the University of Alabama's library school, had earned a degree from the Atlanta University Library School (opened in 1941, after Hampton Institute closed its school two years earlier). She was also a Montgomery native whose ailing mother still lived there. When Pleasant arrived, she quickly sifted through materials sent from the main library, pronounced them "junk," and boldly protested to the board. With help from the Alabama Public Library Service Division, she instead selected her core collection from state library agency titles. On December 8, 1948, the Union Street Branch Library opened its doors to local black residents.

With help from the friends group and local women's clubs, Pleasant was able to meet basic needs the main library board refused to fund. To generate more community interest, Pleasant wrote a library column for the local black newspaper and spoke on the local black radio station. In subsequent years she also opened deposit stations in black neighborhoods, started a story hour, and so successfully established services to local schools that her white board requested the city fund a bookmobile. When the city refused, black teachers carried classroom collections in their cars. But inadequate funding hurt—too many users, not enough materials. "You can go to the branch anytime at all," the main library director wrote in 1952, "and find almost no books on the shelves of the children's room."[17]

That Montgomery blacks were not satisfied with their branch was obvious. As early as 1949, members of the Youth Council of the National Association for the Advancement of Colored People went to the main library to ask for service. As Rosa Parks, secretary of the NAACP's Montgomery Chapter, later recalled, because "the colored library did not have many books . . . a student who wanted a book that wasn't there had to request it from the colored library, which in turn would order it from the main library." And even if it was obtained from the main library, black patrons could not return a book there. For many, this was not only an insult but also an inconvenience because they lived so far away from the "colored" branch. Because their requests were ignored, students returned "again and again" over the next five years, but as Parks noted, "they were unsuccessful in changing the practice."[18] In 1955, however, Montgomery witnessed Parks and others engage in a yearlong bus boycott that represented a seminal event in the civil rights movement. *Brown v. Board of Education,* one legal historian concludes, "was enough for Parks and millions of others to expand their struggle against institutionalized humiliation into other crucial spheres of life."[19] The boycott also catapulted Martin Luther King Jr. into the public eye and was only resolved when the U.S. Supreme Court ordered integration of the public buses in 1956.

While many in the local white community were outraged by the Court's decision, white Montgomery Public Library reference librarian Juliette Morgan saw things differently. In a letter to the *Montgomery Advertiser,* the city's major white newspaper, she objected to the harsh treatment she had observed white bus drivers accord black riders: "Three times I have gotten off the bus because I could not countenance treatment of Negroes. . . . Twice I have heard a certain driver with high seniority mutter audibly, 'Black ape.'" But for this letter to the editor Morgan paid a price. Segregationists "called her at the library. They called her at her home, where she lived alone with her mother. They threatened her. They harassed her. They insulted her with vulgar and obscene accusations," noted a black *Pittsburgh Courier* columnist. Stress became so great that she took a leave of absence, but "she could not sleep, she could not eat. Death came and took her out of her misery." "Plain murder," the columnist called it. Publicly, the library profession hardly noticed. Two colleagues commemorated her in the *Alabama Librarian,* the state library association's major journal; one noted she was an "ardent Democrat and liberal" and "often the eloquent spokesman for a growing group of progressive Southerners," but neither mentioned her tragic experiences. Nor did any of the national library journals, including the *Bulletin of the American Library Association,* carry her obituary. What happened to Ruth Brown and Juliette Morgan undoubtedly had a chilling effect on like-minded white librarians across the South. Morgan was "the last white public librarian [in Alabama] to speak openly in favor of civil rights for black citizens during the movement years," notes library historian Toby Graham.[20]

PEACEFUL DESEGREGATION SUCCESSES

Despite these experiences, public library systems in several southern cities managed to desegregate without demonstration or violence before 1960. In 1947 black leaders approached the recently hired Nashville Public Library director, Robert Alvarez, about using the main library. They argued their branch was poorly supported ("only 1 book in 25 is readable," Alvarez verified upon inspection), and because they paid taxes, because the city had 4,000 black college students, 400 black college teachers and administrators, more than 150 black clergymen, 7,500 black children in public schools, and four black publishing houses, the main library, they argued, ought to serve their information needs. It was up to the library board, Alvarez responded, and in his diary wrote on October 16: "I'm too much a newcomer to the South to try and influence their thought on the matter."

When he brought their request to the board's attention, two members were adamantly opposed. "They were sure that the Negroes were not interested in the library's resources but only wanted to break down an old barrier and gain entry into another white institution long closed to them. . . . These gentlemen felt sure that the Nashville Negroes would overrun the main library once they got their foot in the door." When the board considered a formal petition by prominent Nashville blacks several months later, board members "were of the opinion that now was certainly not the right time to make such a move—what with the South already seriously stirred up over President Truman's civil rights program," Alvarez noted. "As far as two members of the group were concerned, the time would never be right."

A year later, however, after the most vocal opponents of integrated services left a board meeting, Alvarez addressed those remaining: "Excuse me. May I say just one thing more? Lately, we've been having a few Negroes come to the main desk asking to borrow a book. Would anybody here mind if we just gave them the books they wanted and let them go on their way?" As they hurried themselves to leave, the remaining six quickly (and probably absent-mindedly) responded, "No, go ahead and do it." "And with that," Alvarez wrote in his autobiography, "the bars came down and our main library at long last was open to every member of the community. It was my single most exhilarating moment in Nashville." To this decision he gave no publicity and trusted word of mouth to spread news of the policy change. Slowly the number of black visitors increased until one day a desk attendant "rushed into my office to announce that there was a young black man sitting in the reading room." What should she do? "I could see no harm in the young man's being there in the reading room, so I told the lady to just go about her business and let him stay. So that was the end of that, and I don't recall ever catching any flack from anyone."[21]

And it was at the Nashville Public Library, David Halberstam writes, that black civil rights activist Jim Bevel "found a wealth of books on Gandhi" a decade later. "It was a treasure trove for Bevel. . . . With the blessing of the librarian, who, he said, encouraged him to share these otherwise virginal books with his friends, he walked out of the library with them and started circulating them among his friends. The Bevel Lending Library, it was called." Among friends who had access to the "Bevel Lending Library" was John Lewis, U.S. congressman from Georgia since 1987 but in 1960 an American Baptist Theological Institute student who, along with several teenage friends, had been turned away from the public library in his hometown of Troy, Alabama, several years earlier because he was black. In the next few years Lewis would become chairman of the Student Nonviolent Coordinating Committee, receive a serious beating as a Freedom Rider in Anniston, Alabama, in 1961, and serve as an organizer of the March 7, 1965, march across the Edmund Pettus Bridge in Selma that became known as "Bloody Sunday," when he was again beaten. This time, however, the violence was caught on camera and played again and again on evening newscasts across the country.[22]

When Richmond, Virginia, opened a public library for blacks in 1925, the black weekly *New Journal and Guide* complained it was "far out of the reach of the colored people; too far, in fact to be of any service to them." The *Journal* advised readers to use the library of the YWCA Phillis Wheatley branch instead. Six years later, the city announced it would allocate $16,000 for a "colored branch" in a renovated building three times larger than the Wheatley branch. "When completed," the *Journal* reported, the Rosa D. Bowser Branch of the Richmond Public Library (named after a revered black Richmond teacher) "will be equal to any in the South with the possible exception of those found in the Louisville system," but the new location, the newspaper noted, was still miles from black neighborhoods. Not until 1934 did it open, however, and only with the help of federal funds that employed six persons to do the renovation.[23]

Dissatisfied with these services, two years later several black citizens sued in federal court to desegregate the main library, but their suit lost on default. Then, in 1946, the black YMCA's Professional and Business Men's Council requested that the Richmond City Council desegregate the library system. The council listened and on March 12 petitioned the Richmond Public Library board to open the main library to "all Richmonders." On April 14 the library board discussed the petition but deferred action. Rumor had it that board members wanted to solicit the city attorney's legal opinion. The black weekly *Richmond Afro-American* reported that some citizens believed the petition would be "dismissed summarily," but others had higher hopes because several individuals "regarded as liberals are library board members." The *Afro-American* also noted a story published the previous week in the *Richmond Times-Dispatch*, the city's major white newspaper, complaining that the Bowser branch had been underutilized: "However, the story made no mention of the fact that the branch is miles distant from thousands of citizens who are expected to use it."[24]

On May 28, despite a city ordinance that remained on the books forbidding use of the central library by any but white citizens, the board voted seven to two to integrate the central library system and all branches, except for black children under sixteen. "Whereas it has been brought to the attention of the city library board that the Negro citizens of Richmond are from time to time in need of library facilities that are not met by the Bowser Branch," the board resolution read, "therefore be it resolved that the facilities of the Dooley central library be made available to all adults of Richmond, subject to the regular rules of the library." But because facilities were "inadequate to accommodate the city's Negro children," the librarian told the *Times-Dispatch,* he announced plans to open several new branches in local neighborhoods to address youth library needs. "The transition now being made represents all that can be absorbed by present space or facilities at the central library." Weeks later, the board announced plans to open two new branches in black neighborhoods. Not everyone was happy with this arrangement, however. In subsequent months the number of white patrons coming to the central library "decreased sharply," one black newspaper reported.[25]

In 1942 black community leaders asked the Louisville Free Public Library Board of Trustees for more "liberal service." Populations had shifted since the system assigned them two branches in 1905 and 1914, they argued, and even though the board had provided a place for them at the central library in the 1930s if materials they requested were too rare to risk transportation, blacks wanted more. In response, the board gave black readers full access to Reference Department shelves while "continuing to maintain separate seating accommodations for them." Then, in April 1952, the Louisville Free Public Library abandoned segregated services and without incident voted to admit blacks to the central library and all its branches. Elsewhere in Louisville, however, Jim Crow prevailed. Schools and housing remained segregated, and places of amusement such as bowling alleys, skating rinks, and many hotels continued to exclude Louisville's blacks.[26]

In late 1953 Albert Dent, president of the historically black Dillard University in New Orleans, quietly contacted colleagues who had successfully and peacefully desegregated library systems in Dallas and Fort Worth and asked their advice. He then contacted a local "Catholic, a Jew, and a Protestant" and, along with a white integrationist, conspired to have them approach the New Orleans Public Library board to request that New Orleans integrate its public library system. He himself refused to be part of the delegation. A month later, three clergymen approached the board and urged its members to follow models of integration set by Dallas and Fort Worth. On the board sat Rosa Keller, a white liberal on the issue of race whom the mayor had appointed a year earlier; she immediately began agitating for an integrated system at every meeting. Just as persistently, however, the board refused to vote on the issue and instead, in May 1954, dished it to the city council and mayor, who—knowing a decision on *Brown* was imminent—quickly passed it to the city attorney for a legal opinion.

On May 21, four days after the Supreme Court issued the *Brown* decision, the city attorney advised the mayor that "no attempt be made to enforce segregation in any of the libraries." When the board bowed to the inevitable, however, it was with the knowledge that the mayor and Dent had quietly worked out an agreement not to generate publicity about the decision. Instead, Dent later admitted, he had promised to "call the presidents of the Negro colleges and the principals of the Negro high schools" privately "and tell them, 'Did you know the library is open to Negroes now? . . . If you have some students who want to go to the library, tell them to go.'" Concerning the desegregation of the New Orleans Public Library, "nothing was ever published in the newspapers," Dent noted. Unaware of these behind-the-scenes agreements, Rosa Keller apologized to the mayor for having caused turmoil on the board, and the mayor then told her that he knew library desegregation was inevitable after the *Brown* decision. "Like other smoothly achieved victories of the 1950s," one historian concludes, "the integration of libraries was facilitated by elite collusion—by the guarantee of little or no publicity, and by pressures applied by a strategically placed white elite." Despite desegregation, however, in the main library and its formerly white branches, blacks still could only drink from the "colored" fountain and still were not permitted to use the bathrooms.[27]

When he returned home to Monroe, North Carolina, in 1945, after serving in the military, Robert F. Williams joined the NAACP. Because Monroe had no local chapter, Williams walked into a poolroom one day and laid NAACP literature on a pool table. Half those present in the room joined, and shortly thereafter Williams began recruiting laborers, farmers, domestic workers, and the unemployed. "We ended up with a chapter that was unique in the whole NAACP because of working class composition and a leadership that was not middle class," he recalled in his 1962 book, *Negroes with Guns*. "Most important, we had a strong representation of returned veterans who were very militant and who didn't scare easy." The chapter decided to integrate public facilities in Monroe and Union County and, with the support of a Unitarian group of white people, started with public libraries. "In 1957, without any friction at all," he wrote, "we integrated the public library."[28] Yet Williams claimed more than actually happened. More accurately, when the Winchester Avenue Recreation Center, which housed the black branch of the Monroe Public Library, experienced a fire on December 26, 1956, Williams requested that whites open the main library to black Monrovians for their use while the black library was being repaired. Once completed two months later, however, the library reverted to segregated services. The system did not integrate until the mid-1960s.[29] In the meantime, Williams fled the United States in 1961 under seemingly trumped-up criminal charges. He lived in Cuba and China before returning eight years later. All criminal charges were dropped.

After World War II, a "Negro Women's Voters League" formed at the Atlanta Public Library's Sweet Auburn branch began a campaign to register voters and taught citizens how to use voting machines. The league then worked closely with the branch's Friends of Libraries, the local chapter of the American Veterans Committee, the Atlanta Council on Human Relations (ACHR, led by Whitney Young, who would later become a driving force in the National Urban League), and the Atlanta Urban League to desegregate the system. On October 9, 1953, the ACHR petitioned the library board to open the main library to black patrons. The board appointed a committee to study the matter but for the next five years avoided making any decisions. At a May 13, 1959, meeting, however, Director John C. Settlemayer, recently hired from the Minneapolis Public Library and personally opposed to segregated services, told his board that black Atlantans had attempted to use the main library (several of white historian Howard Zinn's black Spelman College students had specifically targeted the library for these efforts) and that when he reported these incidents to authorities, he was told by police no ordinance or law prevented them from being in the library. As a result, Settlemayer asked permission "to instruct the library staff to serve Negro borrowers by checking out materials to them quietly and quickly." The library board delayed, but when the ACHR threatened to sue, it capitulated.

On May 22, Irene Dobbs Jackson, a black French professor from Spelman, "walked through the electrically operated door of the marbled and modern Carnegie Library . . . went to the front desk, and filled out a membership application. She turned it in, and the slim girl behind the desk handed her a new membership card." As Howard Zinn describes it: "The girl's voice was calm. But her hand trembled slightly, perhaps because Dr. Jackson was the first Negro ever to receive a membership card at a 'white' library in Atlanta." On May 24, 1959, Mayor William B. Hartsfield—who as a young adult had self-educated in the Atlanta Public Library and who owed his office to thirty thousand black voters whom the Negro Women's Voters League helped organize—issued a statement to Atlanta newspapers, which until that time were unaware the library had been desegregated: "The Board of Trustees . . . decided to leave this delicate matter of interracial use of the Main Library" to Settlemayer. That decision ended segregation in the Atlanta Public Library system.[30]

Others also desegregated quietly. In May 1962 in Alabama, for example, Huntsville Public Library director Richard J. Hovey informed his board he had been named in an "omnibus integration suit" in nearby Gadsden, where he had previously been public library director. He warned members that similar problems would come to Huntsville if they did not integrate the system. To avoid trouble, the board reversed its segregated practices. "There was no confrontation or angry words in our library," one patron later recalled, "just a quiet changing of the status quo."[31]

THE IMPACT OF LAWSUITS

In 1950 William Hale Thompson, a black dentist from Newport News, Virginia, sued the local public library because he had been denied use on account of his race. On July 19, 1952, the city dropped its practice of restricting its reading room to whites only and desegregated its system. Rumor had it the decision was made to squelch Thompson's suit.[32] When the Miami, Florida, Public Library opened a new central building in 1951 at the same time it desegregated its system, few knew that several months earlier Rev. Edward T. Graham, pastor at the local black Mt. Zion Baptist Church, had written the board of trustees, "Please do not force me to bring an injunction against the opening of this very beautiful library." Integration went smoothly but for minor complaints about blacks using water fountains at the central and one branch library.[33]

On January 10, 1957, black interior decorator Samuel C. Murray and his wife, Josie, entered the Purcellville (Virginia) Public Library to borrow a book on Austrian shades. President Dwight D. Eisenhower's sister-in-law had commissioned their services, but they had never fashioned such ornate shades; they hoped to find information at the library. "The librarian . . . told me I'd have to get permission" from the board chairman, Murray later said, but the chairman turned him down because "to lend him a book would not be in the spirit of the library's founders." Murray's lawyer told the *Washington Post*: "There is no doubt about Virginia state law. It provides that libraries be free to all inhabitants." Murray asserted: "If I didn't pay my taxes they would sell my home. Since I do pay my taxes, I felt I should have the use of the book from the library which is paid for by my taxes." Because of Murray's pressure, library trustees asked the county board of supervisors two questions. If they integrated the library, "Would that have any effect on the appropriations usually given the Purcellville Public Library by the county?";

and would the additional federal funds promised to the county by the recently passed Library Services Act be affected? The county board responded that state law was clear: "If public funds are allocated to this library it must be operated on an integrated basis." Days later, the city council unanimously passed a resolution demanding the library board obey the law. Trustees waffled. One worried: "It can even be a question of closing the library." On March 21 trustees voted seven to five "to open the library to Negroes. They also voted in favor of providing Negroes with bookmobile service." With a decision to "open these hallowed doors," the *Philadelphia Tribune* noted, Purcellville's black community now had access to valuable information in large part because Murray's "unquenchable thirst for the know-how of making French drapes [sic] has made all this possible."[34]

The *Tribune* did not report the backlash evident at the subsequent county board of supervisors meeting, however. Three petitions with 366 signatures supported a $6,000 appropriation for the library. "I feel that the Library should be run according to State law," said a white Baptist minister. "Education is a matter of national security and the library is an integral part," said another. But another petition bearing 44 signatures presented by the Defenders of State Sovereignty and Individual Liberties argued that the library budget "could be lopped off to keep the tax rate down." Discussion that followed showed community discord. "I have not changed in opposing integration of the schools," the library board chairman said, but a 1946 state law "provided library service to all people. . . . Negroes go into banks, stores, and other places of business." Mrs. Clarence Robey, a trustee who organized the library in 1936 and was among the minority, argued against any appropriation: "I am ashamed of what the library trustees did to be the first in the State to vote for integration." Better to appropriate state and federal moneys "for a library for Negroes," she argued. At its meeting a week later, the board approved the appropriation; the library remained integrated, the first victory for the civil rights movement in Loudoun County, a local historian later labeled it.[35]

In 1945, Portsmouth, Virginia, built a new "colored public library," to which the city allocated $1,000 for new books; in addition, the *New Journal and Guide* reported, "several sets of books have been transferred from the white library and hundreds of fiction books have been donated." Named the Portsmouth Community Library, it differed from the Portsmouth Public Library, which grew out of a women's club reading group in 1914 that began receiving city funding in the 1920s and always barred black people.[36] On March 12, 1958, however, Hugo Owens, a black dentist who considered the "colored" library "totally inadequate," asked for a borrower's card at the main library. He was refused because he was black.

On April 8, he and fellow black dentist James W. Holley (both men had been instrumental in desegregating the local golf course in 1956) sent one letter to the Portsmouth Public Library board and another to the city council, asking to make the library available to all the citizens of Portsmouth. On that day the board considered their request but took no action. The board chair later told the *New Journal and Guide* she did not know "if and when the matter would be taken up again." On April 9 the Interdenominational Ministers Forum of Portsmouth endorsed the request to the city council, which considered it at an April 22 meeting but, like the library board, took no action.

The dentists pressed on, seeking to bring the library board together with the city council to discuss the issue. Both parties agreed to meet October 30, but on October 24 the public library board canceled because most members would be "out of town." In the interim the city attorney issued an opinion that the Portsmouth Public Library was an independent entity, and because it was not owned or operated by the city, the board had authority to set its own policy. Owens and Holley persisted. In March 1959 they sent the board another letter requesting integration. This time the board ordered a study and, after completing it, promised to open the library to everyone as soon as it could find larger facilities, indicating it might be the post office when a new federal building was completed two years hence. Because Owens and Holley believed the board had "no intention of living up to its voluntary desegregation promise," they chose another tactic. On November 25 they filed suit in federal district court for the "nauseating practice of denying the use of [central] library facilities" to Portsmouth's black community, alleging that "the conduct of discrimination by the Portsmouth Public Library based on race is humiliating, embarrassing, and grossly unfair. This conduct tends to reasonably suggest and imply that your complainants and other Negroes are inferior." Such conduct was "repugnant" and violated the Fourteenth Amendment. The court gave the defendants until December 23 to respond.[37]

On December 22, the library sought to void the suit. The board denied blacks use of the central library not because of race but "because the present library quarters are so small, cramped, and crowded as to make it impracticable to try to accommodate both races," attorneys explained to the court. "When the library has become housed in the present Post Office building or in any quarters containing comparable space, use of the library facilities will be made available to all persons on a full and equal basis regardless of racial identity."[38]

On February 17, 1960—sixteen days after the first Greensboro, North Carolina, lunch counter sit-ins—the federal district judge held a three-hour hearing on the case. "The question is can the court defer a constitutional right which has now existed since the *Brown* case?" the judge began. "Our defense, if you call it a defense, is a request for time," the board's lawyer argued. The librarian testified that she was willing to serve Negroes but was worried about the "heavy strain" their numbers would place on cramped quarters and especially the potential for trouble between black and white youths using the facility. To that the judge responded, "I have a little bit more confidence in teen-agers on these race problems than I do in adults." But he also warned against demonstrations by "any organized group, or disorganized group, that comes into the library for the purpose of occupying all the chairs and remaining all the time. You just let me know," he told the Portsmouth Public Library director, "and we'll handle them without any trouble."

At the end of the hearing, the judge ruled. The Portsmouth Public Library must admit black people or close up "lock, stock, and barrel." Any library using public funds had to serve all races, he said. "The sooner the good people of Portsmouth face up to it, the better off we'll be." The next day the judge announced the case would remain on the court docket for twelve months "to avoid any possible friction between the members of either race while using the library." The *Philadelphia Tribune* complimented all parties. In its February 27, 1960, "Civil Rights Roundup" column, it noted that elsewhere in the South, "white and Negro youth were battling in the streets over a demonstration aimed at ending Jim Crow seating in lunch counters." In Portsmouth, however, "integration made a quiet gain."[39]

On March 1, African American sheet metal worker Linwood Williams walked into the Portsmouth Public Library, applied for a borrower's card, and when approved, became the library's "first card-carrying colored member," the *New Journal and Guide* reported. In December 1961, three former board members of the Portsmouth Community Library were elected to the public library board by the city council. When the library moved into the remodeled post office in May 1963 (the Portsmouth Community Library had closed in 1962), it also had an integrated staff. "Dedication ceremonies" scheduled for March 17, a *New Journal and Guide* columnist wrote, "could become something of a Dixie model of desegregation."[40]

Before 1960, pressures brought by outside forces such as presidential executive orders, Supreme Court decisions, federal civil rights legislation, and federal funding for library services supplemented pressures from black leaders in various locations across the South to initiate and improve their public library services. Sometimes the solution was the creation of a black branch; sometimes it was the integration of the whole public library system. And to reluctant local whites who wanted to avoid community disruptions such as bus boycotts, desegregating the public library sometimes served as a useful way to demonstrate to local black citizens and to the outside world the white community's willingness to integrate local noncompulsory civic institutions without having to take the ultimate step— integrating public schools.

Few in the white community wanted to experience what had happened in Little Rock, Arkansas, where in 1957 Governor Orval Faubus defied a federal court order to desegregate the all-white Central High School and blocked nine black students from entering. White riots forced President Dwight Eisenhower to send in five thousand federal troops. Ironically, recalled Ernest Green, one of the high school protesters, "a year before we went to Central both the city buses and the public libraries were integrated without any problems," thus demonstrating that segregationist communities differed in where they drew lines of no compromise regarding integrating local civic institutions.[41]

But many in the South's white establishment continued to resist these forces and, specifically regarding public libraries, in ways both sad and repugnant to twenty-first-century readers. In 1956, for example, the Mississippi state legislature directed its Library Commission to spend $5,000 of its annual LSA appropriation for books on "ethnology"—a code word for tomes "proving" the inferiority of black people. Among books purchased was Judge Tom Brady's *Black Monday,* an attack on *Brown* and argument for white superiority. "You can dress a chimpanzee, housebreak him, and teach him to use a knife and fork," Brady argued, "but it will take countless generations of evolutionary development, if ever, before you can convince him that a caterpillar or a cockroach is not a delicacy. Likewise the social, economic and religious preferences of the Negro remain close to the caterpillar and the cockroach."[42]

Another arena of conflict regarding public library materials was the depiction of any kind of race mixing. In 1958, for example, an Alabama state legislator decided that a newly published children's book, written and illustrated by Garth Williams and entitled *The Rabbits' Wedding,* advocated interracial marriage because the front cover depicted a black and a white rabbit. Williams, the white son of English artists, was already well-known. In his lifetime he illustrated more than eighty children's books, including E. B. White's *Stuart Little* and *Charlotte's Web* and Laura Ingalls Wilder's *Little House* series. At the center of the controversy were Alabama Public Library Service Division director Emily Reed and state senator E. O. Eddins of Marengo County, who in 1956—the same year Alabama legislators outlawed all NAACP operations within its borders—had solicited the federal government to resettle Alabama's black people elsewhere in the country. Eddins was particularly disturbed with what he saw as books supporting integration and communism in Reed's library collections.

In May, he took after Reed for stocking *The Rabbits' Wedding.* "This book and many others should be taken off the shelves and burned," he insisted at a committee hearing. When Reed refused, the controversy quickly went national. "Incredible that any sober adult could scent in this fuzzy cotton tale for children the overtones of Karl Marx or even Martin Luther King," teased *Time* magazine. Even Alabama's major white newspapers abandoned Eddins. "We haul many a prop out from under" the "cause" of segregation "when we allow ourselves to appear ridiculous," argued the *Birmingham News*. Although Eddins quickly backpedaled, he continued to press for Reed's resignation. In January 1960, Reed told the press she was taking another position in the District of Columbia Public Library system. "My leaving was not directly related to the incidents of last year," she stated, but few believed her. As with Ruth Brown and Juliette Morgan, no one in the Alabama library community or from the American Library Association—including its Intellectual Freedom Committee—publicly came to Reed's defense.[43]

3

MEMPHIS, TENNESSEE, AND GREENVILLE, SOUTH CAROLINA

In the 1950s, Americans had plenty to worry about. Internationally, Cold War tensions were increasing; the Third World was decolonizing, often violently; and the nuclear arms race was heating up. Domestically, people feared communist infiltration into many of the nation's organizations and saw evidence of this infiltration in every movement that caused local and national stress, including the rise of rock and roll, which infused a youth culture with subversive racial messages. The federal government, its elected officials, and its many agencies, including the Federal Bureau of Investigation, fed this paranoia.

Almost all Americans had televisions in their living rooms by the end of the decade, bringing them news of the excesses of McCarthyism—of much more concern to the nation's library community in the 1950s than segregated public libraries— as well as visual images of racial mixing in the entertainment industry and the desegregation of sports at the collegiate and professional levels; evening news programs covered attention-getting footage such as the hostilities at Little Rock's Central High School in 1957. Civil rights protests fit the bill nicely, and civil rights activists quickly discovered that "direct action" was a powerful way to spread images of Jim Crow humiliations across the South. But a reaction to this media attention was also evident in the growth of the Ku Klux Klan, the establishment of White Citizens' Councils, the rise of shrill voices eager to defend the "southern way of life," and the rhetoric of segregationists such as Robert Byrd, Orval Faubus, and George Wallace. The cacophony they raised tended to mute the voices of moderation, many of which remained buried deep in southern library communities.

Efforts to desegregate Jim Crow facilities such as buses, golf courses, and public parks after the successful Montgomery bus boycott in 1955 met mixed results. "The pattern was that in some places," including Atlanta and Charlotte, both eager to lure new business and anxious about negative publicity, desegregation occurred "after hemming and hawing, and erecting a few roadblocks," argues journalist Fred

Powledge. Some "in the middle"—Mobile, Nashville, and Savannah, for example—"tended toward a little quiet, token segregation." Others, however—often referred to as "hard-core" areas controlled by "segs"—took "segregation forever" positions, and the people who lived there, one *Arkansas Gazette* reporter noted, manifested an "ain't no son of a bitch gonna tell me what to do" attitude. Among them were towns such as Baton Rouge, Birmingham, "and virtually anyplace in Mississippi."[1] Powledge could also have included in this group Memphis, Tennessee, and Greenville, South Carolina, the subjects of this chapter.

MEMPHIS, TENNESSEE

For many people the public library served as a refuge, a place to escape from life's daily toil, an opportunity to transport oneself to some other place, at least for a while. And that's what Jesse H. Turner thought in 1949 when he recommended that his new wife, Allegra, head to the local public library to divert her thoughts from a recent loss. Jesse and Allegra, black Americans living in Memphis, had just married that year. Five months after the wedding, Allegra's sixteen-year-old brother died in a freak train accident, and Allegra went into mourning. Pregnant with her first child and unable to shake her deep depression, she agreed with her new husband that a visit to the Cossitt Library might do her good, and one day Turner dropped her off there on his way to work.

At the time, the Cossitt Library served as Memphis's main library. It was an imposing yet beautiful red sandstone building, Romanesque in style, with a tall turret dwarfing surrounding buildings in downtown Memphis. Opening its doors on April 23, 1893, it was the city's first public library and held a prime location at 33 South Front Street.[2] In the 1930s, the Cossitt Public Library began bookmobile service. Although blacks made up nearly 40 percent of Memphis's population by then,[3] they could use neither the library nor the bookmobile.

Memphis's black population instead was allowed to use the "LeMoyne" branch, opened in 1903 and located at LeMoyne College (now LeMoyne-Owen College), where the main library sent its discards to fill the small space.[4] The LeMoyne branch closed in 1932. Three years later, the library system opened a "Negro Branch" in Church Park Auditorium, then moved it to an old converted store in 1937 and in 1939 to the small "Vance Branch Library." Memphis blacks did not get access to a bookmobile for another fifteen years. But in 1949, if one were seeking a place of comfort with a variety of resources, a place of awe, Cossitt was it, and it was there that Allegra Turner sought solace.

Once inside, she went directly to the public catalog. As she ran her fingers through the cards, a library worker tapped her on the shoulder and asked why she was there. "Using the card catalog. What else?" she replied. Ordered to accompany the library worker, Allegra was led to a small area of the library marked off by a white picket fence and told to stand there while library personnel decided what to do with her. Eventually Allegra received an explanation. She was not permitted to visit the Cossitt Library; instead, she needed to visit the Vance Avenue Branch—the "colored" branch. There, at "her" branch, she could request a book that it did not have, which would then be sent from the Cossitt Library the next day. Allegra left the library humiliated and empty-handed.

For her husband, Jesse, this represented yet another in a string of humiliations he had suffered in his young life. He was born in Longview, Mississippi, in 1919 but moved to Tennessee to attend LeMoyne, a historically black college, where he graduated with distinction. In 1941 he entered the army. There, despite his intellect and education, he experienced racism in many forms, including his assignment to the cooks' and bakers' school, where blacks often received training as servants in the mess hall. Years later, his wife recalled of his army days, "he experienced injustice, consistent put-downs, trickery, and a deliberate waste of his brilliance."[5]

After four years of service—during which time he resisted assignment to cooks' and bakers' school, was promoted to captain of an infantry company, and received a Bronze Star—Jesse began work on a master's degree in business administration at the University of Chicago. It was there that he met Allegra. Frances Allegra Will was the second of eleven children born to Leo and Emma Amar Will of Louisiana. She had been valedictorian of her Baton Rouge high school class and, denied admission to Louisiana State University because of her race, instead earned a degree from the historically black Southern University. Like Jesse, she was working on a master's degree at Chicago.[6]

With degree in hand, Turner returned to Memphis, not only because of his college years there but also because the new Tri-State Bank of Memphis had just opened in 1946. Founded by Dr. J. E. Walker (who also founded University Life Insurance) and his son, A. Maceo Walker, it was the first black-owned bank in Memphis and later played an important role in the civil rights movement. Plans for local sit-ins were hatched in the bank's boardroom, and the vault was often kept open at night to provide bail money for protesters.[7] Turner began work there as a cashier and eventually became its president. He was also the first black to pass Tennessee's Certified Public Accountant exam and was active in the NAACP's Memphis branch, eventually serving ten years as its president. During those early years Turner wrote letters to the editors of local papers, often quoting the Declaration of Independence: "We hold these truths to be self evident, that all men are created equal." But in June 1949 Turner was just beginning his career and married life. Although he did not forget the insult to his wife, it took several years before he was ready to challenge the library's Jim Crow practices. He first began his activism, as did many other black civil rights leaders, with less-threatening voter registration efforts, and by the mid-1950s he was raising money for the NAACP. In the meantime, the main public library had moved into a new facility in 1955.

On June 17, 1957, eight years after the public library insulted his wife, Turner left for work as usual. Allegra recalled that the "day seemed fairly ordinary." But in late afternoon she turned on her radio and heard: "A well-dressed Negro man entered the front door of the main library . . . and requested a library card to borrow books," but was turned away by Jesse Cunningham, library director for the past thirty-two years. Allegra then heard her husband's name as the black applicant. When Turner got home that evening, he described to Allegra how shaken the library employees seemed at his presence. "I could have burst out laughing," he said, "but I didn't let on. Obviously, [the librarian] was hoping that I would just go away."

To the Memphis media, Cunningham explained he had simply acted "on the custom that prevails in this community and the South," and although admitting that no law prohibited him from granting Turner library privileges, hastened to add that the library board unanimously supported his decision. Board members' average age was seventy; two were members of families that had served since the library was founded. Board chairman Wassell Randolph, who had succeeded his father, had been on the board for forty years. Initially he asserted this was the first time any black had asked for a library card, though later, in a deposition, he had to admit that since he began service on the board in 1917, "on four or five occasions Negroes had requested use of the library system." Steeped in Jim Crow southern traditions, the librarian and board members found Turner's request both startling and threatening. Once the story hit the news, Jesse and Allegra Turner received threatening phone calls: "Nigger . . . tell Jesse to have his mammy read to him." "When did niggers start needing books?" "You niggers are getting mighty uppity."

Local white newspapers seemed sympathetic to Turner. They reviewed his credentials to demonstrate why he might need to use the library and concluded that he required certain periodicals and reference works for his position as a bank employee and accountant. The librarian countered that he could get such works through the black branch "if he was a person really trying to do something and not trying to make a scene."[8] But Turner persisted. On July 15, 1957, attorney H. T. Lockard, local NAACP president, sent a letter to board chairman Randolph requesting that Turner and his children be given permission to use the main library and all its branches. He stated that the library's denial was based solely on race. The board met on July 18, closed the meeting to the public, and deferred any action on Turner's request. In October, Randolph sent Lockard a three-page letter asserting that "an investigation has been made to learn the wishes of the people of Memphis, as well as the legal questions," and as a result, the board declined Turner's application for a library card.

What "investigation" the library board made is unknown, but it is clear that the board received at least one response, a twenty-seven-page diatribe dated August 1957. The letter, listed today in the library's records as authored by a black person (an assertion hard to document and difficult to believe), is unsigned. "We . . . negroes," its author claimed, "want you real white people to know that we are not for all of this trouble." The author refers to "negro trash leaders" fomenting the trouble, claiming "we do not want intergration [sic]." He also lambasts black leaders, claiming Jesse Turner "actually hates white people" and has "the big head" because of his education. He says that black people "owe it to the southern white people for our being so prosperous and makeing [sic] it possible for us to be educated, and we are so narrow that we do not apreciate [sic] what the white people have done for us." Turner "has said so many times . . . he will try killing all of old white so and so's." Remarkably, he says "it is unfair for us to want you all to give us the best jobs and place us above your white people this is not in keeping with the Bible and the teachings of Jesus." Regarding race itself, the author says that some blacks "are frying our cursed nappie hair straight . . . . We know all other races look better than our black race but if the Bible is right we know it is—we should stay in our race." He chastises whites, writing, "You all should stop calling our negroes miss mrs. and mr. for they are carrying this to [sic] far. . . . White people should call us by our names as you use [sic] to do [sic] Old Black Turner want you all to call him Mr."[9]

This diatribe became part of the library board's record and, if indicative of other responses, provided the board with ample support to deny services to the black population. But board chairman Randolph pointed out that the black branch would furnish any materials to black citizens upon request. "The . . . library facilities are available equally to all citizens," he wrote, "but, for convenience in management, and to avoid regrettable incidents which have no relation to the circulation of books," blacks would have to continue to use the black library branch.

Randolph also noted that "the records show that books are available at the [black] Library in excess of the use of them." Furthermore, having both black and white library users share a reading room is not "conducive to harmonious relations amont [sic] the people of our City. Forcing people to associate together against their will is the antithesis of freedom." He continued: "For almost a hundred years, Memphians of all races have lived together in growing peace and harmony. Helping hands have been extended from one to the other whenever occasions have arisen, and the public advantages and opportunities furnished our Negro citizens have been gratifying, although Negroes pay a very small and disproportionate part of the cost of these benefits; and the almost complete experience with these shared blessings has shown that self-respecting Negroes and self-respecting White people do not commingle socially. Each prefers his own group." Randolph concluded by saying, "Sadly, recent events have opened wounds which we thought were healed. . . . The library directors . . . are unwilling to increase the tension or widen the breach now so painfully apparent" by permitting Turner to use the library.[10] The board's decision came weeks after white mobs had prevented black students from integrating Central High School in Little Rock and a month after racists dynamited an integrated school in Nashville.

On January 3, 1958, Turner's attorney responded with a brief letter. After speaking with his client and "several other interested persons," he wrote, "we decided that the request made by Mr. Turner can and ought to be granted without any difficulty at all." He asked the board to reconsider.[11] Shortly thereafter, several white faculty members from Memphis universities and colleges appeared before the library board and presented petitions favoring integration signed by seventy professors from Memphis State University, which had begun a "gradual desegregation" program in 1955; sixty-five from the University of Tennessee's Medical School, located in Memphis; twenty-nine from Southwestern (now Rhodes) College; and eighteen Christian Brothers College students.[12] The petitions noted that "such cities as Nashville and Chattanooga in Tennessee, Miami, Florida, and New Orleans, Louisiana, have opened all public library facilities to equal use by all their citizens without difficulty or disturbance." In June the library board voted to stand by its original decision: "In our opinion, the necessity for adhering to this position is greater than when the [first] letter was written, by reason of the increasing public interest involved." The board chair added that plans were in the works for an "extensive research library" to be added to the main library; it would be available to all residents, black and white, although the reading room and all white branches would remain white.[13]

On August 15, 1958, Jesse Turner filed an NAACP-financed class action lawsuit against the library. The suit named the librarian and the board of directors as defendants. Hoping to defuse the situation, Memphis Public Library director Cunningham's newly chosen successor, C. Lamar Wallis, announced that blacks could use the reference section of the main library because "their" own library lacked one, but other sections of the main library and all the white branches would remain off-limits. However, the new rule would not take effect until more than a year after Turner filed his lawsuit.

Turner's complaint alleged violations under the due process and equal protection clauses of the U.S. Constitution. He sought no money damages but instead asked for a "permanent injunction enjoining defendants from enforcing their policy . . . of denying [Negro citizens] the right to use the library facilities and services made available at the main municipal library . . . and at other branches of the Memphis Public Library."[14] The complaint was signed by five attorneys, three from Memphis—H. T. Lockard, A. W. Willis Jr., and R. B. Sugarmon Jr.—and two from New York who had dedicated their careers to civil rights: Thurgood Marshall, who in 1967 became the first black justice to serve on the U.S. Supreme Court, and Constance Baker Motley, who in 1966 became the first black female federal judge. During the 1960s these two New York attorneys played key roles in civil rights litigation by traveling throughout the South to represent other plaintiffs willing to challenge segregation. This was their first, but not last, suit involving the desegregation of a public library.

The *Turner v. Randolph* lawsuit progressed slowly, but what appears to have moved it to a conclusion more quickly were a series of protests begun throughout the South. Memphis was not immune. In 1958, for example, a year after the Little Rock fiasco, the mother of eight-year-old Gerald Young decided to enroll her son at Memphis's Vollentine Elementary School, an all-white school. He was denied admission. Although the *Brown* decision had made new law, it did not provide remedies, nor did it furnish a timetable for integration. Later the Supreme Court made it clear that local authorities had primary responsibility for integration, with federal court oversight, but again refused to set deadlines for such action.[15] As a result, many black communities had to follow the slow path of litigation to force change. And in Memphis, whites were in no hurry. Gerald Young's experience ultimately led to a federal lawsuit filed on March 31, 1960.[16] Not surprisingly, four of the plaintiff's attorneys were the same attorneys representing Jesse Turner in his suit against the library.

Yet not all Tennessee cities resisted change as strenuously as Memphis. Some considered Memphis "among the four most segregated cities in the United States," and it was often contrasted with its more progressive sister, Nashville. Although only 220 miles apart, "to the colored person who knows both cities well," wrote the Baltimore black weekly the *Afro-American*, "the two are as far separated in racial outlook as Cleveland, Ohio, and Cleveland, Mississippi."[17] While blacks could not enter most of Memphis's public libraries, well-known black poet and Fisk University librarian Arna Bontemps served on the board of the Nashville Public Library, which had integrated in 1948. Chattanooga had integrated its public library a year later.

Not Memphis, however, where it was difficult to find any whites willing to speak out against segregation.[18] In August 1958 a local white merchant wrote to library director Cunningham "commending" him for his "stand on the mixing of the races for Library use." The NAACP "and others are pressing harder every day and we must endeavor to resist," he argued. "I am sure that most all White People want the Library facilities maintained as they are." In response, Cunningham reassured him that the "Library Board is definitely committed to the continuance of our policy" but added, "Of course, with a Supreme Court like we have in this country most anything can happen."[19] In December another unsigned diatribe, this one twenty-nine pages, arrived from the same unknown "negro" author, arguing it was God's plan to keep the races separate. In late 1958, when C. Lamar Wallis became the new library director, some wondered whether he would resist efforts to integrate the library; previously, in Virginia, he had been director of the integrated Richmond Public Library. They need not have worried. In a letter written several years later, he assured the city attorney that although his "personal stand . . . is one of moderation, . . . I have a personal dislike for the methods of the NAACP and am perfectly willing to do battle as the Board directs. . . . My sympathy is with legal resistance."[20] He continued his resistance throughout the litigation.

Public protests escalated. In September and again in December 1958, black residents tried to use the Memphis Public Library. In both instances they left after being refused service. On March 19, 1960, however—six weeks after the Greensboro lunch counter sit-ins that catapulted the student sit-in movement into the national consciousness, one month after similar sit-ins at lunch counters in Nashville and Chattanooga, and one day after protesters conducted sit-ins at Memphis lunch counters—forty-one black demonstrators (mostly college students) were arrested at the main white library and one white branch and subsequently jailed, all charged with disorderly conduct, loitering, and breach of the peace when they refused to leave. Among those jailed were five representatives of black newspapers covering the sit-in, including two editors. Bond was set at $352.[21]

Prior to the trials of the library sit-in defendants, hundreds of blacks stood outside the police station singing the national anthem. Many entered the courtroom two hours early. The judge cleared the courtroom of two hundred black spectators before the trial began, allowing only enough to fill available seats. Of the forty-one defendants arrested, thirty-seven were convicted of disorderly conduct and fined $25; one black newspaper editor was fined $50 for "disturbing the peace" by talking to the demonstrators as they sat in the library. The judge called the scene "a mass demonstration that breeds contempt for the law, an open invitation to mob rule, to violence," and affirmed, "I am not going to stand for it." He insisted race had nothing to do with his position. As the defendants left the police station, they filed out through a double row of police holding billy clubs.[22]

The next day, students from LeMoyne and S. A. Owen College—another historically black institution that merged with LeMoyne in 1968—returned to the library and to the Brooks Memorial Art Gallery, open to blacks only on Thursday, when whites were excluded. Police arrested thirteen at the gallery and ten in the library reading room.[23] The arrests added to the total of sixty-four arrests in Memphis that week, consisting mostly of black students.[24] Protests and sit-downs continued into April, with dozens more arrested, reflecting similar activity occurring throughout the South from Galveston, Texas, to Orangeburg, South Carolina, to Savannah, Georgia, to Tallahassee, Florida. Elsewhere in Tennessee, the federal government announced on April 25 that, under the provisions of the 1957 Civil Rights Act, voting discrimination practices in Fayette County (adjacent to Shelby County, where Memphis was located) would cease. And after racists bombed the Nashville home of a black civil rights activist and thousands marched to city hall in protest on April 19, the mayor told the crowd he thought all Nashville public facilities should be desegregated; they were on May 10.[25]

In July 1960, federal district court judge William E. Miller denied Jesse Turner's motion for a summary judgment and set the case for trial in November, over two years after it had been filed. This decision may have been just the push the city needed. The city commission asked the library board to reconsider its "long standing policy" of segregation, but unwilling to make hard choices, on September 9, the board decided that the matter "be referred to the City Commission for decision." Days later, the commission determined that the library should be integrated, and the library board agreed to abide by the decision. On October 13 the city commission, with the library board's approval, issued a statement that "the facilities of the public libraries shall be made available to all citizens of the city."[26] It appeared Jesse Turner had won.

Six months later, library director Wallis reported that integration had been accepted by the public "except for one or two white persons who expressed distaste for the idea on the first day of integration." He did not mention a letter from one white patron dated October 17, 1960, which included the patron's library card, torn in half, with a comment that the "vast majority of your patrons feel as I do but are either too indolent or too hopeless to register a protest." Wallis reported that he expected more blacks to register for cards at formerly white libraries. Although Memphis's population was nearly 40 percent black, "of all persons registering since integration took place, 21% were Negroes." Most of those registering, not surprisingly, were from schools at all levels, elementary to graduate college. And, the librarian reported, he had "only the highest of praise" for their "conduct"; they "have been polite, courteous, and understanding."[27]

But another problem surfaced quickly. Memphis blacks could use all branches of their public library but not all the restrooms. The main library had two restrooms, one for whites, one for blacks (located in the basement and shared with the library's janitors), mandated by section 3044.29, volume 2, of the Memphis Municipal Code: "Where buildings are used by both white and the black races, separate facilities shall be provided for each race. . . . Proper signs shall be affixed on water closets indicating those provided for each race." Because the library board refused to budge on this issue, Jesse Turner refused to withdraw his lawsuit, so once again the parties returned to court, this time in late 1960.

The city raised several objections to Turner's argument that the restrooms must be integrated. First they simply relied on the ordinance, arguing their hands were tied. Later they argued the ordinance was not only binding on them but also both reasonable and constitutional. They asserted that the incidence of venereal disease was much higher among blacks than among whites, and so toilets, which they insisted carried and spread the disease, must remain segregated. A third argument seemed exaggerated, though it was one that another federal court in Norfolk, Virginia, had accepted.[28] They argued that the ordinance requiring separate bathrooms was binding only on those who actually built the library, but it did not *require* whites and blacks to use the separately built bathrooms: "There is no fine or penalty of any kind to be imposed upon anyone if a negro uses a white toilet or a white person uses a negro toilet. The Building Code simply says that the building shall be constructed with separate facilities."[29] The defendants concluded that the issue of separate bathrooms was so trivial that the court need not even rule on it.

Judge Miller disagreed. He noted that the "separate but equal" doctrine had by now "been generally swept away" in education, theaters, housing, parks, golf courses, swimming pools, restaurants, "and in many other areas." Nor did he accept the "spread of disease" argument. He noted, first, that "venereal disease would not be expected to occur to any appreciable extent among that segment of the populations, whether white or negro," that used the public library. Second, no reliable evidence existed that venereal disease could be spread by using the same toilet seat. Ultimately, he found no reason why restrooms should remain segregated.[30] On August 18, 1961, Miller ordered that "all public restrooms . . . in all public library units" in Memphis and Shelby County be operated without discrimination based on race and that the defendants pay all court costs. Shortly thereafter, Jesse and Allegra Turner walked with their three sons to the formerly white main library and registered for library cards. Although by then their oldest child was only ten years old, all five were nonetheless proud to finally be able to use the public library on an equal footing. That fall, Memphis schools began desegregating.

Perhaps inspired by his successes with the Memphis Public Library, Jesse Turner's activism continued. His work with the NAACP had already led to the integration of Memphis State University in the late 1950s, and other NAACP lawsuits and protests sought to desegregate public bus transportation and other public accommodations throughout the city.[31] After learning that a prominent black journalist had been denied service at the airport restaurant, in 1960 Turner filed a lawsuit against the City of Memphis and Dobbs Houses, Inc. He was represented by the same three Memphis lawyers as in his library suit.[32] His effort to integrate the restaurant ultimately succeeded, but he had to take the case all the way to the U.S. Supreme Court. Not until March 26, 1962, did the Court vacate a lower court decision and order "a decree granting appropriate injunctive relief against the discrimination complained of." Although the city argued that the restaurant was private and therefore not subject to the U.S. Constitution's equal protection clause (which prohibits any state from denying equal protection), the Court held that the restaurant was "an integral part of a public building" and that segregation violated the Fourteenth Amendment's equal protection clause.[33]

Jesse Turner died in 1989, but today in Memphis the Jesse H. Turner Park, the Jesse Turner Tower (at the Memphis Regional Medical Center), and the Jesse H. Turner Sr. Memorial Bridge all honor his memory. He was posthumously awarded the NAACP Walter White Award for his contribution to the civil rights movement. Allegra Turner was appointed to the Shelby County Library Board in the early 1990s, on which she served for twelve years.[34] She died in 2008.

While home in Greenville, South Carolina, over Christmas break during his 1959 freshman year at the University of Illinois, Jesse Jackson went to the McBee Avenue Colored Branch, where, the white *Greenville News* noted, "Negroes are afforded . . . the best facilities and access to all the books the meager resources of the Library can afford."[35] Because Jackson could not find the titles he was looking for, however, the librarian wrote a note and sent him to the white main library downtown. "The lady there is my friend," she told Jackson; "she'll handle this for me." But Jackson did not know this practice was hardly routine. "Because 'an appointment' has to be made by the McBee Avenue Branch librarian first," Calverta Elnora Davis wrote in a 1958 Atlanta University master's thesis, "it is rare that a Negro goes to the main library. . . . In 1956 only two African American males did this." This "psychological barrier," she argued, "should be eliminated."[36] Jackson was about to meet the "psychological barrier."

When Jackson got to the main library and walked through the rear entrance, several policemen were talking to the librarian. She looked at his note and remarked, "It'll take at least six days to get these books." "*Six* days?" Jackson responded. "Couldn't I just go back in the shelves and look for them . . . where nobody else would see me?" "You cannot have the books now. That's the way it is." "You heard what she said," growled one policeman. Jackson stormed out the library's rear door, walked to the front of the building, and looked up. "I just stared up at that 'Greenville Public Library,' and tears came to my eyes. I said to myself, 'That thing says public, and my father is a veteran and pays taxes.'" Angry and humiliated, he decided to take action, or, in the civil rights jargon of the day, "direct action." "When I get back home this summer," he promised himself, "it's gonna go public for real. I'm gonna use that library." Although he did not notice, carved into the granite base of a monument to Confederate soldiers immediately in front of the library where he stood was the poem:

> The world will yet decide
> In truth's clear, far off light,
> That the soldiers who wore the gray and died
> With Lee—were in the right.[37]

At the time, Greenville County supported five bookmobiles, but only one served black people and that exclusively.

During Jackson's 1960 spring semester, however, local black high school students preempted him. On March 1, 1960, twenty entered the building, milled about the stacks, and read at tables. This was just a little over a month after the Greensboro lunch counter sit-ins and a day before similar sit-ins in Columbia, South Carolina, that drew protests from five hundred students from nearby historically black colleges, two hundred of whom then marched to the city center. Rather than serve the twenty Greenville students, however, officials closed the library for the day. Two weeks later, seven students returned to do the same thing; this time they were arrested for disorderly conduct but were never brought to trial.[38]

That summer—while reports of sit-ins and demonstrations across the South filled newspaper columns—Jackson and five other students showed up on the steps of the public library on July 14, whereupon police told them they would be arrested if they entered the building. "And so," Jackson later recalled, in order to avoid arrest, "we left." But word about the incident spread quickly. "Third time this year that groups of Negroes have invaded the quiet of the public library," the News and Courier, a white Charleston, South Carolina, newspaper reported.[39] When Jackson returned to his neighborhood and told his clergyman his group had successfully avoided arrest, the clergyman responded, "But that's the *whole point!*" Jackson clearly understood what he meant; two days later he told his mother, "Mama, now I know you watch the news, and I'll probably go to jail this afternoon."

On Saturday, July 16, he was part of a group of eight "neatly dressed" mostly college students—five of them women, two of whom had been arrested on March 16—who entered the library and staged a forty-minute sit-in. When they refused to leave at the library director's request, the director called police. All were arrested for disorderly conduct, held for forty-five minutes, and released on bail paid by Jackson's clergyman. The Greenville News identified all eight—including "Jeff" Jackson—and published two photos of the students awaiting release. "Students obligingly and playfully posed for photographs," the News told its readers. "As far as I know," their self-proclaimed lawyer, Donald Sampson, told a reporter, "we still have a bunch of illiterate white trash in the library that don't know enough but to have these students arrested." A few days later, the local NAACP chapter called a press conference to condemn Sampson's words (he had already received a bomb threat) "attacking the dignity" of library personnel and to announce the NAACP's chapter lawyer would also be representing the demonstrators.[40]

Jackson's stepfather was not happy about the arrests, and his reaction reflects clear differences between generations of blacks—one that grew up in and negotiated life before 1950 in the Jim Crow South, the other from a restless generation that came of age after the *Brown* decision. "I just been watchin' yawl down there at the jail talkin' 'bout not being able to use the library," Jackson's stepfather said. "See that 'frigerator? Enough food in there for you? You ever had to go without a meal around here? Got enough clothes to wear? Thing is, when you out there talkin' 'bout you got to go to jail 'cause you can't get enough to read or eat someplace, that's sort of a *reflection* on me and your momma. . . . I don't think you ever quite thought how it could affect this family. So if you can't adjust to the situation here, maybe you ought to just go away from here."[41] He could not, of course, foresee that his stepson would one day become one of the nation's leading civil rights activists, ultimately receiving from President Bill Clinton the Presidential Medal of Freedom, the nation's highest civilian honor. The Greenville library arrest was Jackson's first among many.

The *Greenville News* found library protests contemptible: "The White people of Greenville County are not going to pay additional taxes to support an expanded institution which is going to be subjected to constant harassment simply because the equal facilities happen to be segregated." Although Jackson could overlook this slight, he was stung by his stepfather's words. Nonetheless, the library incidents in which he participated helped spark other demonstrations by black youths at Greenville lunch counters, swimming pools, and recreation parks that summer. "Our library sit-in," protester Joan Mattison Daniel later recalled, "was a pivotal point in Greenville's history."[42]

At a hearing the day after their arrest, a judge decided to postpone the trial. About seventy-five black spectators then left the courtroom to conduct demonstrations at three local lunch counters. They were turned away at all three, but at the third site, white spectators exchanged words with Charles Helms, a white Atlanta student attending New York's Union Theological Seminary who had been in Greenville for a month to help fight segregated public accommodations. A scuffle ensued, in which Helms lost his glasses. "I was slapped around," he told the *Washington Post–Times Herald*, "but I've been hurt worse playing softball." Nonetheless, police took him into protective custody.[43] Leaders had described the demonstrations at lunch counters days earlier as "spontaneous," then threatened to use the library arrests to file a federal suit to force integration of all of Greenville's public accommodations. One leader noted he had used the integrated Spartanburg Public Library when he lived there and had received "the best of service." He wondered why Greenville could not provide the same.[44]

On July 21 a "fist-swinging street fight" broke out on Main Street when a member of a group of white students struck one of thirty black youths demonstrating at local lunch counters. While a crowd of five hundred looked on, police broke it up and arrested three people (two black, one white). Days later, similar fights involving hundreds of white and black youths broke out at local drive-ins. Understandably, Greenville was nervous. "Time for level heads to take over," the News editorialized, and although the paper worried about "the possibility of bloodshed," it asserted that the white community's "most important objective is to maintain segregated schools." The "violence" resulting from demonstrations "does endless harm to that cause"; for that reason alone, the newspaper said, blacks needed to temper their "outrageous conduct," and whites needed to exercise "more patience."[45]

The editorial had little effect, however. Incidents continued, and as arrests and violence—including rock throwing and shooting at passing cars—increased, on July 25 the city council imposed a 9:00 p.m. curfew on Greenville residents under the age of twenty-one. "We cannot tolerate lawlessness," the News editorialized in support of council action. Local NAACP leaders, also fearing bloodshed, repeated calls for a biracial community committee, which they had been advocating for years but whites had resisted. They nonetheless promised to use their influence to stop lunch counter demonstrations and "marches against the Greenville Public Library." In its report about the curfew, the New York Times noted, "Race relations started deteriorating rapidly after the recent arrest of several Negro students for a sit-down demonstration in the white public library."[46]

On July 28, the NAACP filed suit in federal court to desegregate the Greenville Public Library on behalf of seven plaintiffs (although Jackson was not among them, he hardly faded from subsequent civil rights history) who also asked for a temporary injunction against the library's segregated practices.[47] Although the violence in Greenville diminished, black teenagers continued to conduct sit-ins at local lunch counters. Then, on August 10, executives of major variety store chains, including Woolworth, Kress, and Grant, all with branches in sixty-nine southern communities, announced they would be ending racial segregation at their lunch counters, in large part because local store managers had requested the action. The impact was immediate. Lunch counters in more than a hundred cities eliminated segregated services within a year of the Greensboro sit-ins. And in late August the Greenville city council lifted the curfew.[48]

On August 27, county authorities and county library officials named in the federal suit against the library filed a motion for dismissal. Six days later, city council members voted to close the main library and McBee branch until further notice. "The efforts made by a few Negroes to use the White library will now deprive White and Negro citizens of the benefit of a library," said the mayor. "This same group, if allowed to continue in their self-centered purpose, may conceivably bring about a closing of all schools, parks, swimming pools and other facilities. It is difficult to see how such results could be of benefit to anyone." The *News* supported the move, and worried about "an influx of mixed races and the renewal of strife" that integration of the library would bring. Plaintiffs' attorneys saw the action as an effort to forestall integration. Ten days later, a federal district judge threw out the lawsuit, arguing that the plaintiffs had no case because the library was no longer in operation.[49]

As numerous complaints came in from whites and blacks about the closed library, on September 16 the mayor announced he would seek a meeting with the library and city council to consider the library's future. Two days later, the *Greenville News* published a letter from Dorris Wright, president of the NAACP Youth Chapter and one of the plaintiffs in the federal suit, who pointed out several inequities between the McBee branch and the main library, particularly the number of newspapers at the main library inaccessible to McBee users. "The separate but equal principle is very expensive," he argued. "Integration of the libraries is not only morally right, but it is also less expensive as well." The same day the mayor met with the library board and city council.[50]

On the morning of September 19, and without prior announcement, all city libraries opened. "The board of trustees, with the approval of the city council, has ordered the city libraries opened," stated the mayor. "The city libraries will be operated for the benefit of any citizen having a legitimate need for the libraries and their facilities. They will not be used for demonstrations, purposeless assembly, or propaganda purposes." Although the mayor's statement did not say the library was being integrated, the *News* noted, "the inference was unmistakable." And while the newspaper welcomed the action, it also forewarned: "There is no cause for anyone to either gloat or complain that an integration 'breakthrough' has occurred. The Library simply isn't in the same category of public facilities as parks and playgrounds, swimming pools and the like," and especially the public schools. "Contacts and associations in the Library are brief and lacking in the intimacy which exists in parks, swimming pools, and schools. Each patron goes about his business in the same way as he does at the bank, the post office, or on the public bus."[51]

That first day, "there was no outward show of racial friction as a dozen or so Negro youngsters and adults came and went, some checking out books, others reading or apparently studying and perusing the shelves," wrote a *News* reporter. "Considerably more White persons were at the library during the day, and they went about their business as usual."[52] Greenville Public Library director Charles E. Stow wrote the *Wilson Library Bulletin*—a periodical widely read by librarians across the nation and published by the same company that issued the heavily used *Readers' Guide to Periodical Literature*—that he was "pleased that the library has been integrated, a step which I recommended several years ago. I feel it was extremely unfortunate that the library was closed and it is difficult for me to understand why that step was necessary, since it was reopened so promptly on an integrated basis."[53] He said nothing, however, about another type of segregation imposed on library users ten days after integration, when it was decided to force boys and girls to sit at separate tables—probably a reaction to the possibility that black males might sit next to white females.[54]

Memphis, Tennessee, and Greenville, South Carolina, both had a segregated public library system in the 1950s that local black citizens forced to integrate through the courts following the *Brown v. Board of Education* decision. In Memphis, integration was driven by a disgruntled veteran whose wife had been humiliated in 1949 when she was denied service. In Greenville, integration was compelled in 1960 by black high school and college students stirred to action by similar sit-ins protesting Jim Crow practices across the South. In both cases the public library system functioned as a local platform to mediate disputes—always reluctantly but mostly in nonviolent ways. In both cases, the successful resolution of disputes forced upon them resulted in libraries being one of the first local civic institutions to desegregate, while other public accommodations, especially public schools, remained segregated. And in both, the NAACP Legal Defense Fund took a central role in federal suits filed on behalf of plaintiffs and bore the brunt of white backlash.

4

PETERSBURG AND DANVILLE, VIRGINIA

In Virginia, site of the 1831 Nat Turner slave revolt that so frightened nineteenth-century southern whites and for more than a century festered in the white establishment's public memory, the NAACP filed more civil rights lawsuits than any other state. On the one hand, it was the state represented by Senator Harry F. Byrd Sr., author of the "Southern Manifesto" and leader of the Massive Resistance movement; on the other, it also experienced a lawsuit that desegregated interstate bus travel in 1946, hosted one of the five school desegregation lawsuits that was combined into the case that led to the 1954 *Brown* decision, and witnessed the famous 1967 *Loving v. Virginia* Supreme Court decision that overturned state laws banning interracial marriage. All these events received considerably more public and historical attention than the desegregation of Virginia's public libraries. Two such cases, however, are especially notable; both occurred in the wake of the Greensboro sit-ins.

PETERSBURG, 1960

During the Civil War, Petersburg had witnessed the final collapse of Robert E. Lee's army. In subsequent decades, it developed into a railroad town that by the mid-twentieth century transferred much of the tobacco and peanuts grown in that part of the state to external markets. When Clara J. McKenney donated her antebellum mansion home of high ceilings and marble fireplaces to the City of Petersburg for a public library in 1923 as a memorial to her husband, she stipulated that while whites would have exclusive use of upper floors of the building, "the basement be kept and maintained for the exclusive use of Negroes"—an "enlightened stipulation" for the 1920s South steeped in Jim Crow practices. At the time, Petersburg was 40 percent black. Should the city fail to conform to this and other requirements, the property would revert back to her or her heirs.

The first floor and the basement had equal space when the city gladly accepted the donation. By the time McKenney died in 1942, however, the city had built two additions costing $25,000 to the first floor; both served only whites. Dion Diamond later remembered approaching the twenty-four-room Petersburg Public Library as a black seven-year-old in 1949: "It was easy to walk through the gate and up the steps," he recalled, "but the lady at the door looked at me and said, 'Little boy, you're supposed to go to the side entrance, and down in the basement.'" The basement library, the black weekly *Richmond Afro-American* noted, was a "three-room affair with 14 seats and outmoded lighting fixtures." Perhaps this humiliation played a role in Diamond's later activism as a Freedom Rider, in which he suffered more than thirty arrests. Although young Diamond could request any book in the library, identifying any that were outside the basement was impossible because the library's only public card catalog was upstairs.[1]

But in late June 1959, Rev. Wyatt T. Walker, pastor at the Gillfield Baptist Church, state president of the Congress of Racial Equality, and president of the local NAACP chapter, walked into the Petersburg Public Library front door to request Douglas Southall Freeman's highly laudatory biography of Robert E. Lee.[2] Several reporters he had previously tipped off were there to cover what happened; Walker was refused service and told to go to the basement library. At the time, Petersburg—recently declared an "All American City" by a national magazine—employed no blacks in its police or fire departments, in city hall, or in its public library. Days later, the NAACP petitioned the city council to desegregate the facility. When city officials told the local press that "all books and research material in the city library are available to Negro patrons, for whom there are reading rooms with a special entrance," the chapter petitioned the council to close that entrance and instead substitute "a common entrance for all." On June 30, Virginia Claiborne—daughter of Clara McKenney—wrote Petersburg's mayor to endorse the petition. "The present branch facilities . . . represented human dignity in 1923. The same is not true in 1959," she wrote. Neither she nor the mayor made her letter public.[3]

On February 27, 1960, just four days after a series of unsuccessful sit-ins at Petersburg's Kresge lunch counters, young blacks in groups of 3 to 6 began entering the Petersburg Public Library shortly before noon. Within minutes, 140 blacks, mostly high school and college students with "a sprinkling of adults who were counselors for the students," the white *Petersburg Progress-Index* reported, occupied all the tables and wandered about the aisles. One approached the circulation desk and requested the Freeman biography of Robert E. Lee. When told he could get it downstairs in the "colored" library, "he shook his head and walked off."

Others who requested books were given the same response. To a reporter, Wyatt Walker identified the activity as a "student-organized movement. They came to us." "It is significant that the library was attacked and not the lunch counters," he told the *Richmond Afro-American* later, "for this means that we are opposed to segregation in any form that it takes."

In response to their presence, the city manager immediately closed the library until the council could discuss the matter the following week. At a meeting thereafter, students vowed to continue their protests not only at the library but also at lunch counters and schools. "Regrettable," a *Progress-Index* editorial labeled the demonstration. "These sit-down demonstrations usually are described as orderly. . . . However, the fact that the demonstrators have been drilled in quiet and uncommunicative behavior does not obscure the larger fact that there is something essentially disorderly about these large-scale affairs which appear to have been so carefully planned." The city manager immediately began hinting that Petersburg might have to close the library permanently if forced to integrate because such a ruling would violate stipulations in Clara McKenney's gift.[4]

At a March 1 meeting attended by seventy citizens—including about fifty of the students who had protested at the library three days earlier—the city council heard one of the protestors, C. J. Malloy, a student at the historically black Virginia State College, read a group statement that accompanied their petition to desegregate the library. "Segregation as a part of the fabric of American life is dead," he said. "We stand on the threshold of America becoming her ideal." Council members listened politely, quickly dismissed the petition, then unanimously passed an "anti-trespass" ordinance before announcing a decision to reopen the library on a segregated basis on March 3. Asked by a *Richmond Times Dispatch* reporter what he intended to do, Wyatt Walker responded: "This will in no way intimidate or thwart our efforts for desegregated facilities. If it will be necessary to go to jail, we will go to jail." He noted these kinds of demonstrations had assumed a "pattern across the South" and suggested the possibility of a federal lawsuit. "This reduces the city of Petersburg to a police state," said another NAACP spokesman. The *Progress-Index* saw council action differently. "Law and order will be served," it declared in an editorial. The newspaper echoed the city's position that it was bound by the terms of McKenney's deed. On March 3 the library opened again, without incident.[5]

Four days later, however, seventeen blacks entered the white sections of the library, including six Virginia State College students, two high school students, ministers Wyatt Walker and R. G. Williams, and Walker's wife, two children, and the child of another demonstrator. Mrs. Walker and her children immediately occupied tables in the white children's room. Others took seats in three reading rooms; Walker again asked a librarian for Freeman's biography of Robert E. Lee, by now a running joke among all protesters. The city manager, who had been tipped off about the sit-ins, asked all but Mrs. Walker and the children to leave and advised them they were subject to arrest if they did not. They responded that they knew about the ordinance and were prepared to go to jail if necessary. After they sat quietly awaiting warrants, police arrested eleven demonstrators and took them to the police station. Rather than post bond, five chose jail, where for two nights they slept on the floor. "We are staying in jail to dramatize the full implication of what this hastily enacted city ordinance means" to Petersburg's citizens, said Walker. "We sincerely believe this ordinance violates the guarantees of the bill of rights, the right of assembly and the right of protest." Said one of the students not arrested, "From the moment the City Council passed the anti-trespass ordinance we were committed to a position of civil disobedience." From jail the five inmates issued a statement: "In the light of our democratic principles and current social changes we feel that the city ordinance passed by council affecting 'trespass' laws is untenable, unchristian, and unconstitutional. It would be both timely and wise for our city council to reconsider the petition to integrate the public library."[6]

On the courthouse steps the next evening, in twenty-six-degree temperatures, two hundred Petersburg blacks protested the arrest of the demonstrators. Because officials had turned off floodlights that normally illuminated this public building, one protest leader read by flashlight: "We will be jailed by the thousands and while there make plans for full integration and equal rights behind prison walls." Said another, "It is with regret that a city with a population of approximately 40,000 people cannot afford to own fully and operate democratically a [public] library for all of its citizens without suffering the penalty of being jailed as criminals." Scores of whites stood across the street, many booing, some heckling.[7] The next day the five arrested were freed on bond, just in time to attend a mass rally at Zion Baptist Church; fourteen hundred attended to protest the anti-trespassing ordinance and segregated practices at their public library. "We will rid the City of Petersburg of every vestige of discrimination and segregation," said one rally leader. Martin Luther King Jr. sent a telegram of support. After the rally, lawyers representing those arrested said they would file a federal lawsuit requiring Petersburg to desegregate its public library.[8]

At trial on March 14, as six hundred black supporters "filled the steps leading to the courtroom" and sang hymns and prayed, sixty filed into the courtroom, where they were first directed to take seats on one side, then, when all those seats were full, were herded into three back rows on the other side. The defendants declined to take the stand. City officials did testify, however, including the police chief, who admitted the defendants had been arrested "because they are of the colored race and the city had consigned them the use of a side door." When the judge rendered his decision, he fined Wyatt Walker and R. G. Williams $100 and sentenced them to thirty days in jail for violating the anti-trespassing law. One Virginia State College student was fined $50 and sentenced to ten days in jail, and eight other defendants were fined $50 each. All were released on bond pending appeals.[9]

Immediately after they were sentenced, nearly two hundred supporters formed a thirty-car motorcade to Richmond to file a petition on behalf of the eleven convicted to end segregation at the Petersburg Public Library, which, their petition said, constitutes a "nauseating practice" and was "humiliating, embarrassing, and grossly unfair . . . and unconstitutional." After filing the petition, supporters joined a picket line protesting the discriminatory practices of a downtown Richmond department store.[10] In the meantime, Petersburg's city manager vowed to keep the library open on a segregated basis.

City action surrounding the public library functioned as a catalyst for other Petersburg civil rights activities. Milton A. Reid, a black Baptist preacher, announced his candidacy for city council, an all-white bastion of local power preserved in large part by making it difficult for blacks to vote. A new black organization, the Petersburg Improvement Association (PIA), promised increased numbers of demonstrations at chain-store lunch counters, swimming pools, and playgrounds. The PIA declared a moratorium on the library, however. As "a matter of litigation, there is nothing more we can do about it," Walker said. "We are not going to harass them, as the city manager expressed it. All we did was go there to read." Eight hundred miles away, forty-one African Americans, including five newspaper reporters, were arrested that day at Memphis's public library.[11]

Petersburg blacks braced for reaction. When a *Washington Post–Times Herald* correspondent visited the city that week, she reported that white community leaders actually thought that "the Negroes were satisfied with the patterns of segregation that have evolved since the Civil War," that demonstrations at the library "have been stirred up by outside agitators and will subside," and because white town officials "do not recognize the Negroes as leaders" and were "not taking the sitdowns as a serious protest," they felt no need to establish channels of communication with the local black community. And because of the court case filed against the library, she observed, "an uneasy truce now prevails in Petersburg."[12] That week the PIA sent two letters to city officials asking for meetings to discuss desegregation issues; officials ignored both. On March 21, someone threw a bottle containing an obscene note directed at Wyatt Walker's wife and signed "KKK" at her front window while she and her four children were home alone. It broke but did not shatter the window. "Friends stood guard at the Walker home the remainder of the night"; the next day the family requested and received police protection.[13]

On March 29, Virginia Claiborne, McKenney's daughter, wrote Petersburg's mayor a second letter calling for desegregation of the public library her mother had donated to the city. "In spite of my distaste for some of the tactics used in the present matter," she wrote to the mayor, "I wish to back Petersburg's colored citizens in their move for desegregation of the library, now that they have taken the initiative." On April 4, she made her position public, released her June 30, 1959, letter to the press, and criticized the mayor for not having publicized it a year earlier. Because their relationship with Petersburg blacks in the first decades of the twentieth century was "unique, believing as they did that to be treated with dignity breeds dignity," because "the original and amended deeds of the gift represent a positive, not a negative, affirmation on the only terms then tenable or even imagined," her parents, she told the *Richmond Afro-American*, would stand with her in 1960 were they still alive. When the *Washington Post–Times Herald* asked how this would affect the city's response to the federal suit, Petersburg's city manager replied that the "the deed will be invoked as the city's defense in court." The next day—the same day as local city council elections in which Reverend Reid lost but placed fourth, with the most votes ever garnered by a black candidate—the city asked the court to dismiss the suit because Virginia statutes governing segregation practices had not been found unconstitutional by the state supreme court of appeals.[14]

Angry that it had received no response to two letters to white city officials inviting cooperation, on April 13 the PIA announced a citywide campaign to desegregate lunch counters, schools, and all public facilities. Its first targets would be six segregated lunch counters; it also planned two additional suits aimed at desegregating schools and courtrooms. "The lid is off," said Wyatt Walker. "We go to court to fight segregation and we have to sit in segregated seats." Days later, a Virginia state judge ruled Petersburg's anti-trespassing law constitutional. "It has taken America almost one hundred and eighty four years to build our great nation," argued one citizen in the *Progress-Index*'s "People's Forum," "and there is no use in letting a bunch of overheated Negroes from way up north try to take it over."[15]

As all this whirled around the city of Petersburg, on May 20 federal district judge Albert V. Bryan held a hearing in Richmond on the public library case. Virginia Claiborne testified that she welcomed integration and would not ask for the building to be returned to her mother's estate. The basement room that served blacks was "dingy, dirty, and badly lighted," testified the Reverends R. G. Williams and Wyatt Walker. But the library was "fully available" to blacks, Petersburg lawyers responded. "So long as the library is available to both races, we feel the practice of segregation is valid." No, plaintiffs' attorneys argued, the library was not available to both races. Blacks had no access to the card catalog—and thus did not know what materials the library held—and modern reference books and current periodicals were not available in the basement. Toward the end of the hearing, city officials informed Bryan that if ordered to integrate, they would be forced to close the public library. The city would then bring suit to adjudicate the terms of the deed that had conveyed property to the city. But how would that help Petersburg citizens? the plaintiffs asked rhetorically. "I think it would be a detriment to whites and Negroes if the library would be closed," responded Williams. That the national media had interest in the hearing was obvious when Judge Bryan ordered a United States marshal to confiscate the film of a *Life* magazine photographer who had taken a photo through a window in the courtroom door.[16]

At Virginia Claiborne's prompting, Louis Brownlow, Petersburg city manager at the time her mother gave the building for a library in 1923, wrote a letter made public in early June. "There is not the slightest doubt in my mind that the one condition which your mother insisted upon in the name of your father was that this library should be open to all the citizens of Petersburg, and especially to the Negro citizens," Brownlow wrote. "Mr. McKenney, in his lifetime, took a strong position with respect to liberal and dignified treatment of the Negro citizens of the community."[17] On June 21 the city council reiterated that it was only trying to carry out the terms of the original deed. The *Progress-Index* sympathized with their plight. "Petersburg is receiving the full benefit of advice and lectures from outside sources—newspapers, former officials, and what have you," it editorialized, yet "nothing could be more specific than the provision of the deed calling for segregated use of the facility, whatever the intent may have been and however the intent may be interpreted in this year of grace."[18]

When three Virginia State College students—all among the eleven arrested on March 11—again sought service on the first floor of the public library on July 6, the city manager decided to close it down indefinitely pending a court decision regarding the validity of Clara McKenney's deed. Ironically, officials closed the library three days before hiring a new librarian to succeed the retiring librarian named in the federal lawsuit. "In the meantime," the *Progress-Index* reported, "members of the library staff continue at their posts behind an entrance door which bears the sign: 'Closed until Further Notice.'"[19]

On July 21, a Virginia state judge dismissed charges against the remaining youths arrested on March 7 for violating Petersburg's anti-trespassing law. But protests continued at other public facilities. On July 30 fifteen black students were arrested for trespassing in the white section of the Trailways Bus Terminal restaurant. The next day, three hundred gathered at the courthouse for their hearing. Additional arrests took place as students continued to sit at terminal lunch counters in subsequent days. "Fill the jails," demonstrators shouted as they were led to police cars.[20] On October 6, Judge Bryan announced he would decline to rule on the Petersburg public library case. Because the library was closed indefinitely, he reasoned, issues listed in the complaint no longer existed.[21]

But behind the scenes, matters moved quickly. In what one observer called "a surprise move," on November 4 city councilman William Grossman offered a resolution to reopen the Petersburg Public Library. "We may lose the library if we continue to keep it closed," he said. The city manager cited court cases that dismissed anti-trespassing charges against demonstrators and indicated he could no longer enforce the ordinance. That council members were prepared for the resolution was obvious when they approved it unanimously. Three days later, the new librarian opened the front doors of the library, which had been closed for four months. No Petersburg blacks entered that first day. "The branch library in the basement will continue operation as long as authorities feel there is need of it," the *Progress-Index* reported delicately. "Negro patrons who come into the portion of the library formerly reserved for white persons will be served." When the library opened that day, it became the ninth Petersburg public facility to desegregate since the February 26 Kresge lunch counter demonstrations. "Another victory for the sitdowners," crowed the *Richmond Afro-American*.[22]

That Petersburg was shifting attitudes toward integrated civic institutions was obvious from subsequent events that elsewhere brought bloodshed. When Freedom Riders came through Petersburg on May 5 aboard a Trailways bus at the beginning of their historic journey that witnessed violence in Alabama days later, they met no resistance at the terminal. Instead, they were greeted by locals, many of whom had worked through the Petersburg Improvement Association the previous August to desegregate the facility and had also participated in the events that forced the integration of the Petersburg Public Library in November. Taken together, all these successful efforts—most of which were spearheaded by local black high school and college students—had the effect of softening support for

Jim Crow practices in Petersburg and reassuring Freedom Ride organizers that at least in Petersburg, as one historian argues, their "successful testing of local facilities was almost a foregone conclusion."[23]

DANVILLE, 1960

Less than 150 miles southwest of Petersburg, black seventeen-year-old Robert A. Williams of Danville, Virginia, learned about the 1960 Greensboro lunch counter sit-ins the day after they occurred. He immediately approached his high school friends about how to challenge Danville's segregated facilities. "Based on dinner conversations with my father [NAACP attorney Jerry Williams], and his conversations with other friends about what we could accomplish through the law," he later recalled, "I was able to convince the other students and our adviser that the first attack we should have was against the public parks and the public library."

Williams knew enough about the law to recognize it would be easier to attack publicly funded institutions than privately owned establishments such as restaurants and hotels. He had also followed news about the sit-in at the Petersburg Public Library in March, in which eleven black youths had been arrested for trespassing. In the spring of 1960, his group met with Chalmers Mebane, a black World War II veteran who, like them, wanted to desegregate local public accommodations. "We planned what we were going to do, the routes we were going to take, and the objects that we were going to fight against in terms of the public park and the public library." They also met with local NAACP officials to discuss the "legal aspects of the sit-in demonstrations and what we could use them for and what type of support we could garner from the NAACP Legal Defense Fund."[24]

Danville's public library stood as a testament to the Old South. It was housed in a mansion declared the "Last Confederate Capitol" by a prominent bronze sign on its front lawn. Built in 1859 by Confederacy quartermaster William T. Sutherlin, it served as the executive mansion for Confederacy president Jefferson Davis, who fled there after Robert E. Lee recommended the evacuation of Richmond. It was there that Davis held his last cabinet meeting before the war ended. Danville's black residents did not share whites' pride in the mansion or their interpretation of its past. "The city had the nerve to take pride in the fact that it was here," writes Danville native and civil rights activist Evans D. Hopkins, that Davis "had hidden out for seven days before Robert E. Lee's surrender, after having been run out of Richmond by the Union Army."[25]

For generations the library served only whites, although in the early 1930s the white librarian hired Mrs. Frankie H. Jones, a black assistant, who, ironically, assumed responsibilities when the librarian left. "Because Negroes requested it," a Danville mayor recalled thirty years later, the city opened a branch in the black high school shortly thereafter and transferred Jones there. In 1950 the collection moved to two small rooms in a separate building two blocks away from the white library. Although the new William F. Grastey Branch (named after a revered twentieth-century black Danville educator) "mainly had books discarded from the segregated main library," Evans Hopkins later recalled having spent hours there discovering literature and new worlds, and admiring the beauty of words.[26]

On Saturday, April 2, 1960—the ninety-fifth anniversary of Davis's retreat from Richmond to Danville, two months after the Greensboro lunch counter sit-in, and five weeks after the Petersburg library sit-in—Williams and fifteen friends from the Loyal Baptist Church met at Ballou Park. The police quickly arrived, recorded the students' names and addresses, and closed the park. Williams and his group then walked to Main Street and into the all-white Danville Confederate Memorial Library. The librarian refused to let them take out books, telling them the library was closed. They sat down briefly, then left. "We felt on that day, very, very triumphant— that we had accomplished what we wanted—that was that if we could not use the park and the library, then they would be closed to all."[27]

"Racial calm in this Last Capital of the Confederacy was broken today as a group of Negroes of high school age entered the public library, bringing its closing two hours ahead of the usual time," the white *Danville Bee* reported. In an emergency session the next day, the city council passed an ordinance to limit library usage to existing cardholders because "facilities of the Danville Public Library are overtaxed by the demands of its patrons." In an editorial the *Bee* lamented: "The arrival in Danville of the Negro juvenile Gandhi-like revolt ushers in untold future consequences posing a grave problem to orderly government. . . . The conservative people of Danville deplore this rupture of homogeneous relations between the Negro and the white man of this community, because it brings to an end what, for decades, has been a sympathetic and understanding racial coexistence. It has endured ever since Danville citizens in November 1883 drove out the northern carpet-baggers and convinced the colored people that they had been the tools of unscrupulous self-seekers, just as they are today."[28]

The following week, black teenagers reappeared in groups of four, and when all requested library cards and library privileges, the librarian told them about the new city ordinance and urged them to visit their own library. "Few of the Negro students who invaded the main library," the *Bee* reported, "have ever used any of the library facilities available to them, a check of records disclosed today." The following Saturday night, April 9, Williams and his neighbors watched as crosses were burned on the front lawn of the Loyal Baptist Church and at the home of its pastor, Rev. Doyle J. Thomas, then president of the NAACP's Danville branch. On Sunday morning a local newspaper published on the front page the names and addresses of the students who had attempted to use the public park. Later that day, the Loyal Baptist Church hosted a mass meeting attended by 350.

"Burning crosses on front lawns is not going to solve Danville's present racial complexities," the *Bee* wrote, expressing surprise at discovering "a feeling of dissatisfaction among the colored people of Danville"; the newspaper attributed it to "outside agitators and reformers" who "came here to egg on children to mass acts of provocation." Shortly thereafter, the NAACP voted to file a federal lawsuit to challenge segregation in the public library and other public facilities. Robert Williams's father agreed to draft a complaint, with the help of Danville attorneys Ruth Harvey and Andrew Muse and Richmond attorney Martin A. Martin.[29]

On April 11, the city council met in a special session. A group of "25 leading citizens" had met the previous evening, one councilman reported, "and voted unanimously in favor of closing rather than integrating." In response, the council requested that the mayor appoint a committee to consider the request.[30] But not all Danville whites agreed with those leading citizens. On April 19 thirty-one whites met to organize a "Committee for the Public Library" and sign a petition to the mayor to keep the city library open "without interruption." When asked if the petition meant the group favored integration of the library, its spokesman had "no comment." Days later, the white petitioners announced they had garnered the signatures of "300 additional leading white citizens."[31] On April 13, however, local NAACP attorneys filed the complaint, asking for an injunction to desegregate not only the public library but all public facilities and accommodations in Danville.[32]

The case ended up in the court of sixty-two-year-old federal district judge Roby Thompson. At the May 5 hearing, before a packed courtroom of twenty-five whites and nearly one hundred blacks, city manager T. E. Temple testified that because blacks had "on numerous occasions" in the past used the public library without incident, there was no discrimination. Then why was the library closed on April 2? asked NAACP attorney Martin. "To maintain peace and good order," the city manager responded. "Wasn't it simply because they were colored?" No, Temple said, "it was the manner . . . mass entrances." How many tried to enter the library? Martin asked. "10 or 12," Temple said. That's a "mass"? Martin asked. Many blacks in the courtroom snickered; some laughed. Why were black students not allowed to enter the library on April 6? Martin asked. Because the ordinance the city council passed two days earlier restricted use to library cardholders. Could Danville citizens use the reading room without a card? Martin asked. Yes, Temple replied. "If Negroes go up there this afternoon, could they use the reading room?" Martin pressed. "Yes," Temple responded and after a pause added, "If they have a card." Again, there were snickers from blacks in the crowd. (The city attorney told a Rotary audience weeks later how "exasperated" he was "to hear the snickers and laughter among Negro spectators who filled the courtroom" when he "lost a point.")

The next witness after Temple was librarian Florence Robertson. On those occasions when black people used the library, she said, "we made no distinction and never had any incidents previously." Martin then asked if these "occasions" were "special" and involved black workers sent there by white employers. For many yes, she said, but not all. This time the judge interjected to focus the line of questioning. "The only point is this: Is the City of Danville operating a free public library with public funds and denying some citizens use because of race?"[33] He then ended the hearing. On the following day Thompson granted the injunction, ordering the city to extend full library privileges to Danville's black citizens. When the city announced that it planned to appeal, however, he suspended execution of the injunction for ten days to give the city "the right to apply to a higher court."

The response of Danville's white establishment to these events showed grave concern. What to do? The *Danville Bee* suggested an action unique in the history of desegregating public libraries in the South: call an advisory referendum. "The council is at grips with one of the deepest problems within this generation which has confronted city government," argued the *Bee*. "It is a problem which in the long look ahead far transcends whether the library shall function or whether it shall not function."[34] The city agreed, and on May 14 a local judge set the date for a five-point referendum for June 14, the same day as council elections were sched-uled. Citizens would be asked if they wanted: the entire system closed; facilities closed "if it appears that private facilities will be reasonably available"; the system to be open to all; the city council to work out a "modified plan" to continue to operate the system; or the library closed and books distributed through the book-mobile service.

By calling for an advisory referendum, however, they automatically pushed the issue of closing the library into local election debates. At a forum conducted by the Junior Chamber of Commerce on May 27, for example, four of the six common council candidates vowed to fight integration of the city's libraries. The other two agreed to abide by the decision of the advisory referendum. The topic also preoccupied other public discourse. On May 30, the Rotary Club heard the city attorney say that "to protect ourselves," the public needed to be "awakened" to the issue because the library integration suit was yet another example of how "certain rights of the majority race are being trampled." To prove his case he noted that most of the books in the "colored library" were also in the main library and any book not in the former could be requested from the latter and delivered "within fifteen to thirty minutes. Now, if anyone can tell me what irreparable harm or damages that were going to endure to the detriment of the plaintiffs according to what I just enumerated, I would sure like an explanation." No one in the audience pointed out to him that without access to a public card catalog Danville's blacks did not know what was in the main library that their taxes supported.[35]

On May 16, the same day the council filed a formal notice of appeal of Judge Thompson's ruling, a steering committee formed to organize a private library foundation and mobilize opposition to integrating the library. The effect of the mobilization effort on the council was obvious. On May 19, council members voted to close the city's public libraries and its bookmobiles the next day rather than comply with Judge Thompson's order. As word spread, "there was a rush on the main library . . . by persons desiring books, many of them getting stacks of volumes ranging up to between 15 and 20." Then, on the evening of May 20, the Danville Public Library system "closed without fanfare." Library staff members were not affected by the closing, the *Bee* reassured its readers the same day. On the following day someone tacked a "crudely made sign" on the library's front door that read, "Congradulations [sic] on this intelligent display of true Americanism."[36]

Just two weeks later, a newly formed "Danville Library Foundation" announced it would open a private segregated library to evade the court order. One founder argued: "You cannot appease the NAACP. If we compromise this thing we will have to face it again . . . in some other quarter." Whites who argued that few blacks would use an integrated library were "appeasers. . . . Let us not be misled by these appeasers—these prophets of compromise. Let us organize to demand our constitutional rights." "We believe the people would prefer a private library rather than making any concessions to the NAACP," said another.[37] The group planned to move into a fourteen-room mansion across the street from the main library and expected to pay for rent by selling eight thousand annual public subscriptions at $2 per adult and $1 per child.[38] It planned on spending $9,500 for books and periodicals. The city attorney advised the group it could not simply transfer the public library books to its private use because they had been purchased in part with taxes from Danville's black citizens.[39]

Public opposition began to mount outside Danville. "I, too, feel the old prejudices," novelist William Faulkner told an audience at the University of Virginia commencement on June 3 but added, "When the white man is driven by the old prejudices to do the things he does, I think the whole black race is laughing at him." He opposed closing public libraries in Danville and Petersburg: "I think everyone not only should have the right to look at everything printed, they should be compelled by law to do so."[40] The *Richmond Times-Dispatch* agreed. "Keep Libraries Open," it titled a June 13 editorial. "We expect to resist massive integration of our schools with all legal and proper means. We also oppose the mixing of races in restaurants, hotels, swimming pools, and so on," it argued. "But libraries are in a different category. . . . A library is a place where interracial contact is at a minimum, and where students and readers sit quietly and mind their own business." Virginia public libraries in Arlington, Charlottesville, Fairfax, Harrisonburg, Newport News, Norfolk, Portsmouth, Richmond, Roanoke, and Winchester had integrated, the newspaper noted, most "without any trouble arising. . . . Do the people of Danville and Petersburg wish to place themselves in a class apart, and to abandon the well nigh universal practice of making the wisdom of the ages freely available to all?"[41]

On June 8, the Committee for the Public Library mailed a letter to all of Danville's registered voters. "It is not, as some have said, a question of whether you approve of integration or of segregation, for the matter of the public library should be above this question," it read. "It is simply a matter of whether or not you want your city to have a library staffed and equipped to perform all essential services . . . that a library is expected to perform, or whether you want to do without these services." The Danville Library Foundation countered, "In the final analysis it must be the question of whether you approve of integration or segregation," and if Danville integrated its public library now, it would "give the green light to the NAACP to move further and faster with their plans for total integration. . . . If people vote to close the public library, there nevertheless will be a library available to the white people of Danville."[42]

On June 14, Danville residents went to the polls to vote on the referendum. At the time, blacks constituted 33 percent of Danville's population, though fewer than 10 percent were registered to vote. Of Danville's total population of 46,253, only 5,942 voted—yet not without incident. When polls opened at 6:00 a.m., members of the "Danville Committee on Negro Affairs," a local NAACP organization, began handing pink sample ballots to black voters that advocated for desegregating the public library; it also named five council candidates it supported.

None of the five had been informed of the committee's initiative, however, and although all of them denounced the pink ballot, by noon it appeared the effort was backfiring against the NAACP as "supporters of some of those candidates listed on the pink ballot became so incensed at the tactics used that, they said, they decided definitely to vote for closing the library rather than opening it to all as advocated on the ballot," the *Bee* reported.[43]

Not surprisingly, by a margin of nearly two to one (2,829 to 1,598), voters opted to keep the library closed.[44] "I surely hope the responsible colored citizens of Danville will take their cue from the results of the referendum on the library and drive the NAACP from their midst," said one city official. "It is only in that way that the good relations which formerly existed here between the races will be restored." The *Bee* celebrated "vox populi." "The solidarity of Danville in this matter may have caused some acid remarks by the neo-liberals in coalition with the Negro voters," it wrote in an editorial, "but it has at least reflected the truth that there are still a lot of unreconstructed rebels in Virginia not disposed to accept lightly an invasion of state rights by the federal judiciary, nor the vindictive purpose of alien reformers who hoped by the referendum to trumpet the claim that the onetime seat of the Confederate government had struck its colors."[45]

The issue would not die. The city council was split five to four against reopening the public library until a private library was available, so nearly two hundred people met to organize a petition drive for 5,000 signatures of "white citizens" to reopen the library "on an emergency basis." (One of the organizers teased, "An emergency may last 50 years.") But on June 24, Danville Library Foundation officers exercised a five-year lease on a site for the private library. "This is a community project," said Councilman John Carter, who led the effort. "It is one that can and will succeed. Let's do nothing to interfere with the tasks ahead." At a city council meeting the next day, a spokesman representing the group to reopen the library presented a petition bearing 3,151 signatures, but even after one council member suggested the possibility of reopening it after removing chairs and tables so blacks and whites would have to stand while using the library, no member changed his mind.[46]

The idea of a private library was certainly not welcomed by Danville's black population, but it was obviously not popular with many whites either. Opinions were split, with some concerned about negative national publicity, others about whether the conflict would hurt the local economy by discouraging new industry from moving there. Many of those in favor of keeping the library closed clung to the status quo, arguing that the two races had lived in peaceful harmony until this time and it was only NAACP attorneys who had stirred things up. They insisted the city stand its ground.[47]

This dissension resulted in several citizen initiatives. One group of thirty-one residents, "the majority in the field of medicine, dentistry, research chemistry and two officials of the Dan River Mills," a local fabric manufacturer, petitioned the city to reopen the library on an integrated basis. They began meeting at the home of Samuel Newman, "noted humanitarian and champion of democracy," one library periodical called him, and then opened up negotiations with Danville's mayor, the city manager, the city council, the city attorney, and the head of the Danville Library Foundation. Most of the meetings also included NAACP attorney Jerry Williams. By this time, it was becoming apparent that the foundation was having difficulty raising sufficient funds.[48]

When city councilman D. Lurton Arey presented the group's petition, he proposed that the library be open only on a "vertical plan" that would involve removal of all chairs and tables. Persons of both races would be able to enter the library and apply for specific books. Those books would be delivered to the applicant, who would then exit the library—a "get in, get out" plan. For in-library research the applicant would receive the materials and be assigned a numbered booth in which to study.[49] The idea, later termed "vertical integration" (a term segregationists adopted from economics that had nothing to do with race), may have come from a satire penned by American journalist Harry Golden in a 1956 article and reproduced in his 1958 book, *Only in America*. He noted that blacks and whites seemed to get along fine "so long as they *stood* near each other in grocery stores, dime stores, and the like," but "it is only when the Negro 'sets' that the fur begins to fly." He came up with the "Golden Vertical Negro Plan," in which desks but not seating would be provided for students in public schools.[50] Either because someone in Danville had read Golden's book or because they had reached the same conclusion, the city liked the idea.

While the libraries remained closed, racial tension continued. On September 4, the Ku Klux Klan gathered at a racetrack outside of town, raised the Confederate flag, burned a cross, and listened as imperial wizard J. B. Stoner of Atlanta launched a virulent attack primarily against black Americans but also against Jews, "Judas Iscariot" preachers, Communists, Hollywood, and the U.S. Supreme Court for its integrationist rulings.[51]

On September 13, nearly four months after the city had closed its libraries, the council voted five to four to reopen them on a "stand-by" integrated basis for a ninety-day trial period. (At least one councilman voted yes because of the negative publicity Danville was receiving; he noted that an industrial plant had decided not to move to Danville in part because of the controversy.) All borrower's cards would expire October 1, forcing anyone who wanted to use the public library thereafter to reapply. In addition, applicants had to fill out a four-page form calling for two character references and two credit references over which officials promised "rigid scrutiny." (Similarities with registration forms previously used throughout the South that were deliberately crafted to discourage African Americans from voting were unmistakable.) Finally, all applicants also had to pay a $2.50 application fee. "If all goes well," the city manager promised, chairs and tables would be reinstalled at a later date.

The vote that shifted the majority to reopening the library belonged to Councilman George Daniels, who agreed to the motion because it specified "stand-up service only." Nonetheless, he and Councilman James Catlin vowed to close the library again at the council's next meeting unless the NAACP withdrew its suit. "I'm not willing to vote to open libraries unless the local colored leaders will withdraw the suit," said Daniels. "Why wouldn't they?" commented Councilman John Carter, who remained a no vote and had been a central force in the failed effort to establish a private library. "The NAACP has tonight won a great victory." The implication was clear: withdraw the suit, or Daniels would rejoin the four who wanted to keep the libraries closed.[52] Others noted the negative national media attention Danville had received; in fact, even a widely circulated Soviet Union library journal covered the library closing, referring to the "dubious (from the standpoint of common sense) propositions" included in the citywide referendum.[53]

The move angered the *Danville Bee*, which called it "a surprising development in municipal government" that "certainly violates the principle of consent of the governed." And why the $2.50 fee, especially in view of the fact that the city had invested $38,000 in building a recently completed wing, which the events of the last three months had only delayed? Especially galling was the NAACP's "resounding victory," which could "only open the door encouragingly to new racial triumphs. The NAACP does not have to do anything but to enjoy the privileges of the libraries now accorded them. Its court suit achieved its objective." When the libraries opened the next day, seventy-five whites used the main library but no blacks; twenty-five blacks used the "former colored branch."[54]

Two days later, federal judge Ted Dalton, who had replaced Judge Thompson after his untimely death in July, dissolved the injunction against the city and dismissed the suit without prejudice. NAACP attorneys vigorously protested, especially objecting to the "ultimatum" Catlin and Daniels issued publicly and the new $2.50 fee, which violated the principle of a "free" public library and would disadvantage poor people. The fee was an administrative matter, Judge Dalton responded, and the plan to reopen he thought had been adopted "in a spirit of good will."[55] It appeared the conflict had finally ended.

Unfortunately, the appearance of resolution was deceptive. Florence Robertson, librarian at the main branch, reported that traffic at the library was slow and that only "a few" black people had applied for library cards. Not surprising. As it turned out, the four-page library card application asked the applicant to provide, among other things, birthplace, college degrees, prospective use of the library, last grade of school completed, reading habits, and the hours one expected to use the library and how often. Furthermore, in addition to two character references and two credit references, each applicant had to list the type of books he or she planned to borrow and pay $2.50. The NAACP immediately filed suit, asking Judge Dalton to enjoin enforcement for the new rigid rules, but Dalton dismissed the suit on the ground that the library had been successfully integrated.[56]

Among the first black people brave enough to enter the library was nine-year-old Evans Hopkins. "I remember arranging to ride into town with a teacher after school, and rushing to the main library to delve into the books that had been denied me." Once inside, however, he discovered all of the tables and chairs had been removed. "When I recall the shock of seeing the spitefulness of whites evidenced by the bare floors of that library," he later recalled, "I began to understand how anger turns to rage."[57] Hopkins put that anger to good use in later years as a celebrated author featured in the *New Yorker*, the *Washington Post*, and the *Atlanta Journal-Constitution*, among other publications. Simon and Schuster published his memoir in 2014.

Justifying the new library restrictions, the city manager explained the "stand up feature" would be in effect for only ninety days, a trial period to determine whether it would stay or "return to a normal operation." He added that "within the next few days" patrons would be able to browse through the stacks. And concerning the $2.50 fee, he said, "I understand fully, of course, that the charging of a fee is not in keeping with standards established by professional librarians and yet, we felt that it was a necessary measure in bringing about the restoration of library service to the community." He offered no further explanation. He also admitted that the long list of answers required for a card "may be a departure from the customary type that are contained in an application for library membership," but he argued that the answers "will aid us considerably in planning the library program and facilities for the future." He further justified his position by noting that he had library experience—he had worked in his university library while a student and after graduation had served on the board of visitors for his university, during which time they planned for a new campus library: "We do recognize the great need for adequate public library facilities. . . . Yet there are in our community many, many people who see little or no need for this service. You see, therefore, it is a problem that I believe only those of us on the local scene with previous background and experience can see objectively. Mrs. Robertson [the librarian] and I are trying desperately to keep the public library opened and have the services restored as nearly as possible to normal."[58]

The ninety-day trial period was scheduled to expire December 11. On November 9, the city manager announced that "well spread out" tables and chairs would be returned to the library on December 10 and that the library's 6:00 p.m. closing time would now be extended to 9:00 p.m. Although the librarian exercised discretion in assigning each user to a specific table for research, it appeared that, finally, the newly integrated library had resumed "normal" operations. During the subsequent year the number of library borrowers increased from 1,390 to 6,903.[59]

But the successful integration of the public library did not easily translate to other Danville public and private institutions. Lunch counters remained staunchly segregated, as did Danville schools and most other public and private facilities, despite the Supreme Court's *Brown* decision. On August 23, 1962, civil rights attorneys filed a lawsuit against the city manager, city council members, the housing authority and school board, judges, parks and recreation directors, a hospital, and others. Demonstrations, protests, litigation, and violent confrontations between the police and demonstrators continued for the next year and a half, stretching even beyond the enactment of the Civil Rights Act of 1964. In June 1963 police officers used fire hoses and sticks to disperse a crowd. Events in Danville during this traumatic period made the nonviolent integration of the public library seem almost effortless.

As was the case with Greenville, South Carolina, the integration of public libraries in Petersburg and Danville was forced by black high school and college students inspired by lunch counter and public accommodations sit-ins across the South. As in Memphis and Greenville, public libraries in Petersburg and Danville served as local platforms where the two races mediated their disputes, for blacks mostly through local NAACP chapters. And as in Memphis and Greenville, Petersburg and Danville's public libraries were among the first local civic institutions to desegregate.

Louisville Public Library Children's Room, 1928
(Caufield & Shook Collection, CS 091520, Archives and Special Collections,
University of Louisville)

Sit-in arrest at the Alexandria, Virginia, Library, August 21, 1939
(From the Collection of the Alexandria Black History Museum,
City of Alexandria, Virginia)

Jesse H. Turner
(Photo courtesy of Turner Estate)

Allegra W. Turner
(Photo courtesy of Turner Estate)

Petersburg chief of police W. E. Traylor serves warrant
on Virginia State College student Lillian Pride, March 7, 1960
(*Richmond Times-Dispatch*)

African Americans assemble at Petersburg Courthouse, March 8, 1960
(*Richmond Times-Dispatch*)

Miles College student speaks to Birmingham public librarians, April 10, 1963
(Alabama Department of Archives and History. Donated by Alabama Media Group/
Birmingham News)

Sit-in at the Birmingham Public Library, April 10, 1963

(Alabama Department of Archives and History. Donated by Alabama Media Group/
Birmingham News)

Albany Public Library, closed during the summer of 1962,
with garbage can for book returns blocking front door
(Library of Congress, Prints & Photographs Division)

James "Sammy" Bradford surrounded by police moments before his arrest
at the Jackson Public Library, March 27, 1961

(Library of Congress, Prints & Photographs Division, Visual Materials from
the NAACP Records, LC 95515764)

Police escort the "Tougaloo Nine" from Jackson Public Library, March 27, 1961
(Associated Press photo)

Mug shots of the "Tougaloo Nine" (*from top left*): Joseph Jackson Jr., Albert Lassiter, Alfred Cook, Ethel Sawyer, Geraldine Edwards, Evelyn Pierce, Janice Jackson, James Bradford, and Meredith Anding

(Mississippi Department of Archives and History)

Clara Stanton Jones, first African American president of the American Library Association, addressing the ALA Council about *The Speaker,* summer 1978 (Courtesy of the American Library Association Archives)

5

ALABAMA

In Alabama, efforts to desegregate public library services took a variety of forms and followed several patterns, some violent, most nonviolent. All show in a variety of ways how civil rights activities swirling around them influenced the integration of public library services. They also demonstrate that some Alabama communities capitulated fairly easily to desegregating their public libraries when pressured by protesters; others held out as long as possible.[1]

DEMONSTRATIONS THAT FORCED INTEGRATION

MOBILE

Shortly after the Supreme Court decided *Brown v. Board of Education* in 1954, the Mobile Public Library board affirmed its commitment to a segregated system. As in many systems, however, civil rights pressures and an evolving sense of fairness in the midst of Jim Crow life led the board to plan improvements for the black branch. "This branch library must be kept attractive if we are to keep the negroes from coming to the main library," the library director had written in 1952. Days after the massive protests about segregated public library services in Memphis, the library board met on March 25, 1960, to discuss strategies for the possibility of similar demonstrations locally. Although board members hoped to avoid what they perceived as Memphis's mistakes and deny demonstrators "any chance for publicity," they nonetheless instructed librarians not to provide black people service, even if they were "orderly in behavior."

A year later, several blacks entered the main library and requested service. On April 18, 1961, a "Citizens' Committee" submitted a petition to city commissioners that cited a judge's decision forcing integration of the Danville Public Library in Virginia and demanded all Mobile citizens be permitted "access to lounge, reading, and all other accommodations and facilities of the main library and all branch libraries, bookmobiles, et cetera, sans any form of proscription based on race, color, or creed." As other black groups joined and pressure mounted, in early November board members sought the advice of city commissioners. In the interim, however, they instructed the librarian to "use his best judgment" in dealing with any sit-ins or demonstrations.

On November 8, twenty black youths walked into the main library, sat down at desks and in lounge areas, drank from library fountains, and tried to check out books. After a second day of sit-ins, Virginia Smith, the librarian at the "colored branch," phoned director Guenter Janson to report that teachers at the black high school had told students the main library was now open to them. Worried that hordes of black students would show up at the library the next day, Janson called the board chairman, who met with the mayor on November 10. Desegregate, the mayor advised; he "saw no objection to bona fide use of the library by Negroes."

At a hastily called board meeting November 13, the chairman recounted events of the previous five days, noted the mayor had recommended integration of the library system, recognized no legal standing to justify segregated facilities, and with Memphis and Danville in mind forecast increased numbers of black youths in the library in the immediate future. Caught between "the recent interpretations of the law by the Federal Courts" and "the long-established customs of this community," after an hour's discussion the board approved an interim policy opening the main library to black patrons for reference work and limited borrowing privileges. "The Davis Avenue Branch Library, which has recently been expanded, is designed to provide for the normal and reasonable needs of our Negro citizens," they noted, expecting Mobile's blacks to go there first and withdraw system books through its services. To obtain books that might be subject to "undue delay," causing "undue hardship," however, black people could use the main library and other white branches. The board authorized their librarians—all white—to decide what constituted undue delay and undue hardship.

Because Janson interpreted these instructions loosely, he facilitated the transition to integrated service. Without direct authority he began issuing library cards to blacks from the main library, all without publicity. Within months, the *Wilson Library Bulletin* reported in its March 1962 issue, blacks and whites were "using the library together in complete harmony." Not all of Mobile's white citizens agreed with the policy change, however. One complained about this "clandestine agreement with Negro agitation groups." Another argued, "If we do not want integration in our schools we must not allow it in our other institutions." A third—who on a visit to the library had discovered it "full of Negroes sitting at tables and pretending to do reference work!"—accused board members of being "brainwashed for integration." Although he claimed he could obtain "thousands of signatures protesting this crime," he apparently never acted on the threat. Most Mobilians appeared to have accepted integrated public library service as a fait accompli.[2]

BIRMINGHAM

Although the activities of Birmingham police commissioner Eugene "Bull" Connor and his allies earned the city a reputation for violence and police brutality against black people that bolstered Congress's efforts to pass the 1964 Civil Rights Act, Birmingham's public library showed a different side of the city. By 1953 the city's public library system supported two black branches, Booker T. Washington and Slossfield. In response to one white public library board member's suggestion that local black leaders help increase the use of those branches, leaders organized a "Negro Advisory Committee." The committee quickly mounted a publicity campaign that boosted circulation by 20 percent and the number of visitors by 33 percent. Bolstered by these successes, the committee sought to expand services and pressed the white board for more funds. One trustee suggested a central library for the black community. That would be an unnecessary and costly duplication of services, argued another board member, who then suggested desegregating the main library just for reference and research. To that a majority objected and postponed further discussion of the matter until "such a time as a ruling is handed down by the Supreme Court on the matter of segregation." Obviously, they were waiting for the *Brown* decision.

Nonetheless, the Negro Advisory Committee pressed on. On February 25, 1954, members met with the board. Because no state law or local ordinance existed to mandate segregated public library services, they requested that the public library board integrate the entire system. "Without a single exception," the committee later reported, "every Negro who was at this meeting first expressed the hope" of integrating the system. Barring that, however, the committee wanted a newer, larger central library just for Birmingham's black community. What it got, however, were two new black branches, one opened in 1956, the other in 1957.[3]

In 1961, four years after Bull Connor and his allies had been elected on a platform committing Birmingham to remaining "the most segregated city in America," local civil rights leader Fred Shuttlesworth sued the city in federal court to end segregation in city parks, playgrounds, and theaters. When the court ruled in his favor, city officials vowed to close recreational facilities rather than integrate. Upon being asked whether the city would also close schools and libraries, one commissioner responded, "If they integrate, it will be at gun point." In June 1962, black teenager Lola Hendricks entered the main library to request a book. Librarians refused to serve her "because she was a Negro." They advised her to use the "colored" branches and informed her that if the book she requested was not part of their collections, she could request branch librarians to obtain the book from the main library. The next month Hendricks filed suit in federal court to desegregate Birmingham public libraries; her suit was joined with that of other black Birmingham citizens demanding desegregation of all public buildings and an airport motel.

The following spring, motivated by Southern Christian Leadership Conference (SCLC) speeches by Martin Luther King Jr. and others at the Sixteenth Street Baptist Church that "stirred your blood" and convinced many that civil rights were "worth dying for," students at the historically black Miles College conducted sit-ins at four downtown lunch counters on April 3. Connor's response with billy clubs and police dogs was captured by national media. Days later, Wyatt Walker—at the time, the SCLC executive director temporarily headquartered in Birmingham—recruited fair-skinned Addine "Deenie" Drew to pass as white and case the downtown library to prepare for a public library sit-in like those Walker had monitored in Petersburg, Virginia, three years earlier. Attired like a middle-class white in blue-and-white silk dress and hat, she entered the library unhindered, walked through reading rooms and stacks, and after noting all entrances and exits, left the building to call Walker at SCLC headquarters from a pay phone across the street. The experience was so traumatic, she later recalled, that she had to "look down at my feet and tell them to keep walking." On April 9, she and several other black students entered the library and read undisturbed at desks. Whites stared but said nothing. When librarians took no action, the students left quietly.

Disappointed that they had provoked no incident, Walker planned a second sit-in the next day. On the morning of April 10, he told twelve students in the Sixteenth Street Baptist Church basement to approach the library that afternoon at the same time but from different directions and asked Shelley Millender to speak for the group once they got inside. As they did, two white men approached Millender. "I was really afraid that day," he later recalled, hoping if violence occurred, the media would be there to photograph the incidents. He was unaware the two men were newspaper reporters Walker had tipped off. They followed him into the library and photographed him as he spoke to librarians at the circulation desk, where he asked to join the library. Birmingham had a library for Negroes, the librarian said; Millender should go there. Millender and the librarian then had "quite a little skirmish in terms of rhetoric," Millender later recalled, and when it was finished, he sat at a desk with several other students. Police came but, after several phone calls and much muffled conversation, refused to arrest them. Forty-five minutes later, the students left "voluntarily and without incident or disturbance," library director Fant Thornley later told his board, despite the fact they had to walk through a crowd of young whites. Although several whites in the library uttered remarks such as "It stinks in here" and "Why don't you go home?" the students left without incident.[4] "We were there to get arrested," Millender said; when that did not happen, the students saw no purpose in staying.

At a quickly assembled board meeting the next day, Thornley said he "did not feel that the students had any bona fide desire for library service" and that they "were merely part of the demonstrations taking place throughout the City." At the same time, however, he wanted board approval of his actions the previous day and guidance for what he perceived would be inevitable future sit-ins. "At some length" the board discussed alternatives, and although it rejected any use of the library "for sit-in demonstrations or for the agitation of racial incidents," it approved Thornley's actions and unanimously passed a resolution that "no persons be excluded from the use of the public library facilities" because of race. Their decision came days after local elections had turned Bull Connor and his allies out of office and brought white moderates in and the day before Martin Luther King and 132 other protesters were arrested by Connor (still in office) for violating an injunction preventing them from staging demonstrations—"a flagrant denial of our constitutional rights," King called it. The same day twenty-five young black people were arrested, three for sitting-in at a local restaurant and nine for frequenting the counter at a bakery. In subsequent weeks, millions of television viewers across the county watched visual images of Connor's minions using fire hoses and police dogs on black demonstrators. While incarcerated, King wrote his famous *Letter from the Birmingham Jail*. Then, on September 15, the nation was shocked when four adolescent black girls attending Sunday school died in the bombing of the Sixteenth Street Baptist Church. Subsequent riots led to the deaths of two more black youths.[5]

By "quietly desegregating" in the midst of a violent summer, the Birmingham Public Library actually functioned as a lone mediating site for facilitating racial reconciliation. Perhaps board members approved the effort to counter the national image of violence Connor had helped create for their city; perhaps they feared cameras capturing and the national news media reporting on similar violence in their library. At a July 18 board meeting, Thornley reported "a distinct increase in the number of Negroes using the [main] library facilities," particularly the formerly white branch closest to the black neighborhood. When Thornley testified at the Hendricks case hearing on December 3, he reported that the Birmingham Public Library was an integrated institution. Because the media—national and local—judged this civil action not "news," it largely ignored the library in its coverage.[6]

MONTGOMERY

In the wake of the Montgomery bus boycott of 1955 and 1956, local white politicians ramped up efforts to defend local Jim Crow practices. Many joined the local White Citizens' Council as the city braced against inevitable pressure to desegregate civic spaces. In 1959, for example, rather than obey a federal court order, Montgomery filled the municipal swimming pool with cement, closed its fourteen parks, and sold animals from the local zoo. But these actions did not prevent demonstrations. In February 1960, as students from the all-black Alabama State College marched on the capitol, nine split off to challenge the segregated snack bar in the Montgomery County Courthouse. When turned away by security officers, they proceeded to the public library. There librarians referred them to the "colored branch," and although they permitted the students to apply for borrower's cards, librarians refused them any other services.[7] For the time being, however, civil rights activists chose not to challenge the Montgomery Public Library's segregated services.

On May 21, 1961, three weeks after Harper Lee of Monroeville won a Pulitzer Prize for her novel *To Kill a Mockingbird* (which every generation of high school and college students since has been assigned as required reading), Freedom Riders supported by the Congress of Racial Equality, who were testing a recently passed interstate commerce law prohibiting segregation in transportation facilities, arrived at Montgomery's Greyhound bus terminal. By previous agreement, local police allowed a crowd of two hundred white segregationists shouting, "Git them niggers," to club, kick, and pummel exiting Riders, some of them into unconsciousness, including Freedom Rider and future congressman John Lewis. In the melee, John Seigenthaler, special assistant to U.S. attorney general Robert F. Kennedy, sent there to diffuse a potential riot, was struck in the head with a pipe. He fell to the ground, where he remained unattended and unconscious for hours. Police showed up an hour later to restore order. By then the damage had been done. Once again photos of the beaten Freedom Riders ran in newspapers, and film footage showed on television sets across the country.[8] The city remained tense for months.

In early 1962, Robert L. Cobb, a Booker T. Washington High School student, was working on a scrapbook for a Spanish class. Although he was not a member of the NAACP or the Montgomery Improvement Association (MIA)—a local civil rights organization that had spearheaded the bus boycott seven years earlier—he had received MIA training in nonviolent civil disobedience. On a pretext that neither the school library nor his local black branch library had a particular book about Mexico he wanted, on March 15 he and four other well-dressed friends met at Martin Luther King's Dexter Avenue Baptist Church and took a taxicab to the white library. One stood outside the modern new building, while Cobb and three others entered. "May I help you?" said a librarian in a loud voice as they entered the door, adding, "We do not serve Negroes in this library." Polite but undeterred, they quickly scattered. Some sat at tables; others used the card catalog. Cobb "went straight to the History Department," he later recalled. "I looked for a book on Mexico; I looked at Latin American books." Then he took some notes, returned the books, "went to the news room and started reading a magazine." After fifteen to twenty minutes, library director Farris J. Martin Jr. approached him and his friends and invited the five teenagers into his office for a "closed door meeting."

Although the students refused to give Martin their names, Cobb later recounted their interaction: "When we walked in he shook hands and he said, 'I admire what you are doing' . . . but he said according to the Commissioners, that this library . . . would not be integrated, that anything we said outside these closed doors, that he would deny."[9] But the kindness did not last long. The director told them "if we . . . try to integrate the library he would automatically have the [black] branch library closed." Martin then ordered Cobb and his friends out of the building and threatened to call the police. When the teenagers requested library cards instead, they were told to wait in the newspaper reading room. After fifteen minutes nothing happened, so they left. Three police officers arrived immediately thereafter.

"We have an excellent new Negro library in Montgomery that provides access to any book desired," Mayor Earl James told the *Montgomery Advertiser,* the city's major newspaper, when he heard of the incident. "In view of this fact, today's action can be deemed only outright provocative race agitation and harassment." The mayor made no mention of the fact that the black library held fourteen thousand volumes, the main library sixty-five thousand, and because Montgomery's blacks had no access to a card catalog listing volumes in the main library, they could not determine what was there to request. Nor did he note that in 1961 the Montgomery Public Library annual book budget was $7,554. Of this $3,454 went to the main library, $2,400 to the bookmobile (which served only whites), and $1,700 to the black branch.[10]

Cobb reported his experiences to his father, a longtime employee of the Virginia Carolina Chemical Company, who quickly contacted local black civil rights attorney Charles Conley, a 1955 graduate of New York University's School of Law. Called by one NYU law professor a "radical threat to the status quo," Conley had become well-known in the civil rights movement and served as legal advisor to both Martin Luther King Jr. and his immediate SCLC subordinate, Ralph Abernathy. (Conley later became Alabama's first elected black judge, and Abernathy became president of the SCLC and a leader in the civil rights movement.) Conley's law office on Bainbridge Street— informally known as the "Executive House" because it served as the business center for many of the battles against discrimination—was walking distance from King's church. Because of the violence directed at civil rights leaders, Conley's wife, Ellen, feared for his life and often acted as his chauffeur for late-night office hours. "I'd always insist on getting out of the car first," she said. "If a bullet was coming, it would get me. Chuck had important work to finish."[11]

Conley agreed to represent Cobb free of charge because neither he nor his father could afford legal representation. An informant quoted in FBI files said the city wished to settle out of court; the city attorney knew library segregation had no legal foundation and recognized that the judge reviewing the case was likely to rule against Montgomery. "City leaders offered to integrate their public library with a minimum of publicity, just as Mobile had done," the FBI informant noted, "but Cobb's lawyer insisted on a public trial" to "further the larger movement for equal access to public facilities." Nonetheless, the informant said, both sides worried that "if the library were integrated after a public court battle, the potential for interracial violence at the city library would be greatly increased."[12]

On April 27, 1962, in the midst of a gubernatorial campaign manifesting what one historian describes as "the politics of rage"—and in which candidate George Wallace, after losing the previous gubernatorial election, vowed "no son-of-a-bitch will ever out-nigger me again"—Cobb filed a federal class-action lawsuit against the Montgomery Public Library board, city commissioners, library director, and others. He asked the court to declare that any law, ordinance, or practice of segregation in the public library be deemed unconstitutional. The mayor called Cobb's action "race agitation and harassment." The library director continued to maintain that an "ordinance forbids integration of the library."[13]

Cobb was fortunate to be living in a jurisdiction where Frank M. Johnson Jr. served as federal district court judge. Johnson grew up in rural Alabama, oldest of seven children, son of a farmer and teacher. His father later became a probate judge and served as the only Republican in the state legislature. They lived in the remote hills of Winston County in northwestern Alabama. "Long a Republican stronghold, the county rejected slavery and tried to secede from the state after Alabama left the Union in 1861," the *New York Times* noted in Johnson's obituary. "Styling itself the 'Free State of Winston,' it tried to remain neutral in the Civil War, and eventually sent more men to fight for the Union than for the Confederacy."[14] Johnson graduated at the top of his University of Alabama law school class and entered law practice in 1943 after serving in the army, where he was wounded twice in battle and received a Bronze Star. He had a solid reputation as a criminal defense attorney, became involved in Republican politics, and served as a U.S. attorney for northern Alabama. As an Eisenhower appointee, he arrived on the bench in 1955, one year after the Supreme Court decided *Brown*. Three weeks later, Rosa Parks was arrested for refusing to give up her seat on a public bus. "Johnson's first major ruling was to join the majority on a three-judge panel that struck down the Montgomery bus-segregation law as unconstitutional," the *Times* reported. "He would use that reasoning again and again to create a broad mandate for racial justice in Alabama and across the South."

During his nearly forty years on the bench—first as a district judge, then as a federal appellate judge—Johnson ordered the desegregation of schools, parks, depots, airports, restaurants, restrooms, and other public places as well as the Alabama State Police. For his positions he received "mountains of hate mail and scores of threatening telephone calls," the *Times* reported. "Crosses were burned on his lawn twice. His mother's home was firebombed. . . . For nearly two decades, federal marshals protected the judge and his family." George Wallace, a law school classmate, once called him an "integratin', carpetbaggin', scalawaggin', baldfaced liar" trying to usurp the governor's executive powers. In 1967 Johnson's portrait appeared on the cover of *Time Magazine*, and in 1995 he was awarded the Presidential Medal of Freedom. Despite his reputation in the area of civil rights, however, "almost every lawyer who tried a case before him attested to his fairness." In 1993 Johnson received the American Bar Association's first Thurgood Marshall Award as the person "who most exemplifies Justice Marshall's spirit on behalf of protecting civil rights." The Montgomery federal courthouse is now named in his honor.[15]

In the suit, Cobb was seeking full integration of the city's public library system. At the same time, he argued for integration of the museum (where he had also been turned away) that was housed in the same building. In response, the defendants argued that they did not operate a segregated library or museum but that Cobb and his friends were turned away because they did not have library cards for the main library and were not museum members. Johnson disagreed. "It is apparent to this Court . . . that the main Montgomery Library . . . and the Montgomery Museum . . . are presently being operated upon a racially segregated basis."[16] Nor did Johnson accept the argument that the plaintiffs would have been permitted to use the main library and museum if only they had library cards or museum membership. "There was no evidence that any Negro had ever been permitted use of the museum," he noted, and the evidence "indicated that 'possibly' there was one member of the Negro race who held a library card which authorized the use of the main library facilities"—this in a city of 150,000 people, one-third of whom were black. Johnson did not note that shortly after Cobb filed his lawsuit, the museum board had amended its constitution to read, "Any *white* person of good moral character may become a member."[17] Apparently, the board wanted to make explicit what had previously only been implied.

After hearing testimony on both sides of the case, on August 7 Johnson issued an opinion: "All parties recognize the law is well settled," he noted, "that if the public authorities discriminate . . . in the operation of . . . the Montgomery Library . . . so as to exclude any race . . . then such action is in violation of the Constitution."[18] Johnson referred to "a case almost exactly like" this one decided in Danville, Virginia, in 1960.[19] In that case the court held that segregation in public libraries was unconstitutional. Thus, Johnson granted Cobb's motion for an injunction that prohibited all defendants from making or enforcing any distinction based upon race in the services or facilities of either the library or the museum.

The day after Johnson ruled, city commissioners met in secret with the museum and public library boards. One commissioner not only wanted to close the main library; he also wanted to close the "colored branch." The mayor said he was "besieged with calls urging him to close both the library and the museum."[20] Ultimately, however, officials settled on another "solution." That evening, "several men and women were seen lugging heavy chairs and tables down a flight of stairs and out of sight shortly after sunset."[21] Montgomery's WSFA-TV caught the activity on camera. Tables and chairs were also removed from the black branch. When reporters asked the library board chairman why workers were removing furniture, he commented, "Maybe they're going to wax them (the floors). We'll just have to wait and see."[22]

The next day, both libraries opened without furniture. In the black branch, "kids made a mockery of it," the librarian said, and brought folding chairs and typewriter tables from home. The press—black and white—also chuckled. The *Philadelphia Tribune* condemned "the idiocy of Montgomery white folk in their 'cut-off-the-nose-to-spite-the-face' move" but teased that a pleasant by-product of the order "might be improved posture for the new reader who no longer can slouch in his chair or hunch over his book while reading." "Standing Room Only," teased the *Montgomery Advertiser* in a story headline. It reported that "a large number of whites" used the library that day but no blacks. Several days later, the *Advertiser* noted, "Besides chairs and tables, magazines and periodicals have been removed from racks at the library." At 11:15 a.m. on Saturday, August 11, however, Cobb entered the main library and asked for a borrower's card; librarians issued him one immediately and without resistance.[23]

Letters to the *Advertiser* showed little consensus with library board actions. One writer thought the decision sound. "Just let whoever wants a book go there and get it and take it on home and read it." Ignore the "library situation," advised another. "A fire fanned will blaze; let alone, it will vanish away." Harold Anderson, a lifelong resident of Montgomery whose family had lived there for four generations, lamented that "Montgomerians have been made the laughing stock of newspaper readers from Mobile to Moscow" and assured the *Advertiser* that like "the great majority of our responsible citizens," he was not "pro-integrationist" but a "pro-tolerationalist" for "all public (not private) facilities to be for the use of all law-abiding citizens regardless of race, color, or creed. . . . Please put the library tables and chairs back." "A good library is a direct reflection of the cultural level of a community," said one woman. "Limit the use thereof in any way to any segment of the population and consider the image produced. Not such a pretty picture of Montgomery, Ala., in August, 1962, is it?"

"The latest childish maneuver in regard to the 'race problem,'" a Methodist pastor called it. Reopen the parks and restore "all necessary library equipment," argued another. "To take an opposite course will lead to a long night of ignorance and bigotry for our city." "I consider the removal of chairs and tables from the library a direct insult to the intellectual community of Montgomery and I find the suggestion of closing the library so absurd and irrational that it cannot be dealt with logically," wrote a white high school senior. "Alarming and a sad commentary on the state of civilization in the city of Montgomery," noted a lifelong white resident. "My heart grows cold with the thought that the public library, one of the most important educational assets of Montgomery, might be closed," wrote another woman. "Let us not be blind; keep the library open."

Others disagreed. "Hurrah!" cheered one, "for removing the tables and chairs and reading matter from the library. Now let's go further and close and lock the doors." Said another, "As saddening as the thought is to me, I, for one, would close the doors as tight as the parks and I would never open them again so long as the order to integrate was on the books." "This library move is the first subtle advance," wrote the executive secretary of the Montgomery Citizens' Council. "If we capitulate, the complete rape will occur by fall school time." "If we continue such tactics" to accommodate "those who would change our way of life," argued a white physician, "what is the ultimate plan in regard to public rest room facilities?" "The solution for the pseudo-intellectuals who wish to force the taxpayers of Montgomery to support integration against their will, is to form a *private* corporation to build and maintain a *private* library to be used by Negroes and whatever type of white person who wish to integrate," sniffed a Montgomery housewife. "Us pore [sic], ignorant, prejudiced un-Christian, white people can buy our own books, and loan them to other whites who feel as we do."[24]

"A little integration is like a little pregnancy," an *Advertiser* columnist argued. He recommended to "the gentlemen who propose the integration of our children" the appointment of a "Colored Culture Committee" to conduct "ladies of like hallucinations" through black sections of New York City and Washington, D.C. "If their hallucinations survive these two jolts of shock therapy, let the gentlemen wait huddled in a Washington back alley while the ladies kneel in a Washington church, fully realizing that if they find themselves stabbed, robbed, and raped, it will be of some comfort to them to know that it was only the outward manifestation of an inner desire, aroused by the constant teasing of 'modern woman's' seminudity." Another white male saw the library "incident" as "just another assault upon the white man's civilization."

The *Advertiser* described these letters as "spirited and shrewd" but lacking understanding of "the total picture—the library taken with the city buses, the bus terminals and restaurants, the railroad depot, the lunch counters and trains, and all the facilities at Dannelly Field." Although the "library's vertical necessity" was "unrealistic," it was "quaint enough for a tourist attraction. The condition won't endure indefinitely. When the controversy goes dormant and the Negroes lose interest in agitating the matter, the whites probably will have the library largely to themselves and they will get tired of standing up."[25]

At 9:00 a.m. on August 13—two days after Cobb had obtained his borrower's card—twelve black youths entered the main library to register for their cards. To get in, they had to walk past Ku Klux Klan members milling about on the sidewalks and in cars cruising by. Minutes later, however, uniformed police arrived to keep the peace. At the top of the library steps, director Martin stood next to a detective in front of the door and allowed the youths to enter one or two at a time, "locking the door behind them." Although Martin did eject a newspaper reporter and television cameraman who wanted to record what was going on inside, these new black patrons, the *Advertiser* later reported, were "generally ignored by white patrons." Among the twelve was Robert Cobb, who used his two-day-old borrower's card to check out a copy of *Much Ado about Nothing*. All week, black patrons came by the dozens to check out books. On September 24, FBI informants assessed that the danger of violence over the desegregation of the Montgomery Public Library system was over. Blacks were using the library without incident, and the matter was no longer discussed in the local media. Days later, the library board moved the furniture back into the libraries.[26]

Things were not the same at the Cleveland Avenue black branch, however, where whites employed by or stationed at Maxwell Air Force Base who used the branch were frequently harassed by other whites and where police stationed in front took down their license plate numbers. One officer asked a white patron why she had come to this branch; other white patrons were harassed by phone. Understandably, "they got scared and stopped coming," the branch librarian reported. Perhaps because of this activity, use of the branch by blacks was also down. The absence of chairs and tables made it "difficult for me to study," complained one patron before the furniture was restored in late September.[27]

ANNISTON

On September 15, 1963—the same day four black adolescent girls lost their lives to a bomb placed in the basement of Birmingham's Sixteenth Street Baptist Church—a white mob brutally attacked two black ministers with knives, clubs, and chains in front of the Anniston Public Library. Two years earlier the town had suffered national media attention when just outside the city limits whites stopped and burned a Greyhound bus carrying Freedom Riders.[28] To recover from this negative publicity, town officials organized a biracial Anniston Human Relations Council (AHRC) and looked to it for recommendations to ease racial tensions. For Anniston's blacks, desegregating the public library was high on the list. In June 1963, AHRC members contacted the library board. In July several black people entered the library to apply for borrower's cards—an incident the board chairman later described as "a serious attempt to integrate the main library." After receiving the applications, the board abdicated responsibility to decide about integrating the library by arguing that such matters "should be answered by elected officials of the city." In the absence of a decision, a black minister entered the library in August to consult the *Interpreter's Bible*. "I told him that our library was not integrated," the acting librarian later recounted, and "therefore I could not allow him to use the books in the reading room." Instead, she suggested an office outside the public area. "In other words," the minister responded, "I cannot sit down in here and use" the book? No, she said. The minister then left.

The incident drew an immediate reaction. Fearing negative publicity and possible violence, the city commission advised the library board to desegregate, and at an August 22 meeting the board resolved that as of September 15 "all persons will be served by the library." Heavily influencing the discussions leading to the decision was a desire "to avoid the horrible strife witnessed in Gadsden and Birmingham, the humiliating losing lawsuit that Montgomery experienced and the possible presence of federal troops." In the interim, the board worked on a plan with AHRC to quietly integrate the library. After directing staff not to discuss integration with the press and guaranteeing the council that reporters would not be present, the board assured the mayor, "We do not anticipate any publicity in the absence of any problems." On September 15, they had decided, Reverend R. B. McClain and Reverend Quintus Reynolds would enter the library at 3:30 p.m. and receive service.

By that time, however, white racists had learned of the plans and had assembled in cars and along sidewalks as McClain and Reynolds approached the library. "Where are you going?" shouted one as he grabbed McClain's arm and spun him around. When McClain jerked his arm away, his assailant punched him. Ten whites joined the brouhaha, and while one began striking Reynolds with a chain, others beat and kicked the two ministers, who quickly bolted for their car, a half-block away. As they scurried for cover, about sixty more white men joined the melee, pelting the ministers with rocks and bottles and, once the ministers were inside their car, banging and shaking it. At that moment the ministers heard a crack as the passenger-side window shattered. Although they later surmised it was a bullet that had passed between them, they bolted from the car and ran toward police headquarters. On the way a black driver picked them up and took them to the hospital, where Reynolds was treated for two superficial stab wounds and both were treated for bruises and abrasions. While they received treatment, Anniston police arrived at the library and dispersed the crowd.

Hours later, black youths retaliated by attacking a white man. One struck the man over the head with a bottle, while others kicked him when he fell. "We decided to kill the first white man we saw on 15th Street," one youth later explained. Shortly thereafter, three shotgun blasts shattered windows at a black restaurant. It was a sad conclusion to a day that moderate whites hoped would quietly integrate their public library—"as dark a Sunday as this community has ever known," the *Anniston Star,* the city's major newspaper, editorialized, expressing shock that two respected ministers were attacked by "white thugs who would be far more uncomfortable in a library than in a jail." City officials publicly apologized to McClain, and the mayor visited a recuperating Reynolds at his home. The mayor offered a $1,000 reward for information identifying mob members who had assaulted the ministers, the *Star* added $500 to the sum, and the library board added another $100. "We are not going to let a bunch of hoodlums run the library," the board chairman said. Although the chief of police promised to find the perpetrators, he wanted it known that "he did not approve of the integration of the public library."

On September 16, the board and AHRC desegregated the library. When McClain and a fellow minister arrived by car (Reynolds was still recuperating), board members met them and escorted them into the library. With twenty officers on site to prevent violence, the ministers applied for borrower's cards and checked out books. Some whites stared; others shuffled in and out of the building to report to a larger white crowd about a half-block away. Within weeks, forty-five members of Anniston's black community had borrower's cards as the library weathered a mildly tense adjustment period. On one occasion the white librarian worried about large numbers of black teenagers who "monopolized" space as they tested their newly won library freedom; on another a white teenager scribbled, "Fight Integration," on books and shelf labels.

In subsequent months, police arrested four white suspects in the beating of Reynolds and McClain and five black teenagers for subsequently beating a white man. Among the white suspects, two had prior arrests for race violence—one for assaulting entertainer Nat King Cole in Birmingham in 1956, the other for pistol-whipping two Anniston black women. A grand jury charged one from each group, but at their victims' requests officials ultimately dropped charges against them.[29]

INTEGRATION WITHOUT DEMONSTRATION

SELMA

"Here in Selma the Negroes are contented and happy," one white resident wrote in 1948. "At present the Negro is sitting on top of the world." Not so high, however, as to merit public library service. Although blacks occasionally were allowed to receive a book at the library's back door from a black maid, Selma lacked a "colored branch." Then, after *Brown* and the Montgomery bus boycott, Selma white leaders formed a Citizens' Council to resist any local attempts at desegregation. Assuming she shared their racial sympathies, Carnegie Library board members (many were also members of the Citizens' Council) appointed Patricia Blalock as director in 1963. But Blalock surprised them. In part worried about potential violence at her library, in part disgusted with Jim Crow practices, at her second board meeting she recommended integrated services. "They were all fine people," she later recalled about her board members, "but they were just very strong about this." She persisted, visited board members individually, and told each of the inevitability of integration. Montgomery and Birmingham had recently integrated their libraries, she noted, both after significant civil disturbances. "We need to get it done in a good way, and do it on our own."

In early May 1963, Blalock received "unusual telephone calls" that led her to believe local blacks were planning demonstrations. At a regularly scheduled board meeting, Blalock pressed her case. "I think we need very badly to get this library integrated," she argued, "and I don't believe I can open up Monday until we've made a real decision." Board members delivered their response just before the library opened Monday morning. Gathered with them that morning was the rest of the library staff. To avoid any disturbances, board members said, they would integrate, but "to help the community adjust to integration," they would follow Danville and Montgomery's examples by temporarily removing tables and chairs to minimize racial mixing. Only "as integration in the city progressed" would tables and chairs be returned. Because board members worried about "outsiders," they also insisted on printing new application cards requiring two local references. Finally, they decided to close the library the week of May 13–19—ostensibly for an "inventory," more likely to avoid potential sit-ins—and charged everyone at the library not to speak to the media or leaders in the black community. Although uncomfortable, Blalock agreed to their decision. The library opened Monday morning, May 20, vertically integrated but without incident. Initially few blacks came because most were unaware that Jim Crow had left the building. But six months later, by which time tables and chairs had reappeared, they were regular patrons.

Not without incident, however. One white woman "went into a tirade" when she saw blacks milling about. Better the library close than integrate, she groused. Another white tore up his library card and threw it on the floor. "What's going on here?" said a third, who began shouting racial epithets before being conducted out of the building by a policeman Blalock had called. When others told the mayor to reverse the library board's decision, Blalock offered to take the heat. "Just tell them I did it," she told the mayor. "They can blame me. Tell them you didn't have anything to do with it." Eventually the tension dissipated. "You know, that's not so bad," said a man Blalock called "one of the worst racists in the world" when he saw black people lined up for borrower's cards. When the man who had torn up his library card returned to check out a book two weeks later, Blalock presented him with the pieces she had taped together.[30]

6

GEORGIA

As part of the southern Massive Resistance, in 1956 the Georgia state legislature adopted a resolution to void the Supreme Court's *Brown* decision—ultimately an effort in futility—and incorporated an image of the Confederate flag on its state flag that it did not remove until 2001. But Georgia's experiences in resisting civil rights activists were generally not as violent as those in other Deep South states. Martin Luther King Jr.'s Southern Christian Leadership Conference was born there in 1957, and in 1960 he returned to Atlanta to serve as co-pastor at Ebenezer Baptist Church with his father. A year later, both the University of Georgia and the Atlanta public schools integrated.[1] Although most efforts to desegregate public libraries in Georgia were nonviolent, as in Alabama none occurred in a vacuum. In some cases, integration of Georgia public libraries took place without demonstration; in others, the public library was one of several public and private institutions demonstrators included in a scattergun approach aimed at all local Jim Crow institutions. In yet others, protesters made the public library the primary target. The desegregation of public libraries in Savannah, Albany, and Columbus illustrate all three.

INTEGRATION WITHOUT DEMONSTRATION

SAVANNAH

While Freedom Riders tested Jim Crow throughout the South in the summer of 1961, that July—without public announcement—Savannah desegregated its library system, including its central Bull Street Library in Savannah's Victorian district. "The mayor said city and library officials decided to follow a precedent set by a number of southern cities, including Charleston, Atlanta, Augusta, Jacksonville, Greenville, and Macon," the *Savannah Morning News* reported on July 21, 1961. At the time, the city was contesting a suit to force integration of the library by arguing that Savannah's black people had never been denied access. "The library's reference room has been used by Negroes for a number of years," the *News* noted.[2] Although integration witnessed no immediate increase in black use, "once access was granted," his biographers note, future U.S. Supreme Court Justice Clarence Thomas "became a Bull Street regular."[3]

DEMONSTRATIONS THAT FORCED INTEGRATION

With one exception, 1962 was a relatively quiet period for public library protests across the South. The Greensboro sit-ins and their aftermath in 1960 and the Freedom Rides and their aftermath in 1961 had led to "a challenging period of adaptation and adjustment," notes Raymond Arsenault, "a transitional era that saw the passing of old myths and the birth of new realities of race, region and democracy." And in 1962 the federal government struggled to keep up with events forced the previous year by movement activists, which had been accelerated by the growing power of the Congress of Racial Equality and the Student Nonviolent Coordinating Committee.[4]

THE ALBANY MOVEMENT

The exception to all this was Albany, Georgia, located in Dougherty County, three hours south of Atlanta and fifty miles north of the Florida border. Writing in 1903, W. E. B. Du Bois recalled that in 1860 the county represented "perhaps the richest slave kingdom the modern world ever knew. A hundred and fifty barons commanded the labor of nearly six thousand Negroes." By the early 1900s, however, most of the barons had abandoned their cotton fields and left the area. Former slaves who still lived there, he noted, were "not happy." Almost all were destitute. Many worked for pay, but their income barely covered family necessities. Few were able to save enough to own a home.[5] In 1960 Albany, the county seat, had a population of over fifty-five thousand; more than two-thirds were black, a figure reflecting the legacy of a plantation era when slaves far outnumbered white owners. Singer Ray Charles was born there in 1930, and a large, illuminated revolving statue of him playing his grand piano now serves as the centerpiece for the prominent Ray Charles Plaza. Although the black population greatly outnumbered the white, Albany's public library, built with Carnegie funds in 1906, was still not open to them when the Freedom Riders swept the South.

As in much of the South, the civil rights movement in Albany did not begin in the 1960s. For decades, various individuals and organizations met regularly to discuss how best to deal with the local Jim Crow laws and practices, but they accomplished very little. Then, in September 1961, several field officers from the newly organized Student Nonviolent Coordinating Committee arrived in the area to recruit blacks to register to vote. Students from the historically black Albany State College (now Albany State University) and the local black high school played a major role in these efforts. "We moved into young adulthood in the midst of evidence all around us that the world we lived in could be changed if we were ready to confront and demand it," Albany State student demonstrator Bernice Johnson Reagon later recalled. It had been seven years since the *Brown* decision, she noted, six years since the murder of Emmett Till and the Montgomery bus boycott, and four since federal troops forced the integration of Central High School in Little Rock, Arkansas. And when "the 1960 February 1 Greensboro sit-in led to an expanding student-led movement . . . it was clear" to her "that this was a movement with plenty of room for young people."[6] College administrators suspended many of the students for their participation in voter drives—another manifestation of the generational split among southern blacks—but in the process their suspensions freed them up to become even more involved. City clerks resisted the attempts at voter registration, both actively by requiring difficult literacy tests and passively by closing their offices when it suited them. SNCC next organized downtown picketing, then marches on city hall. As one participant recalls, "These efforts led to arrest—first small groups of school children then larger and larger groups of all ages."[7]

On September 22, 1961, the Interstate Commerce Commission (ICC) issued a ruling that desegregated all interstate bus transportation and facilities. Inspired both by the new ICC ruling and by the activism of Albany students, other members of the black community began to mobilize. "It was at this point that all of the then-known [local] Civil Rights organizations came together in a common cause, to put an end to segregation in Albany," noted local black physician William G. Anderson. "The organizational meeting took place late at night on November 17, 1961, at the home of Dr. Ed Hamilton, a local dentist." Instead of using the name of any of the participating preexisting organizations, the group decided to simply call itself the "Albany Movement." For the next two years the movement staged protests and boycotts aimed at bus stations, lunch counters, and every other segregated facility in town, including the public library.

On November 22, the day after the ICC ruling took effect, black Albany students staged a sit-down demonstration in the bus station to test the law. Five were arrested for sitting in the "Whites Only" section. Three days later, the Albany Movement held its first mass meeting in Mt. Zion Baptist Church (at this writing, the home of the Albany Civil Rights Institute); hundreds attended. When the five students were tried two days later, the black community marched in protest. Then, on December 10, nine Freedom Riders arrived. All were immediately arrested as they tried to use the white waiting room and restroom in Albany's train station.

Thereafter events escalated. On December 12, 267 college and high school students were arrested for protesting the arrests. On December 13, more than 200 were arrested for marching on city hall. Movement leaders convinced Martin Luther King Jr., Ralph Abernathy, and other well-known civil rights leaders to come from Atlanta to Albany to speak to the protesters. They arrived on December 15, planning to stay for a day or two. The next day, however, they led more than seven hundred protesters from Shiloh Baptist Church to city hall. On their third pass around the city square, they were met by police armed with billy clubs and loaded guns. Police chief Laurie Pritchett, dressed in a clean, freshly starched white uniform, picked up a bullhorn and announced, "You are all under arrest for unlawful marching without a permit." No one resisted. No violence ensued. When the local jail was filled to capacity, the remaining prisoners were loaded onto buses and transported to jails in nearby counties.[8]

King and Abernathy's presence in the movement as representatives of the SCLC, as well as SNCC's and the NAACP's subsequent involvement, brought to Albany the much-needed organization and attention that carried the movement forward. At its beginning, movement organizers had no clear plan and no specific immediate goals. As a result, their protests were aimed at nearly every aspect of segregation in Albany. For the next few years the Albany Movement followed the patterns of other southern communities—many individuals arrested, and several churches hosting mass meetings burned to the ground.

As part of this scattergun movement approach, on January 9, 1962, ten suspended Albany State students attempted to integrate the all-white Carnegie Library. Initially, four black men and one black woman entered the library, approached the assistant librarian, and asked for permission to check out books. They were told they needed to go to the black library branch. When they responded that the black branch did not have the books they wanted, library director Virginia Riley emerged from her office, apologized that the black branch did not have the materials they wanted, but said she could not assist them because "no colored people have gotten books here before." When she asked them to leave, they did. Later that afternoon, a second group of five black students made the same attempt. Some entered the reading room; others went into a reference room crowded with white students. Riley told them they could not use the library and suggested they lodge a protest with the library board of trustees. The black students again left peacefully.[9]

The next day eight more students entered the library, sat in the reading rooms, fingered through the card catalog, and drank from the library fountain. Again Riley refused to serve them; she advised them to direct their protest to the library board of trustees. She also noted that if the black branch did not have the materials they needed, the main library would send the materials there. After she asked them to leave the library three times, they left peacefully. Almost simultaneously, the board of directors received a telegram signed by fourteen black people who claimed they were being "denied the right of education" and asked to use the library in lieu thereof. At the time, Albany was in the process of building a new $25,000 black branch library.[10]

Although many in Albany could recall several times when black students from Albany State College and nine other black Albany schools were permitted to use the library without incident before 1960, the movement changed the dynamic. As a result, the library board became intransigent. City officials apparently believed that providing a new black branch—a small, redbrick, single-room building in the predominantly black part of town—would resolve the issue. Like most other black branches, however, its holdings were meager compared to the white library. As for interlibrary loan service, one user noted that it took "two or three days" for the black branch to get a requested book from the white library. "If you have a lesson assignment to get out, it can be an awful lot of trouble." Although the white main library had a bookmobile, it did not serve the black population. Director Riley, a twenty-year veteran at the white main library, told a black *Baltimore Afro-American* correspondent, "We have a segregated system here in Albany and we expect them to take out books through their own branch."[11]

But library protests remained part of the larger movement. As the year went on, protesters appeared to gain ground across a number of fronts. Newspapers around the country paid regular attention to the situation in Albany. In March a bus boycott stopped bus service. In July, King, Abernathy, and others returned for their trial. Charged with parading without a permit, disturbing the peace, and obstructing the sidewalk, they were sentenced to forty-five days in jail or a $178 fine. To make their point, they chose jail. Their cells were in the city hall basement. "This jail is by far the worst I've ever been in. It is a dingy, dirty hole with nothing suggestive of civilized society," King reported. "The cells are saturated with filth, and what mattresses there are for the bunks are as hard as solid rocks." King and Abernathy were placed in one cell, but "conscious of the fact that he had some political prisoners on hand who could make these conditions known around the nation," King noted in his autobiography, "the Chief [Pritchett] immediately ordered the entire cell block to be cleaned."

Three days later, Pritchett arranged for bail, and King was released. Although King objected to being released while seven hundred others remained in jail, Pritchett responded, "God knows, Reverend, I don't want you in my jail." King recalled with some chagrin: "We had witnessed persons being kicked off lunch counter stools during the sit-ins, ejected from churches during the kneel-ins, and thrown into jail during the Freedom Rides. But for the first time, we witnessed being kicked out of jail."[12] Once again, Pritchett defused a potentially tense situation while at the same time minimizing negative publicity. That summer, demonstrations continued as leaders of the movement pressed the city commission to meet with them and negotiate a peaceful end to the protests. City officials repeatedly refused. Mayor Asa D. Kelley was firmly opposed to change and adamantly refused to "deal with law violators."[13]

Protesting the Jim Crow public library remained on the movement's agenda. On July 17, five black youngsters entered the white library and asked for library cards. They were refused and were instead directed to the newly built but much smaller black branch. Twenty others then showed up, but the librarian's husband, who also worked there, stopped them at the door. As they left, one young woman promised him: "Don't worry. We'll be back."[14] A few weeks later, four black teenage boys entered the library and asked to borrow books. While a library worker called the police, the boys began browsing in the fiction room. When police arrived, they dragged the boys out the library door to the local jail, where they were charged with "failing to obey an officer." Director Riley commented, "It does present a sad picture and I am very much distressed," she told the *Afro-American*, "but I do think there are other sides to the picture." She did not identify "the other sides," however.

Frustrated by the continual protests, boycotts, and demonstrations, toward the end of July the city filed an action in federal court to permanently prohibit leadership of the Albany Movement from advocating additional demonstrations. By then, more than twelve hundred arrests had been made since the movement began in December 1961.[15] On July 21, federal judge J. Robert Elliott granted a temporary restraining order banning the movement from picketing, parades, and other demonstrations and scheduled a hearing for July 30 to determine if an injunction should be granted. Three days later, an appellate court reversed the temporary order and encouraged Judge Elliott to schedule a hearing. Many years later, the judge maintained that his ruling on the restraining order had been "misunderstood" and that it was based on a threat against the life of Martin Luther King Jr.: "That was the truth of it. I did it to prevent violence."

Elliott, a fifty-two-year-old Kennedy appointee, had served as a federal judge only a few months when the case was filed. He continued on the bench until 2000 and retired at the age of ninety as the nation's oldest federal district judge. He was born in Gainesville, Georgia, to a Methodist minister and his wife. As a Georgia state representative and House floor leader, he was known for his "fiery oratory," which, one Georgia journalist noted, "helped elect [Governor] Herman Talmadge—one of the South's staunchest segregationists." But when he took office as a federal judge, he swore to uphold the U.S. Constitution. "It was just a matter of doing the job, of doing what was the law," he later commented, "and, therefore my views changed. They had to, and they did."[16] Now, though, his job was to determine whether the Albany Movement should be ordered to cease its protest activities. Given his past, movement organizers understandably viewed him as a "seg."[17]

Hearings began on July 30 and ran for nine days. On August 1, President John F. Kennedy announced during a press conference that he believed the city of Albany should meet with the movement's leaders. The same day, the U.S. Justice Department filed an amicus curiae brief on the movement's behalf, clearly signaling that the federal government would be monitoring Albany events.[18] For the hearings, the movement had the assistance of several well-known civil rights attorneys. Foremost among them was Constance Baker Motley. She questioned Mayor Asa D. Kelley about the segregated Albany library. He maintained that black people did not violate any law if they merely entered the white library, but "if their presence there tends to create a disturbance and there is a probability, because of the presence, of violence or bodily harm, either to the person or to others, and the person refuses to leave when requested by an officer, in my judgment, there would be a violation of the ordinance."[19] Thus, having any black person in the white library created a disturbance for the white librarians and white patrons, so an officer could arrest that person if he or she was ordered to leave and refused. The Albany city attorney adopted the same approach as Kelley, arguing that black people were not being kept out of public facilities. He said that local segregation ordinances were not being enforced and that the arrests were made because of other violations, such as disturbing the peace or refusing to obey an officer.

The next day, the movement sent small groups to test the assertion—by now, both black and white protesters had arrived in Albany from other parts of the country[20]—at parks, swimming pools, a Holiday Inn dining room, and the public library. They were rebuffed at all of these places. Five blacks and one white youth entered the white library and browsed for ten minutes before the librarian asked them to leave. When they refused, Riley asked all white patrons there to leave, after which she locked the doors. The black youths remained until Chief Pritchett arrived and ordered them to leave. Moments later the library closed again—this time permanently. When white patrons arrived later in the day, they found a metal garbage can outside the front door with a handwritten sign: "Deposit books in can."[21]

At the same time, the city closed down its three public parks and the black branch library, all in the interest of "public safety," according to Chief Pritchett. One group consisting of both blacks and whites attempted to play tennis at the "black park," but an attendant there quickly shredded the net with a knife before closing the park entirely. Martin Luther King Jr., "plainly irked by the city's padlocking of the library and parks," the *Afro-American* reported, argued that "it was an act of bad faith on the part of city authorities. . . . Why did they take this step if they stand in court and deny that they are enforcing racial segregation laws?"[22] Unbeknown to King, movement protesters, and the media, at a closed council session the mayor and city leaders had relinquished the power to act to Chief Pritchett. "I can handle it, but I don't want any interference," he told them. He later told civil rights historian Fred Powledge: "When we closed the swimming pools down and we closed the library down, I'm the one who did it. And it was an awesome feeling."[23]

Keenly aware the city would continue to maintain its segregationist ways, the Albany Movement filed its own class-action lawsuit in July, seeking desegregation of the city schools, auditoriums, parks, playgrounds, libraries, swimming pools, theaters, and other public facilities. The city's position was twofold: first, that the four named plaintiffs—all movement leaders—had not themselves been denied any request for integrated service. Thus, the city argued, they could not adequately represent the class for which they sought an injunction in this class action.[24]

Second, the city argued no segregationist policies were currently in effect. Yet the hearing revealed the contrary. Mayor Kelley recalled the petition presented to the city commission in 1961 requesting integration of public facilities. "It was the feeling of the City Commission that the request embraced too much, based on the long-term customs of this area," he testified, "that it was not feasible at this time to consider complete desegregation." Protesters should seek redress in federal court, he had argued. And at the hearings he continued to maintain that "Albany is not yet ready for the use of public facilities involving personal contact" between races. Also presented at the hearings was a 1961 response by the city commission published in a local paper that advised the protesters, "If the Negro leaders of Albany have a sincere desire to help earn acceptance for their people, they can accomplish far more by encouraging the improvement of their moral and ethical standards."[25]

But pressure was building from both sides to find a resolution. Outside the media's purview, some of the city's white business leaders and leading white clergymen were urging an end to the stalemate, and most observers believed that pressure from these white community leaders was key to opening negotiations between the two sides. Weighing in on the side of the protesters was major league baseball's Jackie Robinson, the league's first African American player—now honored in the Baseball Hall of Fame—who had visited Albany after a series of black church bombings and had lent both moral and financial support to the movement. In "Home Plate," a column he wrote for the black weekly *New York Amsterdam News*, he argued it made "no difference" to black people "if someone hates us. It is only when he begins putting his foot on our neck, keeping us from getting a job, walking in a public park, taking a book out of a public library, voting at the polls, living in a neighborhood we can afford—it is only then that we will holler loud and long." Martin Luther King Jr., released in August after yet another Albany arrest, warned, "I am leaving but I will return if there has been no efforts [sic] to negotiate."[26]

Two national television programs—CBS's *Eyewitness* and NBC's *Meet the Press*—featured stories about the Albany events, including footage of young blacks who had been picked up and carted off to jail as they prayed and sang on the library steps.[27] The *Meet the Press* story drew quick objections from library personnel. Director Riley complained the protests were obviously "staged" by young blacks, some of them "disgruntled expelled Albany State College students." She pointed out that blacks in Albany had their own library. She added that the library board had repeatedly asked city commissioners to reopen the library but they refused to do so while the lawsuit was pending. "Your report said that Negro children could get books only by going to some basement," the library's board chairman chimed in. "The implication was that it was a horrible place, or perhaps under this very building in your picture. The actual situation is that the Negroes have had their own branch library for some 15 years. They have a fine, modern building . . . air-conditioned and furnished with new furniture, shelving and a creditable number of volumes." He did not mention that the main branch held over fifty thousand volumes, ten times that of the black branch, which also lacked a card catalog listing the main library's contents.[28]

For several months the Albany Movement ceased demonstrations and protests, creating an "uneasy peace" for Albany residents. On February 14, 1963, however, Judge Elliott issued his ruling. Because he had taken four and a half months to render a decision, some accused him of engaging in a "prolonged judicial filibuster." Their suspicions seemed justified when Elliott dismissed the case. He found that the four named plaintiffs did not represent the entire class and had not shown they had ever been refused service. The plaintiffs' attorneys immediately filed an appeal, but all recognized that months would pass before a decision was reached.[29]

By now, Albany officials may have seen the inevitable. The movement was attracting national attention. Forty clergymen from the North arrived in Albany and were arrested with others as they held a prayer meeting in front of city hall. The local paper described them as black and white, men and women, Protestants, Catholics, and Jews. Some fasted during their jail stay. In the 1962 state Democratic primary election, moderate gubernatorial candidate Carl E. Sanders defeated his opponent, an avowed segregationist, and with no Republican opponent in this single-party Jim Crow state, he inevitably became the governor, a signal to many to end tough segregationist laws and policies.[30] Shortly after the election, more than sixteen hundred white Albany citizens signed a petition asking that the public library be reopened.

For whatever reason, on March 7, 1963, by a six-to-one vote, Albany city commissioners voted to abolish all ordinances that required segregation in private businesses such as buses, taxicabs, and restaurants. In so doing, the commissioners stated that they were "'not interested in desegregating local facilities' but simply conforming to law 'as outlined in numerous U.S. Supreme Court decisions.'" A spokesman emphasized that local businessmen could continue to voluntarily practice segregation: "Now the decisions . . . rest solely with individual citizens, and not with the City of Albany. . . . In our view this will strengthen rather than weaken the existing social pattern of segregation." From afar, Martin Luther King Jr. called the action a "subtle and conniving move to perpetuate discrimination." The commission's action did not directly affect public facilities, given that segregation there was enforced not by ordinance but by local custom. Specific to the library, however, the commission recommended by a four-to-three vote that it reopen on a thirty-day trial basis. Movement leaders had threatened to resume protests if the library opened on a segregated basis, but the city commission opted to cede this decision to the seven-man library board.[31]

On March 11, seven months after the city had closed them—the longest period of time any southern public library had been closed in an effort to resist integration—the black and white branches of the Albany Carnegie Library opened on an integrated basis for a thirty-day trial period. But there were conditions. As in Danville, Virginia, and Montgomery, Alabama, the library practiced "vertical integration." All tables and chairs were removed, the reference and reading rooms were closed, and patrons were allowed only to enter, select their materials, and check them out. A plainclothes detective was on hand to guard against conflict. During the trial period no new library membership cards were issued, so blacks could use the formerly white library only if they had previously obtained cards for the black library.[32] Martin Luther King Jr. called vertical integration an important step to full integration. "The solid wall cracks," he wrote in an op-ed piece for the *New York Amsterdam News*. In addition to the four hundred books white library patrons hungry for reading materials checked out that first day, nine black Albanians also showed up to patronize the collections. "They've all been very nice, and very polite and very quiet," one library official noted. "A year ago, Negroes were being dragged away from the library and locked up," noted a local movement leader. Although he vowed to fight the library's stand-up integration policy, he acknowledged progress in its implementation.[33]

Vertical integration of the public library became, as in other states, the first step toward full integration of the public library. And in Albany the library became the first public facility to be truly integrated. But the editor of the white *Albany Herald* could not restrain himself. "These decisions are disappointing because we see them rendered timidly, without suitable public explanation and in direct reproach of a social principle to which the majority of Albanians had candidly pledged themselves," he wrote. "Neither colored nor white in Albany is ready for this." He argued that library integration was underhanded and wrongheaded, and he attacked both the city commission and the library board: "Somewhere along the line a deal has probably been made with the self-appointed chiefs of the Albany Movement not to assail the libraries with too many colored card holders—at least for the present. But for how long? Who can make a deal with professional racists?" "As for us," he concluded, "we will take the 'old' Albany." Later that month he offered to purchase the city swimming pool and operate it for whites only.[34]

Despite this movement victory, the "old" Albany was alive and well. The tentative integration of the public library seemed the only bright spot amid continued segregationist practices. "I don't know of anything for [the protesters] to be over-joyed about," Chief Pritchett said. Sitting in his newly renovated office flanked by the flags of the United States, the state of Georgia, and the old Confederacy, the chief glanced up from his glass-topped desk and grinned. "You look around and see if anything's integrated," he told a *New York Times* reporter, "and if it is, call me, will you?" He said nothing about the public library.[35]

Indeed, two days after the commission vote, four black teenage girls were arrested and charged with trespassing when they took seats at a drugstore lunch counter. That week, others were arrested as they attempted to use other restaurants and theaters. And in an ironic twist of events, two black teenagers were arrested when they attempted to sit in the white section of a county courtroom. They were dragged from the courtroom, found in contempt, and ordered to pay a fine of $25 each or serve ten days in jail, the maximum allowed under law. The judge, wishing he could have imposed a stiffer sentence, scolded them, "You people have created a situation that borders on chaos."[36]

Two months later, the U.S. Supreme Court rendered four major decisions in one day, all bearing on Albany's continued segregationist policies. In all four the Court struck down the convictions of civil rights demonstrators who had attempted to integrate restaurants, lunch counters, and public parks.[37] In reviewing the Albany Movement's appeal from the February dismissal of their case, the Fifth Circuit Court of Appeals signaled it, too, would not tolerate ongoing segregation, at least where the government played a role. That case, originally filed in July 1962, sought desegregation of not only publicly owned and privately owned but also publicly regulated facilities. No local ordinance or state law required segregation of public facilities—parks, swimming pools, the city auditorium, and the city library—but the local "custom" of segregation was enforced by local police; local ordinances had required segregation of privately owned transportation facilities, theaters, and taxicabs. In both cases government actors enforced segregation. The court first found that the trial judge should not have dismissed the plaintiffs' case for lack of standing. To the court it was clear that these four plaintiffs, leaders in the Albany Movement, had frequently petitioned the city to desegregate, that they had been arrested numerous times, and that "the plaintiffs . . . truly represent the Negro citizenship of the city of Albany."[38]

As to the merits of the complaint, the court clearly and in no uncertain terms found that segregation enforced by government action, whether by arrests for violation of local custom or by segregation ordinances, violated the Fourteenth Amendment. The court therefore issued an injunction against segregation in public facilities and on public buses, in bus and train terminals, in taxicabs and the-aters, and against arrests made for attempting to use the facilities on a nonsegre-gated basis.[39] That left alive private segregation efforts by restaurants and hotels. Almost exactly one year later, the Civil Rights Act of 1964 addressed segregation in those places of "public accommodation." Finally, in 1964, ten years after *Brown v. Board of Education*, Albany public schools were integrated.

The viciousness with which civil rights activists in other cities were treated was never a part of Albany's history. Both Albany's white mayor and white police chief deserve credit for adopting the same nonviolent approaches as the protest-ers. "It was early in the demonstrations that Chief Pritchett, noting that I had been arrested, directed the policeman to escort me to his office. I was impressed with his sincerity and sensitivity," local black doctor and civil rights activist W. G. Anderson recalled. "It was apparent that his strong religious background, his per-sonal moral convictions and his professionalism were being tested by the segre-gation rules he was required to enforce. . . . It is ironic that Chief Pritchett and I became the very best of friends after the movement was over." Like Martin Lu-ther King Jr., Pritchett had studied the life and methods of Mahatma Gandhi and knew that Gandhi had succeeded in fighting the British regime in India through nonviolent means. Unlike Birmingham's Bull Connor, Pritchett believed that a nonviolent response was most appropriate in dealing with civil disobedience. He "knew that to initiate violence on the part of his policemen could do nothing but aggravate the situation and call more press and worldwide attention to the Albany Movement," Anderson notes. "He directed all of his police staff and other police agencies from surrounding communities . . . that no violence would be tolerated."[40]

Not all civil rights historians are so gracious toward Pritchett, however. "Al-bany was the stone wall of segregation, the land of never," argues Fred Powledge. "Albany's police and city government mocked the law while claiming to obey and enforce it." Many credit Pritchett for what they consider the failure of the Albany Movement to achieve all of its goals. And it is true that Bull Connor's brutalism attracted far more national attention and outrage that prompted the federal gov-ernment to take action. But Powledge nonetheless judged the movement a "failed success" because young protesters "brought an end" to "the fear Negroes had of those who would be their masters." Police were "no longer invincible," he argued, governing officials "no longer completely in charge."[41] The Albany Public Library was one manifestation of this success.

While Albany Movement organizers used scattered protests and demonstrations against all forms of local segregation, including at the public library, protesters in Columbus were more focused. Without incident, at 5:35 p.m. on July 5, 1963, one male and six female black youths between the ages of thirteen and seventeen occupied two tables at the white W. C. Bradley Memorial Library. Other patrons said, and did, nothing. Shortly after six, however, seventeen-year-old Cleophas Tyson, president of the NAACP Youth Council's Columbus Chapter, and fifteen-year-old Gwendolyn Smyre left the room to call a wire news service in Atlanta. At 6:45 the remaining five girls left the library, but when they returned at 7:00 with Tyson and Smyre, two library employees blocked the door. Five minutes later the director intervened, and while he talked with the teenagers, other white patrons entering and exiting the building expressed their displeasure at having to walk around them. Tyson asked the librarian to recommend to the local board of education exercising authority over the library that it desegregate the facility. The librarian said he would not initiate a request, but he would recommend library integration if the group—"in a proper manner"—asked for a meeting with the board to discuss their request. The librarian then allowed the group to enter the library but closed it for all other patrons.[42]

Three days later, another group of twelve male and three female black teenagers entered the library at 2:00 p.m., took books from the shelves, sat at tables (several left to make phone calls), then approached the circulation desk one by one and surrounded it. When asked to step aside to allow white patrons to check out books—librarians argued they "stood as close to each other as they could to block the counter"—they refused. Librarians denied them library cards, refused to check out books they brought to the desk, and told them to use the Fourth Avenue Negro library. Instead, teenagers peppered the librarian with questions. Soon police arrived. "They just stood there," the police chief said later. "I read them the state law on unlawful assembly and told them to leave and there would be no case made against them. They just looked at me and said nothing." Because they refused to move, he reasoned, "they were creating a disturbance." Police arrested three (one girl had reportedly "bumped" several white patrons trying to access the circulation desk), and charged four with unlawful assembly in what the city's major newspaper, the *Columbus Ledger*, called a "read-in"—a direct action term that now joined *sit-in*, *kneel-in*, *vote-in*, *ride-in*, and *swim-in* in the lexicon of civil rights activists.

At the hearing, their lawyer argued, "There is no law whereby the people in the library have a right to refuse service because of a person's race." When he asked the assistant librarian why he had refused these teenagers cards, the librarian said it was because they were black. "Then the refusal to issue library cards to the Negroes . . . was based entirely on their race, on orders from your superiors?" "You'll have to interpret that yourself," the assistant librarian responded. After the hearing thirty black people filed silently from the courtroom to the police station to greet those arrested after they had posted bond.[43]

That the protesters did not speak for all in Columbus's black community became obvious the next day when the Adult Liaison Committee, a group of mostly black male clergy and their wives—and representing an older generation—who had been working with white officials, issued a statement: "We feel that real progress can only be accomplished in discouraging activities that tend to mislead and confuse the public in areas that have been finalized or those in the process of being finalized." The committee opposed desegregation demonstrations and called on "citizens who live here" to work for progress through "peaceful negotiations."[44]

The younger protesters ignored them, however, and established a pattern that became obvious the next day, when nineteen teenagers—including Cleophas Tyson—staged their third read-in in four days. Except for one white youth who elbowed a black male, the group left an hour later without incident when a black funeral director entered the library and asked the group to leave. But thirty-nine well-dressed teenagers—"some appearing to be no more than 10 or 12 years old," the Ledger reported—arrived in different-sized groups at 1:00 p.m. the following day, selected books, and sat down at reading tables. Some of the girls used the women's restroom, but none gathered around the circulation desk. An hour later, they all walked out of the library in single file.[45] At a read-in the following day—twenty-three demonstrators arrived around noon and left at 3:30—one white thirty-year-old and a black seventeen-year-old got into what police called a "pushing scuffle," in which the black youth struck the white man twice after being shoved, the second time with clenched fist. Six officers stationed at the library arrested both. The black seventeen-year-old was later fined $37.50 for disorderly conduct; the white thirty-year-old was acquitted.[46]

The incident, combined with several disturbances between white and black youths at city parks and swimming pools, heightened community fears. "The time has come when parents of both races have to have a heart-to-heart talk with their young sons and daughters," the Columbus Ledger editorialized, "to help them become aware of the dangers of rash actions in a tense situation, of the importance of conducting themselves in a dignified, calm manner." On July 20 the NAACP Youth Council and its adult leaders hammered out an agreement "to explore the possibility of ending segregation here without demonstrations." While they discussed the matter, the main library and the Fourth Street branch remained closed.[47]

Whether these read-ins forced the Muscogee County school board to consider integration of public libraries is uncertain. After a special committee of the board issued a series of recommendations on July 17, the full board voted on August 2 to desegregate Columbus public libraries and schools. To apply for a borrower's card at the library, however, black patrons first had to go to the Fourth Avenue branch, which forwarded the application to the main library with a certificate of good standing. The staff at the main library then investigated the applicant and, if he or she was judged "satisfactory," issued a borrower's card good at any Columbus public library. Although no black readers showed up in the main library in the two days following the decision, seven did apply for library cards on July 20.[48]

7

MISSISSIPPI

When the Supreme Court handed down the *Brown v. Board of Education* decision, Mississippi had the highest concentration of blacks of any state in the Union (42.3 percent), and it was there that black people endured the nation's harshest Jim Crow practices. Mississippi also led the nation in lynchings. Led by racist organizations and government agencies such as the White Citizens' Councils that arose throughout the state—Indianola established the first on July 28, 1954—and the Mississippi State Sovereignty Commission, established by the state legislature during the Montgomery bus boycott, "segs" in the state not only fought to perpetuate segregation; they also protected those who inflicted violence on civil rights activists. Sandwiched between the 1954 *Brown* decision and the 1964 murders of three civil rights workers in Neshoba County near Philadelphia, for example, were the assassinations of George Lee, an NAACP member and voting registration advocate, on May 7, 1955 (no arrests were made, and the coroner declared the death from "unknown causes"); Chicago teenager Emmett Till, who was visiting family in Money, on August 28, 1955; Herbert Lee, a voting rights advocate murdered by a state legislator who was never tried for the crime, on September 25, 1961; and Mississippi NAACP director Medgar Evers on June 11, 1963 (not until 1994 was White Citizens' Council member Byron De La Beckwith convicted for the murder).

After Congress passed a Civil Rights Act in 1957 to strengthen black voting rights—only 4 percent of Mississippi's eligible black voters were registered, the lowest in the country—the nation's black press began to pay more attention to injustices against Mississippi's black population. Editors had a lot to report. When NAACP state secretary Medgar Evers criticized the conviction of a black man as a "mockery of justice" in 1958, he was jailed and fined $100. Shortly thereafter, a white lawyer who had raped his children's black babysitter was given a suspended jail sentence, but a black man accused of raping a white woman in 1959 was lynched. Additionally, black parents who signed petitions protesting school segregation six years after *Brown* were frequently fired from their jobs.[1] Yet in some Mississippi towns—either because they observed events surrounding the Jackson Public Library in 1963 and recognized Jim Crow public libraries had a limited life span, or because they considered it a less objectionable compromise in a larger game of resistance that stopped at the schoolhouse door—white officials integrated their local public library without demonstrations by black youths.

Across the South, white public librarians were conflicted about how they should respond to desegregation activities. Mississippi librarians were no different. Many were for segregation, some openly, most quietly. Yet others were sympathetic toward the integration of public library services but worried that open confrontation would lose them their job and friends, as happened to Ruth Brown in Bartlesville, Oklahoma; subject them to harassment, as in the case of Juliette Morgan at the Montgomery Public Library; or damage progress toward what they saw as a greater good—providing any public library services to Mississippi blacks.

In early 1961, for example, African American Frankie Bethea wrote the Mississippi Library Commission to request assistance under the Library Services Act of 1956 to develop a public library for black people in McComb. Commission director Lura G. Currier sent back two letters, one an official refusal, the other an unofficial response written as "an individual librarian" that shows how conflicted and fearful were sympathetic public librarians working in the Jim Crow South. "If there is anything that I can do to help you . . . as a private citizen and as a professional librarian whose entire life is devoted to getting books for people to read, by all means let me hear from you. Any advice I can give you, any work I can help you do, any plans I can assist you with are yours for the asking," she wrote. "I am enclosing an envelope addressed to me at my home for your convenience in the event that I can be of any assistance to you."[2] It is telling that librarians such as Currier felt so alone; their professional organization, the American Library Association, seemed to offer them no assistance at all.

INTEGRATION WITHOUT DEMONSTRATION

GREENVILLE AND MERIDIAN

"Desegregation was often carried out under a blanket of non-publicity, by agreement with local newspapers," notes historian Gavin Wright.[3] That's what happened in Greenville, Mississippi, where city officials "quietly integrated" the public library in the spring of 1964. Even a year later "many Negro people don't know about it," and because others were shy about testing its reality, a librarian noted, "it will take some time before any degree of comfortable library use is reached."[4] Similarly, on July 2, 1964, the day the Civil Rights Act was signed, the Meridian Public Library integrated "without fanfare and without disturbance" and absorbed the black branch into the library system, the librarian later wrote. "It seems probable," library historian Karen J. Cook suggests, "that, due to the absence of fanfare, few if any in the African-American community were aware of the sudden change in the library's status."[5]

DEMONSTRATIONS THAT FORCED INTEGRATION

JACKSON

Among NAACP branches that organized and mobilized throughout the South following the early 1960 Greensboro lunch counter sit-ins was an NAACP Youth Council established at the historically black Tougaloo Southern Christian College (now Tougaloo College), four miles north of Jackson. And it was there, in early 1961, that a group of college students under the guidance of Medgar Evers planned Mississippi's first sit-in demonstration to take place at the main library of the Jackson Public Library system. If whites attacked, Evers admonished them, "do not retaliate. Follow the principles of nonviolence."[6]

Shortly after she opened the Jackson Public Library on the morning of March 27, 1961, acting director Frances French was asked by reporters from United Press International and the *New Orleans Times-Picayune* if she was aware a group of black students was coming to the library that day. She was not, she said, but after the reporters left, she immediately phoned the police. Contact us when students arrive, they responded.[7]

While she was talking to police, nine Tougaloo students—four women and five men, all of them NAACP members—were preparing for their first sit-in. NAACP mentors told all to dress well, sit quietly in the library, and avoid violence at all costs. The four women wore dresses, the men dress shirts and ties, some in sport coats. First they visited the black George Washington Carver branch and requested books they knew were not there. At about 11:00 a.m., they walked to the main library on State Street. "I went into the library and I stood up by the card catalogue and was thumbing through it," Ethel Sawyer, one of the students, later recalled: "After I didn't see the . . . title of the book I wanted, I went over and sat at one of the tables, and I had other textbooks with me that I read up until the time I was interrupted." (Once arrested, she noticed the book she had taken from the shelf was upside down in front of her, an embarrassing sign of her nervousness.) "One or two" of her colleagues "were at the reference table," she noted, while "others were thumbing through the card catalogue. Some were seated at the table."[8]

Youth Council chapter president Joseph Jackson Jr., however, approached the circulation desk. With his heart thumping and his body going numb, he later recalled, he stammered a message he had memorized. "Ma'am, I want to know if you have this philosophy book; I need it for a research project at Tougaloo College." "You know you don't belong here!" the library assistant yelled, adding, "You go back to your library!" "When I saw the expressions on those white people's faces," Jackson remembered, "it was a hush."[9]

Ten minutes passed. During that time, acting director French called the local police, then approached the students and asked, "May I help you?" We're doing research, they responded. "There's a colored library on Mill Street," she said. "You are welcome there."[10] She suggested they visit one of the two black branches, as was the "custom" in Jackson. Immediately thereafter, a "group of policemen and plain clothes men came in and told us to get up and get out of the library, that we were welcome to use the colored branch." But "nobody moved," Sawyer said. "About a minute later, I think, the same person [she later learned he was chief of police] . . . told us that we were under arrest."[11] Six officers placed all the students in squad cars and at the station charged them with breach of the peace because they had failed to leave the library when ordered. They were booked into the local jail, where each was held on $500 bond. Because the students had notified the press in advance, reporters were able to capture the events in photographs and stories. The same day, after hearing of the arrests, students at the black state-supported Jackson State College (now Jackson State University) staged a protest outside the campus library. Some attempted to march downtown but were stopped by the police. They disbanded only after the college president threatened them with dismissal.[12]

In jail that evening, the Tougaloo students worried. "Reflecting back on Emmett Till, the history of lynching connected with Mississippi," Joseph Jackson later recalled, "the later it got that night, I was in fear of my life." He began rehearsing what he would say if the Ku Klux Klan came for them. "Please, Mr. Klansman, don't hang me. I have a wife and two little children in Memphis, Tennessee, and if you release me this night, I promise you I will never, ever come back here to Jackson, Mississippi, and violate your Jim Crow laws." His colleagues teased him for his naïveté. "Well, that sounds very good," one responded, "but you know what the

Klansman would say? 'Nigger, you should have thought of that before you entered our segregated public library!'"[13]

A few days later, the Tougaloo students were taken to the courthouse to be tried, and again reporters were ready. Several blocks away, hundreds of whites were marching through city streets under a huge Confederate flag. At the courthouse, however, a hundred black supporters had gathered to cheer on the group who were now referred to as the "Tougaloo Nine." The possibility that the two groups would collide increased the potential for violence. Fourteen police officers, two with German shepherds, lined the courthouse stairs, turning away black observers after the small courtroom section reserved for them had filled. When the crowd began to applaud the nine students as they arrived for their trial, the chief of police yelled: "That's it! Move 'em out! Get 'em!" Police set upon the crowd with nightsticks and dogs, as once again reporters captured the event with cameras snapping. In the melee, Medgar Evers and several women and children were pistol-whipped (some required stitches for their injuries), two black ministers were bitten by the dogs, and Willis Randall Wren, age eighty-one, who only went to the courthouse "to hear the case," suffered a broken arm when police beat him "with a club."[14] For Jackson, Evers later argued, the brutality exercised on black people supporting the library protesters set broader desegregation activities in Mississippi "in motion." "This act on the part of the police officials brought on greater unity in the Negro community and projected the NAACP in a position of being the accepted spokesman for the Negro people."[15]

On the evening of March 29, fifteen hundred people attended an NAACP-sponsored mass meeting to protest police brutality. One headline quoted a telegram sent to Mississippi's governor by the NAACP, which had formed "Operation Mississippi"—an "all-out and continuous" drive to eliminate discrimination in the Magnolia State, NAACP secretary Roy Wilkins announced. "Call Off Dogs . . . Slavery Is Over," it read. SNCC officials sent a telegram of protest to the governor as well, calling the police response "barbarous and uncivilized." Another article compared the response to South African apartheid, except that the "Jackson gendarmes swung night sticks and loosed vicious dogs" instead of rifles and guns. Perhaps most significantly, however, the U.S. Justice Department launched an investigation into the police actions.[16]

White segregationists defaulted to their canned response. In his daily column, for example, a white *Jackson Clarion-Ledger* staff writer complained: "A quiet community has been invaded by rabble-rousers stirring up hate between the races, and following are the 'unbiased' publicity media feeding an integrated North the choicest morsels from the Mississippi carcass. . . . There will be little acceptance of the NAACP demands that white people fraternize with Negroes." And, he warned, "the Negro who has so long held the guiding and helping hand of the white may lose that hand as he climbs the back of his benefactor and teacher to shout into halls where he is not welcome."[17]

Amid the din, the Tougaloo Nine went to trial two days after their arrests. They were quickly found guilty of breach of the peace under a 1960 law that criminalized any refusal to disperse when ordered to by a law enforcement officer. Each student was fined $100. Their thirty-day sentence was suspended on the condition that they "participate in no further demonstrations." None of the students testified, but a police captain said they had been arrested because their presence at the library could have caused "trouble." But the Tougaloo Nine fueled long-dormant resentment that quickly spread to other institutions and public accommodations. On April 19, four members of Tougaloo's NAACP chapter took seats on a city bus in the section normally reserved for whites. They were promptly arrested and charged with breach of the peace. Operation Mississippi was under way and included not only protests and demonstrations but also legal challenges to Mississippi's segregation of public spaces, including its libraries, parks, zoos, golf courses, playgrounds, and auditoriums.

In the midst of all these activities, Freedom Riders arrived by bus in Jackson on May 24. Wary of drawing national media attention, white officials had learned from Birmingham and Montgomery not to expose Riders to mob violence. Instead, in the process of arresting them, police showed Riders courteous treatment before the public, but after they were convicted and many Riders refused bail, Mississippi judges sent them to the notorious Mississippi State Penitentiary, known as the "Parchman Prison Farm," where outside the public eye they were strip-searched, denied mail, and for the duration of their sentence housed in filthy conditions, poorly fed, and constantly harassed by prison guards. The "Farm" itself was run like a slave plantation and inspired a number of blues songs because of its horrible conditions.[18] Jackson remained tense that summer. On July 6, Martin Luther King Jr. spoke to a crowd of fifteen hundred Jacksonians, most of them black. "Segregation is dead," he declared. To combat local segregation practices, he shouted, "let the Negroes fill the jail houses of Mississippi!" The crowd roared.[19]

While demonstrations like these continued for the remainder of the year, NAACP attorneys prepared their suit for the library protesters. On January 12, 1962, they filed a class action lawsuit in the U.S. District Court. Representing the plaintiffs was Jack H. Young, a self-taught black civil rights attorney who lived in

Jackson with his wife, Aurelia, and their two children. He had been sworn into the Mississippi Bar in 1952 and immediately became the point person for the civil rights movement in Jackson. His home served as the central meeting place for activists who streamed into the state in the late 1950s and early 1960s. Aurelia Young noted in her diary: "Our house is no longer like Grand Central Station; it seems more like International Airport. It is the only place in Jackson where people are integrated."[20] As usual in civil rights cases filed during this time, the NAACP furnished attorneys to assist local attorneys in the field. In this case two attorneys assisted Young—Robert L. Carter and Thurgood Marshall. Carter served as an attorney for the NAACP Legal Defense and Education Fund Inc. and later as legal assistant to Marshall; in 1956 he became general counsel for the NAACP. Future Supreme Court justice Thurgood Marshall had already experienced library desegregation cases by serving on Jesse Turner's counsel team in Memphis.

The complaint named three plaintiffs, though it also requested that the action be certified as a class action on behalf of "others similarly situated" as the named plaintiffs. Eighty-one-year-old W. R. Wren, who had suffered a broken arm during the police attack, was one of the named plaintiffs, along with sixty-six-year-old Reverend L. A. Clark and fifty-six-year-old Mary A. Cox, both victims of beatings and dog bites. It is unclear why none of the arrested students were named as plaintiffs, given that attorney Carter had earlier written Young to include both children and adults among the plaintiffs. It is possible, however, that none of the students were willing to subject themselves to the rigors and dangers involved in filing the suit. It is also possible their status as students only temporarily living in the Jackson area weakened the case. The suit proceeded with the three older plaintiffs.

The defendants included Jackson's mayor, the chief of police, the director of the parks and recreation department, and the chairman and each member of the library board. The lawsuit challenged Mississippi segregation statutes and alleged violations under both the Fourteenth Amendment and civil rights statutes. The case itself involved numerous depositions and evidence, both oral and documentary, and revealed much about the state of segregation in Mississippi in the early 1960s. The state painted a picture of blacks and whites living in harmony, voluntarily living among "their own," and using their own facilities and schools, all by choice.

The plaintiffs instead focused on a Mississippi statute that explicitly prohibited integration. After the U.S. Supreme Court declared in *Brown* that separate schools were inherently unequal and mandated integration, the Mississippi legislature adopted Senate Concurrent Resolution No. 125. It stated that the Supreme

Court had acted unconstitutionally and impinged on state sovereignty and that in Mississippi the Court's school integration decisions were "unconstitutional, invalid and of no lawful effect." Following the resolution, the legislature passed Mississippi Code Section 4065.3, which mandated that the entire state executive branch, including local governments, police, county education superintendents, "and all other persons falling within the executive branch of said state and local government," give "full force and effect" to the resolution. Mississippi officials were "required to prohibit, by any lawful, peaceful and constitutional means," compliance with the Supreme Court's "integration decisions." Furthermore, they were ordered to prohibit "the causing of a mixing or integration of the white and Negro races in public schools, public parks, public waiting rooms, public places of amusement, recreation or assembly" in the state. Finally, Mississippi law section 2056(7) made it a crime for two or more persons to conspire "to overthrow or violate the segregation laws" of the state "through force, violence, threats, intimidation, or *otherwise*." Conviction could result in a fine of at least $25 or imprisonment for one to six months, or both.[21]

Depositions and live testimony at a March 12, 1962, hearing produced ample evidence of widespread discrimination in Jackson. In the weeks following the arrest of the Tougaloo Nine, other black youths were arrested for various transgressions. At the hearing, witnesses testified that blacks could not use the "white" playgrounds, auditoriums, and other public recreational facilities. James Hopkins, a Jackson State student arrested for sitting on a bench in the Livingston Park Zoo, testified that although blacks were permitted to use the zoo, they were not permitted to sit down. The city attorney responded: "Friction between the races does not arise as long as the two races are mixed on a stand-up basis, . . . like in the bank and elevators and the post office. . . . But in places where there is occasion for them to be seated next to each other, friction usually often does occur. Hasn't that been your experience?" Before Hopkins could respond, the attorney noted that "since your arrest and before this lawsuit was filed, all the benches have been taken out of Livingston Park"—another form of "vertical integration."

The library board chairman, also a local judge, testified that the students were trespassers in the library because they were not residents of Jackson. If they had been, "I would say legally they were entitled to come into the library . . . that is, if they don't come like these people came—planned it and notified the press before they came."[22] But other evidence demonstrated the students had not been asked about their residency—at least one was a Jackson resident—and also that they had been told to use the black library, which operated under the same residency rules.

The chairman was obviously grasping at straws. He also admitted that no written rules or regulations prohibited blacks from using the library.

Jackson's mayor testified that segregation was entirely voluntary. He claimed Jackson "never had any of the trouble they have had in other cities" because Jackson had built facilities for both races. He cited the black golf course, "built over the years at the *insistence* of some fine negro citizens who *kept coming* to me. . . . We knew it would cost a lot of money but we went right ahead and did it." Apparently he considered the cost of preventing Jackson's white citizens from having to share their golf course with black people worth the duplication of services. The mayor placed the blame for recent "trouble" on outside "agitators" who had stirred things up. Before their arrival, he said, the peaceful coexistence resulting from voluntary segregation "made this city the outstanding city, frankly in the whole world."[23]

The mayor's view of his outstanding city did not mesh with evidence presented by members of Jackson's black community. Reverend Clark testified that race separation was not voluntary. When asked if "your people prefer to live in neighborhoods with other members of your own race," he said no. Mary Cox testified that she had tried to purchase tickets to a *Porgy and Bess* production at the local white auditorium, but her money was returned, and she was not permitted to attend. And W. R. Wren described how police broke his arm with a club at the courthouse. "That is the reason," he said, "I haven't been going to your places."[24]

Chief of police W. D. Rayfield testified that Clark, Cox, and Wren were arrested not because of their race but because of "fear of public disturbance"; in other words, he feared that whites would be disturbed and this might create controversy. He claimed a breach of the peace occurs "where one or more people by their actions or intentions congregate or do something that their mere presence where they are resented would constitute a breach of the peace." He admitted the defendants were not doing anything to provoke a disturbance, "but the resentment and the reaction of . . . those white people in there, I could tell they had a hostile attitude toward those people." Thus, fearing that the whites might attack the blacks, Rayfield arrested the blacks. When the judge expressed skepticism, the chief continued, explaining that the blacks came into a city where residents "were getting along very nicely." Demonstrators intended "to cause something and to test out something," he said, so he decided to remove the source of trouble. And "they were the source, to my way of thinking. Why not remove the source? And your situation cleared up." He stood his ground, arguing that the black students' mere presence in the library constituted a crime because they had come "with an intention and purpose, giving it notoriety." The city's final argument was based on an affidavit from the executive secretary of the state board of health, who stated that in Mississippi black people had more communicable diseases than whites; they had more than twice as many cases of tuberculosis; and particularly troublesome, they had many more cases of venereal disease. If the races mixed in places like public libraries, he argued, the rate of both diseases among whites would increase.[25]

The case initially focused on what might seem a fine point of law—whether or not it should be tried by one judge or by a three-judge court. Lawyers for the plaintiffs argued strenuously for a three-judge court, required only when the constitutionality of state statutes was at issue. The city argued that if there was any discrimination, it was not because of the statutes, and thus a three-judge court was improper. The debate had an important subtext, however. Sidney C. Mize, the local federal district judge, was not a friend to black people. If a three-judge court were required, two of the judges would be drawn from the Fifth Circuit Court of Appeals, and the plaintiffs stood a better chance of reaching a friendlier audience. Judge Mize had established a well-deserved reputation as a segregationist during James Meredith's attempted integration of the University of Mississippi the previous year. Mize had repeatedly delayed decisions on Meredith's application to "Ole Miss," regularly ruled against Meredith's attorneys, and ultimately ruled in favor of the university, finding that it had not discriminated nor had it denied Meredith admission on the basis of race. At the prospect of facing the same judge, Jackson plaintiffs were not optimistic.

In their initial January 12, 1962, complaint, the plaintiffs requested a three-judge court, and by law they were given the expanded court, at least until that particular issue could be resolved. A month after the March 12 hearings, however, the judges issued their ruling: Judge Mize would hear the case. The panel agreed that the defendants had not relied on the three state statutes in denying blacks use of public facilities (the plaintiffs had already conceded this), but they also opined: "If any one or more of the statutes should be construed to permit or encourage the denial to plaintiffs . . . the use of public recreational facilities, including public libraries, on an integrated and equal basis solely on the grounds of race and color, then it would be so plainly unconstitutional as not to require a three-judge court."[26] By means of this statement the court's two appellate judges—including Judge Richard T. Rives, who had served on the appellate panel that reversed Mize's opinion in the Meredith case—clearly signaled to Mize that the court would not tolerate segregation in public facilities.

Judge Mize now owned the case, and on May 15, 1962, he rendered his opinion. He first asserted that the three plaintiffs were all older residents and had not themselves been denied the right to use any public facility in the city. Jackson was "a clean, progressive city" with 150,000 people, one-third of whom were Negroes, he said. It was known "for its low crime rate and lack of racial friction except for the period in 1961 when the self-styled Freedom Riders made their visits." As Jackson "rebuilt from the ashes of the Civil War," however, "its white citizens occupied one area, and its colored citizens chose to live together in another." Because this situation had evolved without friction, Mize said, "the city duplicated its parks, playgrounds, libraries and auditoriums in the white and colored areas." As a result, "members of each race have customarily used the recreational facilities located in close proximity to their homes. The defendants believe that the welfare of both races will best be served if this custom is continued. They do not claim the right to require or enforce separation of the races in any public facility."[27]

Although Mize cited "no evidence of the arrest . . . of any Negro . . . before the Freedom Riders aroused strained racial feelings in 1961," he acknowledged that "two colored girls [members of the Tougaloo Nine] had testified that they were arrested after they refused a police officer's order that they leave the North State Street [main] library." But these arrests were not because of segregation, he asserted; rather, it was because they were not there to use the library in good faith. They were not Jackson residents, and because they notified the press and television stations "of their intentions to break the customary racial use of the library facility," it was clearly a "deliberate attempt to create racial friction." They were, Mize said, "isolated publicity stunts."[28]

In his conclusion, Mize entered a declaratory judgment that the plaintiffs were "entitled to an adjudication of their personal claims of right to unsegregated use of public recreational facilities." But he also held that the defendants did not deny that right; they were simply encouraging voluntary separation of the races. Thus, he refused to enter an injunction against them. Instead, he noted that the "individual defendants . . . are all outstanding, high class gentlemen and in my opinion will not violate the terms of the declaratory judgment. . . . They know now what the law is . . . and I am definitely of the opinion that they will conform."[29] While refusing to blame local officials for any of the strict racial segregation of the past, Mize signaled that times had changed and he could no longer stop integration in public facilities, including the local public library. Shortly thereafter, the Jackson Public Library quietly desegregated.

Unlike other states in the South, Mississippi witnessed the birth of a number of bootleg libraries in 1964 that were established specifically for its black citizens. In order to more effectively coordinate civil rights activities—particularly voter registration drives—throughout Mississippi, in 1962 a coalition of civil rights groups formed the Council of Federated Organizations (COFO), with SNCC's Robert Moses serving as director and the NAACP's Aaron Henry serving as president. In the summer of 1964, Moses led COFO's "Freedom Summer Project," which brought hundreds of white volunteers, mainly from the North, to Mississippi to register black voters and train black activists for the civil rights battles sure to come. But some Mississippians reacted to Project activities and personnel with violence. That summer, for example, three civil rights workers—Mickey Schwerner, Andrew Goodman, and James Chaney—were murdered, scores of others were beaten and arrested, and churches were burned to the ground. As a result, the Freedom Summer Project helped focus America's attention on the plight of black Americans in Mississippi and is credited with leading to the 1965 Voting Rights Act.

Besides organizing college students, teachers, lawyers, clergy, and local citizens to register voters, COFO also ran summer "Freedom Schools" and in the "Community Centers" that housed them established nearly fifty "Freedom Libraries," staffed largely by volunteers and stocked largely with donated books and periodicals. For many Mississippi blacks, these libraries constituted their first contact with library books. One student later recalled, "I read Richard Wright and W. E. B. Du Bois" for the first time. "From all that, I knew that I could be somebody and that I was somebody and that I could excel."[30] In most cases (and unbeknown to their managers), these libraries replicated the model for black public library services established nearly a half-century earlier by Louisville librarian Thomas Fountain Blue—hosting story hours, poetry readings, and songfests; providing materials that fostered pride in black history and culture; and opening their spaces for community meetings and organizations. Rita and Mickey Schwerner opened a Freedom Library in Meridian in January 1964; local black teenager James Chaney helped build the shelves, and within months, through donations, the collection numbered ten thousand volumes. While these Freedom Libraries provided valued new services to many black communities, their existence also exacerbated feelings about Mississippi's segregated public library services. "Once local residents had been exposed to the information and entertainment value of books," argue library historians Donald G. Davis Jr. and Cheryl Knott Malone, "they might be moved to sit in at the local public library."[31]

In the summer of 1963, Sandra Adickes, a white New York high school English teacher, volunteered to teach in a Virginia Freedom School. The following summer she volunteered for a Freedom School in Mississippi, this time with her friend Norma Becker. Together the two recruited forty teachers. All packed their bags when their New York school term was over and headed into the steamy Mississippi summer. Adickes taught classes in Priest Creek Baptist Church in Palmers Crossing, then in a Hattiesburg suburb. She relied on textbooks contributed by northern publishing company workers.

Years later, when asked what they most remembered about the Freedom School summer, Adickes's students replied, "The books." For them, access to books was a new experience, one that changed their lives.[32] "It was after the passage of the Civil Rights Act," one student later recalled. "We discussed in class what it meant to us as kids; it meant we could legally do things that we couldn't previously do. . . . We talked about the fact that we'd been reading all summer." Thus, it was natural that they would question why they were not permitted access to books in most branches of the Hattiesburg Public Library system. Fully aware of the significance of the new Civil Rights Act, six of Adickes's students decided to celebrate their "freedom summer" by testing it at the white main library. They invited Adickes to join them, and she agreed.[33]

Students could have gone to the black branch that, like many other communities in the South, had opened the previous year to accommodate public library service needs of black communities within Jim Crow society. But the Hattiesburg Public Library board's decision to open the separate branch angered director Carlton Rochell. "I am disgusted, frustrated, cynical and unwilling to back petal [sic] or compromise myself any further," he wrote Mississippi Library Commission director Lura Currier. "After recent, rather heated, conversations with the Board, Mayor, Commissioner, and supervisors, I cannot bring myself to see one brick laid which might involve me in the original sin of Mississippi." Rather than follow the dictates of city officials, Rochell resigned in 1963. Currier's response reflects the dilemma in which Mississippi librarians who favored library services to blacks found themselves. She wrote: "I have decided to stay with this until they run me out. . . . Your comment about Mississippi's original sin . . . was interesting. . . . If I had taken that attitude . . . I would never have given any Negro a book at all. . . . So many, many times I have asked myself: am I making things worse by setting up a branch library for Negroes? Then, I come back to the statement made by the

Negroes themselves in Starkville. 'It is not a question of whether we have books with the white people; it is a question in this day of whether we have books at all. Perhaps some other day we will have the other question to answer but for now this is the best we can do and we are glad to have this.'"[34]

Hattiesburg Freedom School students were not satisfied with the new black library, a one-room facility largely containing "rejects from the public library downtown that should have gone into the garbage," as one student described them, "like our [segregated public school] textbooks at the time." On Friday, August 14, 1964—ten days after the bodies of fellow Freedom Summer workers James Chaney, Mickey Schwerner, and Andrew Goodman were found on a farm near Philadelphia, Mississippi—Adickes and six of her black students, five girls and one boy, all wearing blue denim SNCC "Freedom" shirts, took a bus from Palmers Crossing to the main white library, thirty minutes away. "Our class was a very aggressive freedom class," Jimella Stokes-Jackson later remembered. "It was the time and our spirits were that we're going to change this so our children won't have to."[35] "Going to the library was important, not frivolous," student Diane Moncure Sutton later recalled. "Walking down Main Street [to integrate it] was a good feeling."[36]

They entered the library, approached the circulation desk, and asked for library cards. The librarian refused, citing "custom" and noting that the library board had "decreed that the library not be integrated." Students then sat down at a desk, read newspapers, and waited. Stokes-Jackson heard the librarian call someone on the telephone. "I need some help down here," she said. Shortly thereafter, the Hattiesburg police chief arrived, closed down the library, and forced Adickes and her students to leave. "We'd known all of our lives that we could not go to the [main] library," Stokes-Jackson said, "but we hadn't been confronted with 'You are not good enough to use this library.'" The experience galvanized the group. "I was hurt, but not beaten," Stokes-Jackson recalled. "If anything it was a rush."[37] The police chief had acted on direct orders from the mayor, who explained to the *Hattiesburg American* later in the day why the library had closed: "We decided to have a pre-school inventory of all our books. We hope to be finished with it by Monday and open again then." He said nothing about the fact that the library had closed for an inventory earlier that summer.[38]

By this time it was noon; the group decided to eat lunch. They walked to Woolworth, but because it was crowded, they continued to the Kress store. There they found two empty booths and sat down. When the waitress came, she refused to take Adickes's order. When Adickes asked why, the waitress replied, "Well, I am not going to." Adickes asked, "Why not?" "Because," the waitress answered, "my manager told me not to serve you." "Do you realize that this is a violation of the Civil Rights Act?" Adickes responded. "Yes, but my manager told me not to serve you," the waitress said. "We have to serve the coloreds, but we are not going to serve the whites that come in with them."[39] At that point, Adickes and her students left. Immediately outside the store, Adickes was arrested and charged with (and later convicted of) vagrancy, despite her assertions that she had $95 on her person and that she was regularly employed as a New York teacher at an annual salary of $7,200.[40]

In the meantime, other Freedom Summer students drew inspiration and energy from this initial volley at the public library. Although the police had closed the library on Friday, August 14, it reopened the following Monday. That day William D. Jones, a black New York schoolteacher, along with some of his Freedom School black students, decided to enter the white main library. Jones was born and reared in Birmingham, Alabama, where he lived until the early 1960s. He was an air force veteran of both World War II and the Korean War. Not until his mid-thirties did he move to New York and begin work as a public school teacher. In 1964 he volunteered to serve as a Freedom School teacher in Mississippi. In classes that summer, he and his students regularly discussed Hattiesburg's segregated facilities, so after Sandra Adickes and her students had been removed from the library, Jones and some of his students decided to try again. Ben Achtenberg, a white Harvard University senior, and two other white Freedom School volunteers agreed to precede them and serve as observers.

About 1:00 p.m., Jones and six students, ages nine to seventeen, walked into the public library and waited patiently at the front desk while the librarian spoke on the phone. When she hung up, the students, one by one, politely asked her for "a specific book pertaining to Negroes." The librarian told the first few students that the book they requested was unavailable but that she might be able to obtain a copy and send it over to the black branch library for the students to claim there. She explained they could retrieve the book only at that branch: "Yes, that is your branch." Several students remained standing at the front desk. Others left the desk, selected a book or magazine from the stacks, then sat down and began to read quietly. When the librarian noticed the seated students, she left the desk to confront seventeen-year-old Jerry Wilson. "Do you intend to stay in here and read?" Wilson answered yes. "All right, I'll just have to call the city [police]," she responded. She returned to the desk, made a phone call, and was soon joined by other white women and a white man, all probably library employees.

At one table sat nine-year-old Cynthia McCarty, studiously reading a gardening magazine. "She sat majestically with her chin barely able to reach the edge of the table where she had laid the open magazine," Jones later testified. "I observed her in admiration, compassion, pity and amusement for a few minutes, then I asked her and the next older girl, Dorothy Jean, to go with me to the children's section on the opposite side of the room. We went over and I directed them to a shelf containing story books for children." Each selected a book and started to walk with it toward the librarian's desk.[41] At that moment police chief Hugh W. Herring and another officer confronted the two young girls. "Are those library books?" "Yes," the girls offered. In a harsh voice he ordered, "Put them back." The girls immediately returned the books and once again sat down at a table and resumed reading magazines.

One officer began questioning the white observers, while the other asked the black students for their names, addresses, and ages. Chief Herring then began to harass Jones. "Are they [the students] your children? . . . I mean are you their father? . . . If you aren't their father, what are you doing with them? . . . Do you have their parents' permission to have them with you?" Two more officers arrived. Chief Herring pressed Jones for his name and questioned him about his employment. "I told him that I was employed as a teacher in the public schools of Bellmore, New York, and showed him a faculty member card that certified it," Jones said. "He copied information from the card, then inquired further as to the particular school, its name, address, the subject and grade that I teach. I answered the question fully, having the cumbersome task of spelling out almost every word. Upon hearing that I taught French to fourth grade pupils, he laughed incredulously and derisively. Then he asked me what I was doing in Hattiesburg, and I told him that I was a Freedom School teacher. He asked me whether I was paid for this and I replied no."

Chief Herring then announced he would arrest Jones for vagrancy. Jones couldn't help himself. He laughed at the notion, having already told the chief that he had been fully employed the past year and had a contract for the coming year, which he offered to show the chief. "It's funny to you, isn't it?" Herring asked. "All of you people are funny to me," Jones answered. "You make me laugh." When asked how he could possibly be charged with vagrancy, Herring explained, "You aren't employed around here, you are just hanging around without means of support." Jones was promptly arrested, along with the three white observers, all charged with vagrancy. The children were ordered to return home.[42] Again the library closed, and the mayor said it would remain closed until "we have had time to study the situation. We don't know when it will be reopened."[43]

Those arrested on August 17 needed lawyers willing to represent them and judges willing to listen. In Mississippi before 1964, both were hard to find. Fortunately, along with the many teachers who came south to teach in Freedom Schools in the 1960s, so did other professionals interested in racial equality. This included committed lawyers, most of whom, like the teachers, were volunteers working without pay. Among them was Eleanor Jackson Piel, a 1943 graduate of the University of California, Berkeley, School of Law. Piel's mother was a California concert pianist who had married a Jewish man. At an early age, Piel observed the anti-Semitism that her father regularly experienced. She also experienced sexism in the legal field. She was the only woman in her law school class, and no law firm would hire her after graduation. Not surprisingly, she spent her career representing those who weathered other forms of discrimination, first labor organizers and later political radicals.

After civil rights workers Mickey Schwerner, Andrew Goodman, and James Chaney were murdered, Piel—who knew the mother of one of the young men—joined other lawyers in the National Lawyers Guild, an organization working for political and social change, and headed to the South. There she met Sandra Adickes,[44] agreed to represent her, and, as a result of that friendship, also learned that William D. Jones and the three white observers had been arrested at the library on August 17. She agreed to represent them as well and to challenge their vagrancy arrests.

The first step for most of the civil rights cases was to remove them from Mississippi state courts, whose judges were not inclined to view such cases favorably. Federal judges, appointed for life, were deemed not as susceptible to local pressures as judges whose reelection depended upon winning the majority of a popular vote. Yet, as demonstrated repeatedly during the 1960s, some federal judges who lived and worked in local communities and shared local sentiments were not inclined to challenge local Jim Crow practices, even those declared illegal by federal courts and federal law. Generally, it was luck of the draw. For Adickes, Jones, and the others, their first draw was unlucky. Because of the vagrancy charges, their cases had to begin in state court, so their first step was to remove the cases to federal court. Their petition for removal landed on the desk of federal district judge William Harold Cox.

Cox had been appointed to the federal bench by President John F. Kennedy after intense campaigning on his behalf by Senate Judiciary Committee chairman Senator James Eastland of Mississippi. He and Cox had been roommates at the University of Mississippi. Eastland reportedly told U.S. attorney general Robert

Kennedy, "Tell your brother that if he will give me Harold Cox, I will give him the nigger," referring to Thurgood Marshall, whom Kennedy was hoping to place on the Second Circuit Court of Appeals. Cox did not disappoint his patron. He strenuously fought integration efforts, and though many of his decisions were reversed on appeal, his decisions generally delayed justice for many months. In one voter registration trial held in March 1964, Cox referred to a group of black witnesses as "a bunch of chimpanzees." Cox also oversaw the trial of those accused of murdering the three civil rights workers in 1964. That trial took place the following year, after an extensive federal investigation. Cox immediately dismissed the charges against seventeen of the nineteen indicted. After the U.S. Supreme Court reversed him and reinstated the indictments, the cases finally went to trial in 1967. A jury convicted seven of the defendants. Cox then sentenced the defendants to terms of three to ten years for the murders. "They killed one nigger, one Jew, and a white man. I gave them all what I thought they deserved," he remarked.[45]

This was the judge positioned to determine if the Hattiesburg Public Library vagrancy cases would remain in federal court or be remanded to state court. For the defendants, staying in federal court was their best hope of obtaining justice, albeit on appeal. But for the federal court to have jurisdiction, the defendants had to demonstrate a "federal" interest; vagrancy charges stem from state, not federal, law. But the defendants had a federal component to their petition that formed the foundation of their plea. They asserted that the conduct of the government officials violated their rights as guaranteed by both the U.S. Constitution and the newly enacted Civil Rights Act of 1964. Cox was not convinced. When the state moved to remand the cases back to state court, he granted the motion. The defendants were probably not surprised. That year in open court Cox had commented on the new Civil Rights Act, "I don't know anybody down here who don't oppose it."[46] The defendants immediately appealed to the Fifth Circuit Court of Appeals, an area then encompassing Alabama, Florida, Georgia, Louisiana, Mississippi, and Texas. This time they got lucky. The case was assigned to Judge Elbert Parr Tuttle.

Tuttle was born in California, raised in Hawaii, and attended a racially diverse school in Honolulu.[47] He also attended New York's Cornell University for both his undergraduate and legal education. As a young man, he joined the army, served in World War I, then enlisted again in World War II at the age of forty-five. He served in the military for five years and was wounded in hand-to-hand combat on Okinawa. As a Georgia National Guard captain, he was once sent to Elberton, Georgia, to help face down an angry lynch mob determined to dynamite the town jail where two black detainees were being held, ostensibly for raping a white woman.

He first lobbed tear gas into the crowd, then turned fire hoses on them, but the mob refused to disperse. Finally, he and other Guardsmen managed to disguise the two defendants and spirit them out of the jail for safekeeping during their trial. Tuttle was badly shaken by the experience.[48]

It was in Georgia that Tuttle met his wife, and after law school graduation in 1923, they agreed to locate his law practice in Atlanta. At the time Georgia had only one political party, the all-white Democratic Party, and even though Tuttle had political ambitions, he refused to join. Instead, he attempted to build a viable Republican Party presence in Atlanta, and President Dwight Eisenhower rewarded his efforts in 1954 when he named Tuttle to the Fifth Circuit Court of Appeals. In 1961, just in time for some of the most significant civil rights decisions of the time, Judge Tuttle became the Fifth Circuit's chief judge.

Among other 1960s cases, Judge Tuttle ruled that Martin Luther King Jr. and others were free to conduct civil rights demonstrations in Albany, Georgia, during which time the Albany Public Library desegregated; the all-white University of Mississippi had to admit African American James Meredith; recently elected African American Julian Bond had to be permitted to be seated in the Georgia House of Representatives after white legislators twice refused to seat him; and the all-white University of Georgia had to immediately admit two black students, including Charlayne Hunter (who later become PBS and NPR correspondent Charlayne Hunter-Gault). Tuttle "led the way in disarming the southern states of the most effective weapon in their arsenal—delay," his biographer argues. Although angry segregationists called him a "judicial activist," he often said that the civil rights cases were "the easiest cases I ever decided. The constitutional rights were so compelling, and the wrongs were so enormous." In 1981 Judge Tuttle received the Presidential Medal of Freedom.[49]

Although it took more than three years—the arrests in 1964, removal to federal court shortly thereafter, remand back to state court in 1965, and then the long process of appeal—in late 1967 the four vagrancy defendants were finally before a judge who bore no hostility to civil rights cases. Perhaps Mississippi anticipated an inevitable decision; perhaps enough time had passed that it was clear the tide was turning. In any event, the state did not even bother to file a brief in the appellate case. On February 5, 1968, Judge Tuttle reversed Judge Cox's decision to remand the cases to state court. He held in no uncertain terms that William D. Jones and his students had a right to "enjoy equal public accommodations in the Hattiesburg City Library and a restaurant in the nationally known Kress store." He referred to the "utter baselessness of any conceivable contention that the vagrancy statutes prohibited any conduct in which these persons were engaged." And not only did he decide that the cases should not have been sent back to state court; he also ruled that the charges of vagrancy against the four should be dismissed. The case was over.[50]

But for the Hattiesburg Public Library, the case was moot. When the library reopened in November 1964, it claimed an integrated system but required Hattiesburg blacks who wanted to use the "white" library to "make a special application subject to review by the entire administrative board." Ben Achtenberg, one of the observers arrested, reported: "As far as I am able to determine, no Negro has so far succeeded in obtaining a library card."[51] Months later, however, the library board reversed its practice, gave Hattiesburg blacks library cards, and integrated the library.

INDIANOLA

In 1954 Indianola became the first southern town to establish a White Citizens' Council, and at the time of the passage of the Civil Rights Act in July 1964, its public library still did not permit access to its black citizens. In September, however, eleven black teenagers (including three from the Council of Federated Organizations) approached the white public library. Six blocks from the library they were met by thirty police officers—"most of them deputized," Baltimore's black weekly *Afro-American* noted—who then walked next to them. Not surprisingly, by the time they arrived, the library had locked its doors; it remained closed for several days. But two weeks later black seventeen-year-old Alma Jean Dillard approached the library, now open, with her black friend, twenty-four-year-old Sam Randle, to ask for a book on the Mississippi state constitution. The librarian instead gave her application forms, told her to fill them out, and asked her to return on October 1, by which time, she said, the library board would have made a decision about whether to approve their applications. It "may prove to be the first crack in the solid wall of segregation in this small Delta city," opined the *Afro-American*.[52]

But Alma Dillard did not get a library card on October 1. Instead of integrating the white library, city officials decided to open a "Negro" library. "They cleaned out a former grocery store in the Negro section of town, put in three tables, one large dictionary and four hundred books, and opened it for the Negro community," a COFO official later recalled. "The [black] community did not accept it. The dedication ceremony was met by one hundred pickets demanding that the facility be closed." A subsequent boycott "has been one hundred percent effective ever since the building opened." To encourage use of the black library, city officials gave teachers in the black school cards that advertised the facility. "Many cards were torn up by the children; parents went to the school to protest." Instead, Indianola's black youths continued to picket the white library and ask for library cards there. Clubbings were common, victims frequently spent three or four days in jail, and several lost jobs "because of their requests for library cards," one observer wrote.[53]

On March 4, 1965, the Indianola Freedom School and its Freedom Library— "which had painted on its front a black and white handshake"—was burned to the ground. The black community suspected that arsonists "knew that the Freedom School was to blame for all the 'freedom' trouble" at the white library. "So get rid of the school and you get rid of the trouble." City officials, however, afraid of negative publicity and potential violence, decided it was in Indianola's best interests to integrate the white public library without an announcement by the end of the year. Like many others, they temporarily removed all the chairs so that users— black and white—could not sit together. After a trial period without incident, however, chairs and tables were returned. Nonetheless, public schools remained segregated.[54]

VICKSBURG

In the Vicksburg Freedom Library in 1964, COFO officials hung a sign that read: "Do *you* have a card for the (heretofore) white library. Why not? Go get one. One Man—One Book."[55] Yet not until February 1965 did five Vicksburg black students enter the city's main library and go to the stacks to retrieve books. When one asked the white librarian for assistance, she replied, "The colored books are in the other library," and asked them to leave. "Other library" referred to the underfunded, dilapidated Jim Crow branch in the black neighborhood, not the nearby Freedom Library. When the students refused, she called the police, who took them to the station for questioning. Within a month, however, the main Vicksburg Public Library decided to follow Greenville, Meridian, and Indianola's example and buckle to the pressure to integrate, and on March 15 it issued library cards to teenagers Eddie Thomas and Henry Coleman. Nonetheless, the system supplied separate cards for the two libraries, thus requiring black patrons to carry two. Public schools remained segregated, now more than ten years after *Brown*.[56]

* * *

On March 7, 1965, Mississippi Library Commission director Lura Currier wrote the editor of *Harper's Magazine* that the state had signed a Statement of Compliance with the federal government that with one exception, which was not mentioned, "all of Mississippi's public libraries" were now open to Mississippi "Negroes" and thus were eligible to receive federal funds.[57] The successful journey to integrated public libraries in the Magnolia State had been long, painful, and often dangerous, and like the desegregation of most other southern public libraries, it had largely been forced into the media and the courts by Mississippi black youths who braved dogs, billy clubs, jail time, and constant police intimidation; who refused to be pushed around; and who had the courage and determination to insist on their rights in order to bend history in their direction.

8

BLACK YOUTH IN RURAL LOUISIANA

Although it was in Louisiana that Homer Plessy pressed a case against segregation in the last years of the nineteenth century that resulted in the Supreme Court's "separate but equal" decision, Louisiana's post-1950s civil rights history appears less violent than in other Deep South states. Baton Rouge experienced a bus boycott in June 1953, but city officials and black leaders reached a compromise that satisfied both sides a week after it started. The same year, Louisiana State University desegregated under court order. The New Orleans Public Library had quietly desegregated shortly after the *Brown* decision, and four years later "Whites Only" posters disappeared from New Orleans streetcars. And after a crisis in New Orleans schools in 1960 was resolved—a photo of six-year-old Ruby Bridges, a black child, surrounded by U.S. marshals, descending the steps of an all-white grade school she had just desegregated, quickly circulated in newspapers across the country—desegregation proceeded peacefully, considerably ahead of most other southern cities and towns.

Some explanation for this situation can be found in Louisiana's more diverse nature—its French and Spanish origins, its Creole and Cajun cultures, the uniqueness of New Orleans, and its strong Roman Catholic influence—but most of these elements pertained largely to urban areas of the state. Outside those areas, race relations were different, more like other southern states. Despite the experiences and successes of activists between *Brown* and the August 28, 1963, March on Washington, historian Benjamin Muse notes, "many small towns and rural areas had been virtually untouched by the Civil Rights Movement."[1] In Louisiana's rural parishes, whites held onto Jim Crow longer and more tightly. "Only the very brave and the very foolhardy" in Louisiana's small-town black neighborhoods "raised their voices or put their heads above the parapet," writes historian Adam Fairclough. "Getting along with the white man was an essential survival skill that parents drummed into their children at an early age. As long as blacks accepted their place in the racial order, whites could be remarkably friendly."[2]

The desegregation of public libraries in rural Louisiana looks similar to that of other libraries in the South, with one major exception. In rural Louisiana, the Congress of Racial Equality determined to use public libraries to "test" Jim Crow practices. On August 24, 1963, for example, a CORE Task Force worker from East Feliciana Parish noted in his weekly field report that "among areas to be investigated are . . . the public library—Negroes aren't allowed in the main building, and have a bookmobile of their own."[3] In a January 1964 field report for Pointe Coupee Parish, the local CORE leader reported that he intended to "test the white library in New Roads, and, if necessary, will lead a read-in, coordinated with other CORE groups' actions across the Sixth Congressional District."[4] Then, immediately after the Civil Rights Act passed on July 2, 1964, CORE publicly announced it intended to test it in twenty-two Louisiana towns and that public libraries would be an important target.[5] At each site, local black youths were the "testers."

OUACHITA PARISH

On Thursday, July 9, 1964—a week after the Civil Rights Act passed—eighty-eight black youngsters sponsored by CORE's "Freedom Registered" program attempted to integrate ten places in Ouachita Parish in northern Louisiana, where Monroe serves as its parish seat. The black youths were served at four lunch counters, a movie house, a gas station, and two restaurants but were denied service at five other restaurants and lunch counters. Rather than serve blacks, a second movie theater shut down. In addition, sixteen black youths took seats in the front of city buses. Claiming mechanical problems, city buses temporarily stopped service in late afternoon.[6]

Also among the places they challenged that day was the Anna Meyer Branch Library, part of the Ouachita Parish Library system, where twelve Monroe black youths entered the front door at 2:30 p.m. Eighteen-year-old Dorothy Higgins went to the back of the library, glanced at a few books, and sat down at a table with a *Reader's Digest* next to seventeen-year-old Jimmy Andrews and fifteen-year-old Etta Faye Carter. No one disturbed them while they were reading.[7]

Nineteen-year-old Bennie Roy Brass used the card catalog to search for a book on Louisiana history. Upon finding one, he sat down at a reading table near the librarian's desk, where, like others, he read undisturbed. A few minutes later, however, Brass approached the circulation desk and asked to apply for a borrower's card to check the book out. The female desk attendant said he could read the book in the library but he could not check it out. "Just as I finished asking," Brass later wrote, "a white boy of my age came to the desk and checked out a book to take home." Again Brass asked for a card; again he was denied. This branch did not issue cards, he was told. Go to the main library, the desk attendant said, but don't expect to get a card there either. "The only way I could at all get a card was to go to the [black] Carver Branch." Could he use the Carver branch card to check out books from any library in the system? No, the librarian said. Brass would also have to go through Carver to get the book. "I told them I had come in person to eliminate the transfer problem."[8]

At this point "a male clerk" appeared from a back office to ask Brass if he wanted a borrower's card. Yes, Brass replied. The attendant looked under the counter, said he could find no forms there, and offered to go back to the office to look for one. Through a glass window Brass could see the attendant talking to the head and assistant librarians. When he returned, he said he could find no applications there either. Again Brass asked for a library card; again the clerk said he would have to go to the Carver branch. When Brass asked a fourth time for a card, the clerk shouted "No!" Brass answered, "Well, I'll wait until I get one," and returned to his seat to read.[9]

Police arrived fifteen minutes later. One went directly to the head librarian's office, and brought her back to the table where Brass and his friends were reading. The policeman then said: "You will all have to go because the lady said she will not be able to give you library cards. Are you going to leave?" "I and my friends have come as citizens of Monroe to use our public library," Brass responded. Minutes later, the chief of police arrived and asked the black teenagers to leave; five did. The seven who remained were arrested for disturbing the peace and trespassing. Brass returned his book to the shelf, then waited at the front door while police cars were brought up. "Where are the grown-ups?" the chief asked. "They send children down to do the work." "I'm the one who wants to read good books," Brass responded, and "besides," he was "not a child."[10]

Outside the building, white CORE Task Force worker David Kramer watched events transpire with camera in hand. He and his colleagues had actually alerted the police to what was about to happen in hopes of photographing events. First, he took pictures of the five youths who chose to leave, but when police began bringing the "testers" out, a deputy sheriff protested: "Don't take my picture; I've got my rights too." Kramer ran to a car containing several white CORE Task Force workers, including Mike Lesser, but before they could lock all the doors, the sheriff grabbed the camera and tried to remove the film. Unable to do so, he invited

Kramer to accompany him to the police station, where he could retrieve the camera. Am I under arrest? Kramer asked three times but got no answer. He decided to accompany the sheriff.

Once inside the cars, police formed a cavalcade and stopped all traffic to the station, where the youths were separated for interrogation. The assistant chief took Jimmy Andrews into his office; a deputy sheriff took Dorothy Higgins to a judge's bench. Why did you go to the library? he asked her. "I told him that since the civil rights bill had passed I wanted to use the library to check out some books. And that the books I wanted were works by Edgar Allen [sic] Poe and a novel, Burn Killer Burn, by Paul Krump." Do you know who CORE Louisiana project director Ronnie Moore is? he asked. "No," Higgins replied. How about CORE Monroe Chapter director Mike Lesser? When Higgins replied yes, the sheriff pressed. When and where did you meet him? Had she been involved with any other "tests"? Who was "the white guy with the camera"? How long have you been a member of CORE? Why "don't you let the older people" protest? Don't you know "that someone would have to work to support all of the children that your mother has and that the Welfare has to take care of"? "We are not on welfare," Higgins responded.[11]

Bennie Brass "was pulled roughly to the back of the courtroom" by other officers, where he was peppered with questions:

Who got you into CORE?
Did you have to pay to join CORE?
Are you a communist?
Who's putting up the money for CORE?
Are they going to pay you?
How much are they going to give you?
Did you eat at a lunch-counter this morning?
Did Ronnie Moore pay you?
How did the police know you-all were coming to the lunch-counter and library?
Who told you to come down to the library—Moore or Lesser?
We know you're not doing this for nothing.
Did you have to pay for your badges and cards?
Did you all have some meetings this morning?
We know you were there at the Ritz: What was that meeting?
They are paying Moore and Lesser; you're being short-cutted.
Do you go to church?

Brass answered the questions "truthfully to the best of my knowledge," but when asked for a fifth time if Moore or Lesser had sent him, Brass said he had gone to the library "because I was dissatisfied with the present library conditions and wanted to see if the Civil Rights Bill meant anything to the whites in the South. I attempted to explain my action to the officers," he said, and told them "of all the Negro problems I was aware of." He then quietly explained "that the Negro people were not satisfied with present conditions." He talked for "many minutes," he later wrote. "Many officers gathered about to hear me. They said they agreed with me."[12]

The seven arrestees were then fingerprinted and photographed. In the process, one officer said that if the arrestees had listened to the librarian when she told them to leave the library, none of this would have happened. When Dorothy Higgins said the librarian had not told them to leave, the officer said she did. No, Higgins said, she did not. The officer then "told me to shut up." "Since she's so smart," another said, "put her in [a cell] by herself so she won't see nobody, hear nobody, and talk to nobody for about three days. Maybe when she gets out she won't be so smart." While all this was going on, David Kramer was attempting to retrieve his camera. "The camera incited local people," the chief of police told him. "He wanted me to promise that I would no longer use it." After Kramer refused, the chief said police would not press charges against him (never mentioning for what) and gave Kramer back his camera. He later discovered the film had been exposed.[13]

All seven were then transferred to juvenile detention home cages before officials called their parents. "In jail I spoke to my fellow prisoners about Freedom Registration and about our Civil Rights testing," Brass later wrote. "They wholeheartedly approved of it." On the third day of their incarceration, on their way to breakfast, "some vile remarks were made to us by whites. My fellow prisoners wanted to fight the whites, but we calmed them by telling them that violence would only mess up our cause." When released later in the day, "the detective who escorted us said the only thing left to do with you all is to put you in the river." Three were released on $200 bond each, four to the custody of their parents.[14]

"Testing" at the Ouachita Parish Public Library continued. On July 14 six black youths approached the main library. On a "CORE Testing Form," black activist Diane Gordon reported what happened next. "A policeman and the librarian met us in the walkway, the librarian said what do you want? I said a library card, the librarian said here is a card to the Carver Branch Library." (The library administration had obviously rehearsed a response for the next testing.) Three took the card, and to the three who did not, the librarian said they could not enter: "I was told not to let you come in the Library, I don't want to have you arrested for trespassing, you made your point. Go home now, I don't want to have you all arrested." "We said thank you very much," Gordon wrote, "and left."[15]

But six days later—"in a quiet and orderly way"—fifteen black youths tested all three white branches of the Ouachita Parish Public Library. The premise was the same. They wanted library cards and access to the collections and services of all the parish's public libraries. The response was the same; they were denied service, and when they refused to leave until they were given cards, they were arrested for disturbing the peace and trespassing on library premises. Among those arrested was sixteen-year-old Alice Smith.[16]

While Smith remained with her friends at the detention home, a Ouachita Parish sheriff's deputy approached her parents at their house. Why haven't you visited her? he asked. She has not committed a crime, her father responded. But you have to go see her, the sheriff responded. Alice hadn't committed a crime, her father repeated, and the only way he would go was if he was arrested. Two days later, at 1:00 p.m., two sheriff's deputies came to the house with arrest warrants for Smith's parents. The charge? Contributing to the delinquency of a minor. They were taken to jail, placed in separate cells, and individually interrogated. They "wanted us to admit that we influenced Alice to sit-in," Oliver Smith later recalled. "The juvenile officer also asked if Alice were released, would we permit her to do it again." "That was Alice's decision," her father replied. As he was released, the jailer yelled to his subordinate, "Let that nigger man out."[17]

While this was happening to the Smiths at the parish jail, at 2:30 p.m. sixteen-year-old Tommy Robinson led three black teenage friends to the steps of the Anna Meyer Branch of the Ouachita Parish Public Library. Police blocked them as they tried to enter. The librarian asked them what they wanted, and Robinson said "library cards." Why did you come here? the librarian asked. "Because the Civil Rights Bill says that I can go into any public place," Robinson said, and "this library is a public place." "She said that she did not want to have her library integrated," one protester later wrote, "and she told us we would have to go to the Carver Branch library to get cards." Robinson said they would not leave without cards. "Are you refusing to go?" the policeman asked. "Each one of us said yes," one of his friends later reported. Police then arrested them for disturbing the peace and took them to the detention home.[18] At about the same time, fifteen-year-old Joseph Profit led three of his teenage friends into the West Monroe Branch of the public library. Inside the door they were met by the librarian and two policemen. What do you want? the librarian asked. "Library cards," Profit responded. The librarian said, "I will not have this place integrated," and told them to go to the "Colored Library." When the youths refused to leave, all were arrested for disturbing the peace and taken to the detention home.[19]

That same afternoon, thirteen-year-old Lettie Bess led three of her friends into the main library, where she was met by "two ladies," who said, "The library wasn't integrated yet." Bess asked them for a copy of the Civil Rights Act. If she really wanted it, one lady responded, "we should stay outside and she would bring it to us." Do you have a library card? one lady asked. Bess responded no. At that moment the police arrived and arrested the four teenagers for trespassing on public property; one was also charged with contributing to the delinquency of a minor. "Who brought you to the library?" one detective asked on the way to the station. The four youths refused to answer until they saw their lawyers. At the station one officer asked Bess if she knew David Kramer. "Must be a new kind of drink," Bess replied. Shortly thereafter, state police took her and her fellow testers home.[20]

That these responses had been rehearsed is obvious from undated notes in the CORE Papers (now at the Wisconsin Historical Society), which were likely written by a task force worker. "General procedure," the notes began, was "know your part thoroughly" and "don't lose your temper or your head." For all the Louisiana public library sit-ins, youthful testers showed exemplary behavior. For the "library," the notes continued, testers needed two things—a borrower's card and the title of a "particular book." Possibilities recommended for the book title included a history of Louisiana, a history of Monroe, the municipal code, and the U.S. Constitution. (Lettie Bess's request for a copy of the Civil Rights Act likely was her own idea.) If they encountered opposition, they were to ask for the person in charge and refuse to leave unless that person appeared. Once that person showed, testers were instructed to remind him or her that their parents were taxpayers, that the library was a public accommodation as well as a municipal institution, and that "refusal of service" violated their "rights of citizenship on both counts." Throughout, testers were instructed to "conduct yourselves quietly." When arrested, testers should "go limp" if experiencing force, only answer questions on "vital statistics," and at the police station request one phone call each. In jail they were to choose a spokesperson and to set up a daily schedule that included exercise, prayers, singing (not at "late hours," however), and "quiet times."[21]

On July 28 three black teenage testers filed suit in the Monroe Division of the federal district court to declare the segregation practices of the Ouachita Parish Public Library unconstitutional. On August 3, twenty-two Ouachita Parish black teenagers—all of whom admitted to being CORE members—facing criminal charges for disturbing the peace, criminal trespass, and contributing to the delinquency of a minor as a result of library sit-ins asked federal district judge Ben C. Dawkins Jr. to assume jurisdiction of their cases. They claimed charges against them were an outgrowth of the city's and county's segregationist practices and a violation of the 1964 Civil Rights Act and the Fourteenth Amendment.[22] Although the *Ouachita Citizen*, the parish's major newspaper, reported none of these events, local KNOE-TV did give the sit-ins and court proceedings some coverage on its evening news program, shortly before closing its broadcasting day with video showing black Americans picking cotton to the tune of "Dixie."[23]

In the meantime, white city officials resurrected plans to relocate the Carver branch and in December 1964 reopened it in a new 5,278-square-foot building constructed on the black high school campus at a cost of $66,921. To no avail, however. The new facility did not satisfy local civil rights activists, who continued to protest Jim Crow practices by harnessing the language of the Civil Rights Act. A year later white officials acquiesced, and when the Ouachita Parish Public Library finally desegregated all its facilities in 1965, the plaintiffs dropped their suit.[24]

JACKSON PARISH

On July 22, 1964, in Jonesboro, fifty miles southwest of Monroe, six black youths attempted to enter the Jackson Parish Library at 10:45 a.m. "Good morning, may I help you?" a librarian asked as she met them at the door. "We asked her for library cards," one later reported. Are you Jackson Parish citizens, and have you lived in the parish for at least six months? the librarian asked. "We answered yes, and asked for library cards again." In response the librarian told the youths about the bookmobile service they could use, which would be in their neighborhood the following Thursday. When one youth asked if she was "denying us use of the library," the librarian reiterated information about the bookmobile. Are you the head librarian? they asked. No, she responded, she was the bookmobile librarian; the head librarian was not in the library. She then asked them to leave. Instead, "we asked to see the head librarian. She told us to wait just a minute, but she didn't make an effort to go get the head librarian." Minutes later two men entered, one carrying a book, one with a camera. When she saw the camera, the librarian shouted, "Wait just a minute!" At that point the parish sheriff came out of the back room, and three policemen came in the front door. As the teens turned to leave, the sheriff shouted, "Wait, get their names!" Are we under arrest? the teens asked. "No," the sheriff responded, "give us your names and ages." One policeman told his colleague, "Brooks, you had better get these children back across town and fast." A third addressed the youths directly. "You'd better get back to the 'freedom house' and sing some songs because you are gonna get in trouble up here."[25]

The following day, the president and secretary of the Progressive Voters League, a local black organization, wrote the Jackson Parish Library board chairman. "We believe that an open library is most important for the education and health of all the citizens of this community. . . . Citizens of color have been turned away from this tax-supported public facility. This fact constitutes a denial of this class of citizen's constitutional rights, and is clearly an insult to the Negroes of this community." They sent copies to the U.S. Department of Justice and the U.S. Commission on Civil Rights.[26]

On July 27 thirteen-year-old Larry Robinson was one of five black youths who began picketing the library by carrying signs stating their right to use the building. Fifteen whites observed them silently. Minutes after the picketing started, police showed up. "Move out," one said; "the library is closed and it's not for your use." When the youths refused to stop, one officer retrieved a leashed German shepherd from his squad car. When another officer ordered them to follow him across the street, the group complied quietly, then scattered when ordered to do so. When they reported to their white CORE Task Force worker, however, he gathered them together to re-form the picket line in front of the library. Again police came, this time wielding blackjacks and with more police dogs. One officer told his colleagues not to release the dogs but said to the picketers: "I will ask you to leave once." No one left. "I'll ask you to leave twice." Same response. "I'm gonna ask you one time, I'm gonna ask you two times, I'm gonna ask you three times." Still no one left. "Now you are all under arrest," he said, and he took them to the police station. While conducting them into a cell, one arresting officer told them, "You are here because you violated a city ordinance." Three times the CORE Task Force worker asked: "Which ordinance?" and each time the officer ignored him. Two nights later, seventeen-year-old Will Farmer reported, they were singing in their cells at about 10:00 p.m. when three officers charged into the cell block. One shouted: "Shut up! I don't want to hear another damn word out of you niggers."[27]

On the morning of July 20, black CORE Task Force workers Catherine Patterson and Daniel Mitchell from the Jonesboro Freedom House showed up for the testers' arraignment. They were immediately arrested for contributing to the delinquency of a minor and placed in the same cell block as those arrested at the library. When they all began singing about ten o'clock that evening, five officers stormed into the cell block. One opened the cell door and said, "OK, you niggers, come on out." But "no one moved." Will Farmer described what happened next. One officer "then pulled us out of our bunks and out of the cell. We, the thirteen of us, were taken to a 6' long and 4' wide padded cell and put in it." The officer said, "If you niggers aren't quiet now I have an even worse place." When he began to close the porthole on the cell door, a white trusty "said we would suffocate with the port-hole closed." A second officer responded: "I don't give a damn if they suffocate. As long as they act like animals, we'll treat them like animals." Nonetheless, he left the porthole open. When they got out of the cell the next morning, one officer said, "Maybe you niggers will act like people this time." At no time during their incarceration were any of those detained informed of charges again them; most learned on a local newscast that they had been arrested for disturbing the peace. "To the best of my knowledge," Robinson stated later, "I at no time disturbed the peace. The picket line was moving in an orderly, quiet manner."[28]

Eventually, however, the Jackson Parish Library buckled to the inevitable. On December 16, five black teenagers entered the library at 9:30 a.m., approached the desk, and asked for library cards. "They were received politely and secured cards with no trouble," the black New Orleans *Louisiana Weekly* reported. One new card owner asked for particular books on Negro history. Although the librarian told him the books were not in the collection, she volunteered to order them. By closing time that evening, 236 members of the Jackson Parish black community had obtained library cards, and several were still in line. That evening, members of the Jonesboro Freedom Movement—a "militant group," the *Weekly* called them— hosted a mass meeting and vowed to continue efforts to integrate local restaurants, parks, and theaters. At the library the next morning, however, patrons found all the chairs and tables had been removed. They were returned several months later.[29]

AUDUBON REGIONAL LIBRARY OF ST. HELENA AND EAST AND WEST FELICIANA PARISHES

The series of incidents that brought most attention to library desegregation in Louisiana's rural parishes occurred in the Audubon Regional Library system in St. Helena and East and West Feliciana Parishes. The Audubon Regional Library is located in Clinton, less than ten miles from the Mississippi border and thirty miles north of Baton Rouge. At the beginning of 1964, black people living in this area still could not access the library building. Instead, their only access to public library books was a blue bookmobile; a red bookmobile was reserved for whites. Both were supported by Library Services Act funds through the state library agency.[30] When white residents applied for a library card, they received a red one, no doubt to match their red bookmobile. When blacks registered for a card at the blue bookmobile—the only place they could register and the only place they could retrieve and return a book—they received a blue library card with the word *Negro* stamped on it. Louisiana CORE members helped to organize voter registration drives and protests against segregated swimming pools and other public places, and they also focused on the Audubon Regional Library system's segregated public libraries. As one Louisiana newspaper noted when reporting a local library sit-in, it was "a CORE type integration attempt."[31]

On March 7, four St. Helena Parish black teenagers approached the Greensburg branch of the Audubon Regional Library system. The librarian saw them coming up the walk, recognized what was happening—CORE blamed "talkative Toms and Sallies" for leaking word—immediately locked the door, and posted "Closed" signs in the window.[32] The group left. "The street was crowded with negroes and whites," a CORE observer reported, "the majority of the merchants was standing on the sidewalk talking with spectators. The sheriff could not be found anywhere." Four days later the youths returned and met the same response. Through the window the group saw the librarian make a phone call. Moments later she unlocked the door, came out, relocked it, and walked across the street to a drugstore.

On a third attempt, on March 13, the four teenage boys decided to pair off rather than approach as a foursome. As two of them walked in front of the drugstore across the street, the pharmacist came out and said: "I'm sorry boys, but you are too late. Come back tomorrow and you may have better luck." As they left, however, he added: "I wish you —— Niggers would come to my place." When the pair crossed the street to meet the other two (they were approaching the library from a different direction), they learned it had again been locked against them. They decided to walk to the courthouse, and without incident they drank from the "white" water fountain. They then returned to the drugstore for some ice cream, where the pharmacist met them at the front door. "I am tired of fooling with you —— Niggers!" he shouted, then rushed to his car and pulled out a .32-caliber automatic pistol. "Git away from here and I don't mean maybe." The youths left.

Three days later the group made a fourth attempt and once again found the library closed. Although they did not go to the drugstore across the street, they did go to the courthouse, where they again drank from the "white" water fountain. This time, however, the white janitor grabbed one of the boys and shouted, "There's a fountain over there for the Niggers, and if you —— Niggers can't drink from that fountain, get out of here, and don't be caught back in here no more."

He then called for help from a friend upstairs: "Come down here and help me get these —— Niggers out of here!" When the group walked to the courthouse front steps, the janitor went to a closet for a lead pipe and ran to the front door. "If you —— Niggers come back here again," he threatened, "I will kill every one of you." At that point he struck one of the boys with the pipe. The boy was taken to a local hospital, treated, and released. Days later, after several white merchants queried the parents of the testers if they knew their son or daughter was "trying to use the library," CORE organized a "selective buying campaign" against the pharmacist. "Rallies are being held every Wednesday night to support the selective buying campaign," a task force worker reported.[33]

On March 7, four black teenagers approached the public library in West Feliciana's St. Francisville, where no black citizens had registered to vote for sixty-one years. When some had made the attempt to register earlier that year, they were met at the courthouse by a mob of white men armed with guns and knives. Later that week, night riders shot at the homes of several of them, and two were beaten with a rifle butt.[34] But the teenage library testers had been well trained. "For the past two weeks we have been preparing the young people and the community leaders in West Feliciana [Parish] for the upcoming library action," a CORE Task Force worker wrote in early March. The chapter chairman had been "lining up bond, both cash and property," but was having difficulty because so few black citizens in the parish owned property. If arrested, participants pledged to stay in jail until their trials and prepared for their ordeals by conducting sociodramas and discussing nonviolence. Post-arrest plans included a prayer vigil in front of the jail and a "stepped-up boycott." "It is hoped that the library action will provide an issue around which we can mobilize the people to boycott," a task force worker noted. "We then hope to do extensive canvassing and leaflet distribution to spread the word about the campaign."[35]

One of the CORE observers who had been stationed near the library to record events told the youths that the library had been open that morning but had closed at noon. Although three police cars were stationed outside, the group decided not to attempt to use the library, "since if they were arrested by the Sheriff's deputies, there wouldn't be a clear-cut case against the library now that it was closed." Instead, "after consultation with the project coordinator in Clinton," the teenagers drove to East Feliciana Parish.[36]

The Clinton branch remained open, but the local sheriff had been notified that morning that there might be "trouble." All morning he watched and waited and finally saw five students enter the library. With four of his black friends, East

Feliciana resident Henry Brown walked in, apparently the first blacks ever to do so.[37] The library was not large; it consisted of a small front "adult reading room" with two tables and a chair, a stove, a card catalog, several open bookshelves, and the branch assistant's desk and chair. Offices were in the back room.[38]

As soon as he observed the students, the sheriff called his deputies and ordered them to the library. In the meantime, Brown requested two books, one a copy of the U.S. Constitution, the other *Story of the Negro,* a children's history text written by Fisk University's head librarian Arna Bontemps.[39] Katie Reeves, the white branch assistant, checked the card catalog for Bontemps's book and told Brown that the branch library did not have it. She said that she would order it from the state library and that it would either be mailed to him or he could retrieve it from the blue bookmobile. Shortly thereafter, Reeves asked the five to leave. When they did not, she tried a second time, and when that didn't work, she called in the regional librarian, who issued the same order.

The youths remained, Brown sitting at the table and the others standing near him, doing and saying nothing. Five minutes later, the sheriff and his deputies approached them and ordered them to leave under threat of arrest. When they refused, they were all arrested, taken to jail, and charged with disturbing the peace. The basis of their arrests was a Louisiana statute: "Whoever with intent to provoke a breach of the peace, or under circumstances such that a breach of the peace may be occasioned thereby, crowds or congregates with others" in a "public place or building . . . and who fails or refuses to disperse and move on, when ordered so to do by any law enforcement officer . . . or any other authorized person . . . shall be guilty of disturbing the peace."[40]

While in jail, Henry Brown received the copy of the Constitution he had requested, but with it came instructions that he return the book in person to the blue bookmobile or mail it back to the East Feliciana Public Library.[41] On March 11 police also arrested white CORE Task Force worker Mimi Feingold as a material witness to the trial; a local judge set her bond at $1,000. "Request an immediate investigation," one CORE fieldworker cabled the U.S. Department of Justice in Washington, D.C. "We believe that this is an act to prevent further voter registration instructions and CORE activity."[42]

At their trial on April 9, the five black youths were found guilty of disturbing the peace. Henry Brown received a sentence of $150 plus costs or ninety days in jail. The other four were assessed a fine of $35 plus costs or fifteen days in jail. At the trial, however, the librarian of the Audubon Regional Library system surprised everyone by announcing, "Negroes are allowed to use the library if they are citizens of one of the three parishes." But *use* had taken on new meaning. A week after the trial, all three of the initially targeted Audubon Regional libraries closed their doors, claiming they intended to cut costs and at the same time improve library services through a telephone reference and request service: "The patron can now dial a special library number . . . at no charge. . . . Reference questions are answered immediately or by return call; books are mailed or sent by book-mobile."[43] If users wished to browse, they were required to do so when the book-mobile arrived in their area every few weeks. Black people still had to use their blue bookmobile, white people their red bookmobile.

The plan was so bizarre, a West Feliciana CORE Task Force worker argued, that he hoped "adverse reaction . . . will be enough to open the branches up again." Perhaps he had picked up on complaints from the white community. One white resident observed, "It was strange that no one had ever heard of the plan before now, and the announcement came so soon after the attempt to integrate services there." Many other library patrons, the white *East Feliciana Watchman* reported, expressed "dissatisfaction at the proposed limited service to be offered by phone and mail."[44] Later the city's attorney revealed that the white women who staffed the branch libraries "weren't paid much" and that once the demonstrations began, "they wouldn't work . . . because they anticipated that it would be trouble and they didn't want to have any part of it and that was the reason. They were just scared to work in there."[45] While the *Watchman* reported these events in March and April, the librarian's regular weekly *Watchman* column carried no mention of them. Instead, she kept reporting on "interesting books." On April 24 the *Watchman* also reported a Ku Klux Klan beating of a Baton Rouge newsman who was covering these events.[46]

Although Henry Brown and his four codefendants appealed, *Brown v. Louisiana* followed a different path from much civil rights litigation in the South. Often local lawyers called in NAACP lawyers, who then filed a civil rights lawsuit in the near-est federal court. This time, however, local attorneys worked with Carl Rachlin, a white New York City CORE attorney, and filed no lawsuit, instead choosing to appeal the disorderly conduct charges all the way to the U.S. Supreme Court. Rachlin led the way. Born in Brooklyn, he had graduated from New York University and Harvard Law School and became a well-known civil rights and labor lawyer. At age forty-six, he became general counsel to CORE and served in that capacity for seven years. In 1961 he successfully overturned the conviction of six Freedom

Riders who had entered a "whites only" waiting room in a Louisiana bus terminal. In 1964 he helped form and lead the Lawyers Constitutional Defense Committee, which enlisted lawyers to defend civil rights activists in the South.[47]

Local Louisiana attorneys were also involved in the defense. New Orleans attorneys Robert F. Collins, Nils R. Douglas, and Lolis E. Elie drove the 110 miles north to represent the five defendants, while Murphy W. Bell came up from Baton Rouge. All were attorneys with backgrounds in civil rights litigation. Black attorney Robert F. Collins became the most well known. He had been forced to file a lawsuit just to gain entrance to the all-white Louisiana State University Law School and, after graduating from law school in 1954, became heavily involved in civil rights litigation with both CORE and the NAACP Legal Defense Fund. In 1977, President Jimmy Carter appointed him to the United States District Court.[48]

In 1965, when *Brown v. Louisiana* finally made it to the Supreme Court, all the attorneys were keenly aware that the time had come for change. They reminded the Court in their brief that the March 1964 arrests came just four months before passage of the Civil Rights Act, which had put an end to Jim Crow segregation. They argued that the arrests and convictions violated the defendants' constitutional due process and equal protection rights. The state, on the other hand, argued that "the issue is simply whether any person, or group of persons, have any right to use a facility such as a public library room as a place in which to loiter or create a nuisance," said Clinton district attorney Richard H. Kilbourne, "to the extent that the employees . . . or those wishing to make a bona fide use of it, are embarrassed and disturbed." He asserted that the library did not discriminate, that anyone could use the library, and that the defendants were treated courteously but that they had been arrested because they "had no reason to loiter about the premises."[49]

During the Court's oral argument, however, Kilbourne stumbled when justices asked about the library's policy of issuing different library cards to whites and blacks and permitting blacks to use only the blue bookmobile. Justice William O. Douglas remarked, "That looks like a segregated library system." Kilbourne's response did not help his case. "In Clinton, Louisiana—well, I always felt like we had more integration than probably any place in the United States, I mean, just from the way people live. But . . . segregation and integration seems to mean different things in different parts of the country."[50]

It apparently meant different things to the members of Court as well because they split five to four in the opinion issued on February 23, 1966. Both the majority and dissenting opinions recognized the library as a special place, unlike lunch counters, bus terminals, and public streets, where other protests had occurred.

Justice Abe Fortas, a Lyndon Johnson appointee just four months earlier, who wrote the majority opinion, called it "a place dedicated to quiet, to knowledge, and to beauty . . . [a] hallowed place." Justice Hugo Black, who wrote the dissent, noted that public libraries are "dedicated to reading and learning and studying" and recognized "the extremely necessary purposes underlying their existence."[51] Both sides wanted to protect the quiet and peacefulness of the public library. The most significant difference in the opinions was how each side viewed the conflict that had occurred in this special place and where the blame for that conflict might lie.

Dissenters saw no racism in the arrests. Justice Black blamed the protesters for disrupting the "peace and order" required to achieve the purposes served by the public library.[52] He seemed frustrated by the protesters' continued demonstrations, a frustration that was exacerbated by the location of this protest: "Public buildings such as libraries . . . are maintained to perform certain specific and vital functions. Order and tranquility . . . are essential." He noted that the protesters had received courteous service at the library desk. Brown had requested a book. The librarian had informed him that the branch did not have it, that she would order it, and that he would receive it in the mail or by bookmobile. She had asked the protesters to leave, but they refused. "There simply was no racial discrimination practiced in this case," he stated. He bolstered his statement with the testimony of the librarian, who "testified unambiguously that there was no racial discrimination practiced at her library," and with the state attorney's oral argument, in which he "stated frankly and forthrightly that there would be no defense had Louisiana denied these petitioners equal service at its public libraries on account of race."

Black was offended that the protesters had interfered with the "normal, quiet functioning" of the library, even after they received courteous and complete service. Even though no one else had been in the library, he nevertheless asserted that the library's "normal activity was completely disrupted." His frustration was clear. "It is high time to challenge the assumption, in which too many people have too long acquiesced," he argued, "that groups that think they have been mistreated or that have actually been mistreated have a constitutional right to use the public's streets, buildings, and property to protest whatever, wherever, whenever they want without regard to whom such conduct may disturb." He then warned, "If one group can take over libraries for one cause, other groups will assert the right to do so for causes which . . . may not be so appealing to this Court." States would be "paralyzed with reference to control of their libraries," he warned, and "I suppose that inevitably the next step will be to paralyze the schools." Finally, Black differentiated the merits of the protests and the means used to effectuate them: "It is an unhappy circumstance . . . that the group, which more than any other has needed a government of equal laws and equal justice, is now encouraged to believe that the best way for it to advance its cause, which is a worthy one, is by taking the law into its own hands from place to place and from time to time. . . . The crowd moved by noble ideals today can become the mob ruled by hate and passion and greed and violence tomorrow."[53]

Justice Fortas, however, directly blamed the Jim Crow racism practiced in the area's public libraries. "It is an unhappy circumstance that the locus of these events was a public library," Justice Fortas said. "It is a sad commentary that this hallowed place . . . bore the ugly stamp of racism. It is sad, too, that it was a public library which . . . was the stage for [the] confrontation." Fortas added, "This is the fourth time in little more than four years that this Court has reviewed convictions by the Louisiana courts for alleged violations, in a civil rights context, of that State's breach of the peace statute." In previous cases involving lunch counters, bus depots, and a street protest, demonstrators had been orderly, with no evidence that they planned or intended disorder. "In none," Fortas noted, "were there circumstances which might have led to a breach of the peace chargeable to the protesting participants." In the present case he found that the protesters had been lawfully in the library—"Negroes could not be denied access since white persons were welcome"—and "were neither loud, boisterous, obstreperous, indecorous, nor impolite. . . . They sat and stood in the room, quietly, as monuments of protest against the segregation of the library." Fortas held that protesters had "the right in a peaceable and orderly manner to protest by silent and reproachful presence . . . the unconstitutional segregation of public facilities." They could not be punished for doing so. He admitted that libraries may regulate library use but that they "must do so in a reasonable and nondiscriminatory manner." The convictions were reversed.[54]

At the time of the Court's decision, the Clinton library building remained closed, all the while offering telephone reference and bookmobile service. Both the majority and dissenting opinions made it clear that when it reopened, it should do so on an integrated basis. Months later it did open on an integrated basis, and by the end of the year all Louisiana public libraries were integrated. Around the same time that the Supreme Court rendered its decision, the American Library Association Council, which had filed no amicus curiae brief in *Brown v. Louisiana,* voted to continue welcoming into membership all libraries, including those that discriminated against black people.[55]

9

THE AMERICAN LIBRARY ASSOCIATION

Careful readers may have noticed that in narrating the stories and presenting the histories of public library integration between the 1954 *Brown* decision and the passage of the Civil Rights Act ten years later, very seldom did we cite professional library literature or note actions taken by professional library associations— national, state, or regional. This was not by design but, rather, a telling point. For the most part the American Library Association—and certainly southern state library associations—chose to ignore the issue of public library segregation rather than challenge, confront, or even discuss it until compelled by protests against segregated public libraries across the South.

The history of this neglect is long. In March 1899, for example, as the ALA planned its annual conference for Atlanta—the first time since organizing in 1876 that the ALA had ventured into the South—a member asked about the possibility of a session on public library services to "Negroes." Ninety percent of the country's black people lived in the South, and since Emancipation black literacy had grown from 20 to 60 percent, he said. ALA president William Coolidge Lane of Harvard was cautious. "I am somewhat afraid to tackle [it] & sh'd not want to say anything about it at present," he demurred, though he did suggest W. E. B. Du Bois, a Harvard graduate and Atlanta University professor, as a potential speaker. Planning committee member Anne Wallace, who was the Atlanta YMCA Library director and hoped for a Carnegie grant for a public library, objected immediately: "To bring it in its crude shape before the national association, where partisans could make political capital out of it, would prove inimical to both white and negro interests." Days later, Lane wrote to ALA officials that "the question of Negro Education, or the Negro in Relation to Libraries, we will leave untouched altogether." Wallace had ample reason to be concerned. On April 23 a black man was lynched in nearby Newman for killing a white person—many blacks said he acted in self-defense. Two thousand people watched, many arriving on a special excursion train from Atlanta. Several in the audience tore the body apart after the victim died; one Atlanta grocery store owner proudly displayed the victim's knuckles in his store window.[1]

In coming decades, the ALA continued to ignore Jim Crow practices. Just after World War I, ALA executive secretary Carl Milam told members from the South that the Carnegie Corporation had conceded their position on race issues and now required communities seeking grants to base their appropriations "only upon the white population of the towns." Milam, born in Kansas, raised in Oklahoma, and director of the segregated Birmingham, Alabama, Public Library system for several years before World War I, was also quoted as saying that the idea that "negroes have the right to ask for the privileges" of a Carnegie library was a "misconception."[2] In 1922, interested parties organized an ALA "Work with Negroes Round Table" that met for two conferences and did a survey of public library services to black Americans but little else. The roundtable did not survive the decade.

Partly in response to the survey, the Carnegie Corporation announced in 1925 that it would follow an ALA recommendation to fund a library school at Virginia's Hampton Institute (now Hampton University) to train black librarians for the "colored branches of city library systems" across the country.[3] New York Public Library Schomburg Center director Ernestine Rose, who was white, and Howard University's E. C. Williams, who was black, protested strongly, albeit privately, to the NAACP, arguing that "before long colored librarians from all parts of the country would be debarred from the regular schools and shunted off to Hampton," which would "probably mean a lower standard at the school . . . and a distinct disadvantage to colored librarians." The NAACP agreed and protested to the ALA and the Carnegie Corporation against the establishment of a "segregated library school." Despite NAACP opposition, however, the Hampton library school opened in September, and for the next thirteen years its graduates took jobs mostly in southern segregated and northern ghettoized public libraries serving black patrons.[4]

In 1936 the association published Tommie Dora Barker's *Libraries of the South: A Report on Developments, 1930–1935,* which contained a seven-page chapter entitled "Library Services to Negroes." "These extensions of branch library service to Negroes and erection of buildings, are recorded with a feeling of apology rather than of complacency," Barker told her readers, "for wherever public library service is maintained from public funds for the whites, it should, as a matter of course, be maintained for Negroes also."[5] Nevertheless, throughout these decades the ALA remained largely mute on the issue of segregated public library services in the South.

The same year it published Barker's book, however, and just prior to an annual conference scheduled for Richmond, Virginia, ALA officials circulated a letter indicating that its black members could attend but would be seated in segregated sections of meeting rooms and would not be permitted to attend meal functions or visit conference exhibits or register for conference hotel rooms. After the conference, black librarian Wallace Van Jackson wrote to the *Library Journal:* "The segregation of Negroes" at ALA meetings was "a shameful slide backward. What is worse, no single meeting or group at the Richmond conference so much as brought up the matter for discussion to say nothing of passing a resolution of protest." The *New Republic* projected the matter to a national stage. "The explanation is made rather plaintively that these restrictions were not the fault of the ALA, but part of a law of Virginia. Query: Why should any civilized association, with Negro members, undertake to hold such a convention in Virginia or any other state that makes such distinctions?"[6] Not everyone agreed. Jesse Cunningham, head librarian of Memphis's public library, wrote a letter to the *Library Journal:* "Liberal provisions were made for Negro librarians to attend sessions at Richmond. . . . It is just unfortunate that emphasis was placed on the negative side of Negroes attending meetings where food was served. No Negro attending a meeting in Richmond would expect this. It is not the custom. . . . What does Rhode Island or New Jersey know about the Southern Negro?"[7]

Clearly embarrassed, the ALA Council eventually passed a resolution that "in all rooms and halls assigned to the American Library Association hereafter for use in connection with its conference or otherwise under its control, all members shall be admitted upon terms of full equality." The resolution represented the first time the ALA took a public position against race discrimination.[8]

At its June 1939 annual conference, the ALA approved a "Library Bill of Rights" (LBR) largely as a reaction to pressure brought by right-wing groups in California, Illinois, Indiana, Massachusetts, and New York "objecting to what they called 'subversive' literature in public libraries."[9] Principle no. 1 read: "Books and other reading matter selected for purchase from public funds should be chosen because of value and interest to people of the community, and in no case should selection be influenced by the race or nationality or the political or religious views of the writers." Principle no. 3 read in part: "Library meeting rooms should be available on equal terms to all groups in the community regardless of their beliefs or affiliations."[10] Yet when Buddy Evans and four other black teenagers in Virginia protested at the Alexandria Public Library two months later, neither the library press nor the ALA saw segregation as an issue addressed by the Library Bill of Rights and made no mention of the events.

Although all state library associations sent appointed members to ALA conferences as chapter representatives, black librarians from the South were not permitted to join those associations. As a result, some black librarians organized their own and applied for separate chapter membership. In 1943, for example, the North Carolina Negro Library Association became the ALA's first black chapter. In the mid-1950s, however, the ALA took a stand against this practice by stating that only one association per state could have representation in the ALA and that association had to admit all members who applied, regardless of race. Some complied; North Carolina's black association dissolved when the North Carolina Library Association agreed to admit black members in 1955. Some had already tried but met resistance. In 1950, for example, the Alabama Library Association conducted a mail ballot on the question of opening membership to black libraries. When over half of the respondents answered favorably, albeit in a low return, nine black librarians submitted dues to become members. At the association's subsequent annual conference, however, one white university librarian carped, "Who is it that is stuffing these Negroes down our throats?" Because his reaction was echoed by others, the association decided to refund black librarians' dues and take them off its membership rolls. Other state library associations, such as those in Georgia and Mississippi, continued to deny membership to black librarians in their states and, like Alabama, lost their ALA representation.[11] And the ALA showed it had learned a lesson from 1936; in 1954 it rejected Miami Beach as a conference site when it appeared that blacks would be discriminated against in public facilities. Two years later, however, the ALA did meet there once it had been assured that local hotels and restaurants would not segregate its members.

Yet, despite a significant number of protests at public libraries across the South, the library press largely overlooked Jim Crow public library practices as a professional problem. Not until 1958, for example, did the subject heading "Segregation and the Library" appear in the *Library Literature Index,* the profession's main reference tool to record its bibliographical output and one of a number of resources produced by the H. W. Wilson Publishing Company. And not until events in Danville, Greenville, Memphis, and Petersburg—after civil rights activities across the South appeared on the front pages of the nation's major newspapers and became lead stories for major network evening news programs—did the library profession begin to focus significant attention on the issue. Nonetheless, what actions it eventually took were always peripheral to local efforts to integrate public library systems.[12]

By reading library literature, which almost always put a positive spin on the issue of race in librarianship, librarians across the country with any interest in the subject had reason to see "progress." A 1953 Southern Regional Council report entitled "No Segregation Here," for example, found that fifty-nine cities and towns allowed blacks to use the main library freely, twenty-four offered limited service, eleven supported one or more black branches, and three systems had black representatives on their library boards.[13] At Atlanta University, however, Virginia Lacy Jones, dean of the School of Library Service, encouraged her students to write master's theses on race in individual public libraries of the South. While many of the theses provided detail for the present study, the vast majority were never read by contemporary library professionals. One can imagine the sense of frustration Atlanta University students felt as they shared their findings with each other and their subsequent disappointment with a profession that claimed to be in favor of free access but did very little to bring it about in the South. The soaring rhetoric about intellectual freedom and opposition to censorship that resonated in ALA conference speeches—especially in the 1950s, as the association took public positions against McCarthyism—did not match the reality they experienced and the research they generated.

But events such as the Montgomery bus boycott ultimately forced the issue. In the late 1950s, ALA Intellectual Freedom Committee members asked several librarians from the South if an ALA statement supporting the integration of public library services would be helpful. Their responses hinted at the limits of what the ALA could do. "One of my chores has been to keep publicity about this situation at a minimum," said one librarian managing an integrated library. "I believe the answer to the question of extending use to the Negro race in communities which are still segregated is through the Negroes themselves. . . . This is the only actual approach which would produce results and no amount of speaking or beating of the chest by ALA will do much to aid and abet such a situation." Another librarian managing an integrated institution argued, "Such a statement would stir up the rabble rousers, a noisy minority in the South, which would interrupt the rapid progress being made." Said a state librarian from the South: "Statements by outside agencies such as ALA will do more harm than good because they are deeply resented and further inflame already hot tempers. We fervently hope that such a mistake can be avoided."[14]

But events nonetheless forced the ALA to act. An excerpt from the ALA Executive Board minutes for March 27, 1960, reads: "It was suggested that ALA will sooner or later be asked to state its position on the situations reported in Petersburg, Virginia, and Memphis, Tennessee, related to integration. . . . It was recognized that the Association while striving for service cannot, nor does it attempt to, intrude on local jurisdiction."[15] On May 17 the ALA appointed a special "Committee on Civil Liberties" to "recommend an ALA policy statement on the civil rights of individuals to have access to libraries and the resources contained therein."[16]

With the subject in the public eye, in his September 1960 issue of *Wilson Library Bulletin,* editor John Wakeman enumerated the ALA's reactions to racial incidents in Danville, Memphis, and Petersburg and the "teen-age violence" that followed the Greenville sit-in. Starting with shifting the Miami Beach conference from 1954 to 1956—"a complete success," he labeled it—he also noted how the North Carolina Negro Library Association had quietly dissolved in 1955 because the North Carolina Library Association had agreed to integrate so that the ALA would retain it as North Carolina's only ALA chapter. From this evidence Wakeman concluded, "Surely then, ALA's record is that of an organization opposed to segregation, and as effective as its structure permits." For fear of retarding integration and making more difficult the tasks of southern librarians opposed to segregation, he advised against "intervention in local situations."[17]

The *Wilson Library Bulletin* Wakeman edited was a publication of the H. W. Wilson Publishing Company, which also issued the *Readers' Guide to Periodical Literature* and such staple library bibliographies as the *Fiction Catalog* and *Public Library Catalog,* both issued quinquennially with annual supplements to help librarians identify the best books for library acquisition. Books recommended in these bibliographies were selected from book reviews in periodicals that the *Readers' Guide* indexed, which local public libraries then subscribed to primarily because they had been indexed. The fact that the *Readers' Guide* and other Wilson indexes largely overlooked African American newspapers and periodicals such as the *Chicago Defender* and the *Colored American* in their indexing practices effectively limited the ability of public library users across the country to access African American perspectives on civil rights issues that did not appear in the mainstream media before the 1960s and thus reinforced the perception of American life that dominant white Anglo-Saxon Protestant cultures defined. Through the middle of the twentieth century, other members of the nation's library press reflected similar values.

Wakeman's editorial, which had followed private conversations about the ALA's tepid position on the issue of segregated libraries in the South with *Library*

Journal editor Eric Moon, sparked Moon to react—the first time the thermometer of professional discourse on the subject showed any heat. Like the *Wilson Library Bulletin*, the *Library Journal* was not an official organ of the American Library Association and often functioned as a major ALA critic. In a December 15, 1960, editorial he entitled "The Silent Subject," Moon noticed that "segregation and integration are two words which appear not to have crept into *Library Literature*," and even under existing subject headings "Negro and the Library" and "Public Libraries—Service to Negroes," *Library Literature* for 1959–60 listed none of the events taking place at segregated public libraries across the South. The index did list seven Atlanta University theses, a 1955 *Library Journal* article on "Library Service in Mississippi," and the "No Segregation Here" report mentioned earlier. "A vacuum," Moon called coverage of the subject.

To fill some of that vacuum and start a professional dialogue on the subject, Moon published in the same issue an article entitled "Segregated Libraries" by Rice Estes, a black librarian at Brooklyn's Pratt Institute who was born and raised in South Carolina and had suffered many of the humiliations Jim Crow imposed on black people. Estes's words were sharp and to the point. "So far no library association seems willing to do anything about the most pressing domestic issue the nation faces today, the integration and education of our Negro citizens," he said. "Instead, librarians are piously declaring that they will not become involved in local problems. The term 'local' is never defined." Estes noted how librarians were ready to organize a book campaign for residents of Ghana, but when denied service in Danville, Virginia, black people "were left without a librarian's voice lifted in their behalf." "As effective as its structure permits?" he quoted Wakeman. "I challenge this statement." Millions of black Americans living in the South were denied access to public libraries that their taxes helped support, and "the American Library Association has been completely ineffective about the issue. It has never even passed a resolution on the subject. It has never commended the efforts of Negro readers and organizations who have tried to end library segregation by doing everything from making a mild request to staging library sit-ins. It has not attempted to bring a law suit or lent its name as *amicus curiae* to any group bringing a suit."

Estes recalled visiting a southern library recently, where he asked a librarian how blacks were serviced. "Oh," she responded, "they are not interested in reading." Had she never read Richard Wright's *Black Boy*, he wondered, especially the part where he describes how he illicitly obtained books from Memphis's public library? "If only this passage could be reprinted and sent to every trustee of every library in the South," wrote Estes, "surely fruit would be borne." At the end of Estes's article, editor Moon reprinted the *Black Boy* passage Estes referenced and noted that Wright had recently died of a heart attack in Paris at age fifty-two.[18]

Moon's editorial and Estes's article effectively initiated the debate, and for the next several years—as news of protests and demonstrations against segregation of public facilities in the South saturated the media—ALA discussion of "integration" took priority over "censorship" as an issue of professional ethics. "I, for one, was only vaguely aware of the existence of segregated libraries in the South, and was astounded at the extent of the problem," *California Librarian* editor W. R. Eshelman said in his January 1961 issue. "Yet the subject of segregated libraries is rarely discussed and virtually unmentioned in our professional literature. If federal funds are being used to extend segregated library service, we are compounding the problem."[19] Eshelman seemed unaware of how the 1956 Library Services Act funds for which the nation's library community lobbied so hard were being allocated by southern state library agencies.

In its February 1961 issue, *Library Journal* published a "selection" of scores of letters to the editor. "Orchids to Mr. Rice Estes," wrote one Virginia community college librarian. Estes's article "left me with a very guilty feeling about my own individual failure to speak out against segregated libraries," said an Ohio reference librarian, "and I am sure many other librarians feel the same way." "I salute the editor of Lj and Mr. Rice Estes for their criticizing the pussyfooting of the ALA on the issue of segregation in our public libraries of the South," argued a Rutgers University periodicals librarian. "That this subject has first been broached in Library Journal rather than in the ALA Bulletin [the *Bulletin of the American Library Association* had been the ALA's official organ since 1905] should, I think, cause some room for thought by American librarians," argued a Long Beach, California, public library director. Ruth Brown, at the time director of the Sterling Public Library in Colorado, who had been fired as the Bartlesville, Oklahoma, Public Library director in 1950 for her efforts to desegregate public facilities, asked: "How can a librarian read [Richard Wright's *Black Boy*] and not be influenced, and how can anyone fail to see that freedom to read must include all who have that desire? I could not see then and have never understood why the ALA carefully seemed to avoid this angle."[20]

"How can an issue on which the United States Supreme Court has taken action be regarded as 'local'?" asked an Ohio State Library employee. "It is embarrassing and humiliating to think of our allegedly progressive profession sitting on the side lines in agreeable politeness throughout this period of national shame since 1954," said the Yale University Library director. Joseph Wheeler, Enoch Pratt Free Library director from 1926 to 1945, welcomed the "fresh breeze" that "blows through" *LJ*'s December 15 issue: "Oh my, I've spent 58 years listening to the smug librarians who don't want to change."[21] Wheeler said nothing, however, about interviewing black children's librarian Augusta Baker in 1933, when he "made it very plain that they weren't hiring Negro librarians." "Our interview wasn't the happiest one," Baker later recalled. Nor did he mention that a year later the library opened separate "Colored Men" and "Colored Women" washrooms because whites had complained about sharing toilets with blacks.[22]

Criticism of the ALA was justified. Discussion of integration before 1960 in the association's archives is thin. During the 1950s the *ALA Bulletin* editor said nothing about desegregating southern public libraries, "perhaps under orders from the executive director of the association, an unrepentant southerner," W. H. Eshelman later speculated.[23] While the ALA and its Intellectual Freedom Committee (IFC) carefully watched book censorship activities in southern libraries and corresponded with white librarians running them, existing correspondence shows that ALA officials and southern librarians very seldom referenced issues of segregation, except for some discussion of the eligibility of black librarians for membership in state library associations. Part of the problem was confusion surrounding the issue of professional jurisdiction. For example, although the IFC decided to collect data on segregation in southern public libraries in the fall of 1959 and the following spring sought similar data from the South's state librarians, IFC chairman Archie McNeal nonetheless felt "the committee was functioning outside the scope of its original charge and beyond the limits of the Library Bill of Rights."[24]

At its 1961 midwinter meeting, the ALA Council accepted a recommendation from its special "Committee on Civil Liberties" and adopted an addition to the Library Bill of Rights: "The rights of an individual to the use of a library should not be denied or abridged because of his race, religion, national origins or political views." In his March *Library Journal* editorial, Eric Moon welcomed the discussion, applauded the change in the Library Bill of Rights, and called for a survey that would give the IFC more information on segregated libraries. "Surely, *here* is a worthwhile project for the Council on Library Resources [CLR], one which is at least as important as the kind of charging machines libraries should use," he wrote. "The CLR financiers, the Ford Foundation, whose declared objective is 'to advance human welfare,' might well see this as an advance toward what" a Ford Foundation vice president "recently called 'the ideal library of the future.'"[25]

The debate found its way into other venues. Was National Library Week, scheduled for April 16–22, really "for all"? Harold C. Gardiner asked in the Roman

Catholic periodical *America*. In the six years since *Brown*, Gardiner noted, "scant public attention has been paid to the integration of public libraries." He called on the ALA, the National Book Committee, and Catholic organizations across the country that participated in National Library Week "to take the lead in making next year's observance truly a national affair—for all."[26]

Behind the scenes, ALA officials scrambled. Much of the news about libraries across the nation in the 1950s came to the association from news clipping services, and because sit-ins and demonstrations at public libraries were often not covered in white-owned southern newspapers, ALA officials had difficulty following events. But even direct communication often failed. "In the case of the Danville, Virginia, Library," the *Newsletter on Intellectual Freedom* editor wrote to Chairman McNeal on January 12, 1961, "I did not succeed in obtaining information from the librarian, who declined even to send me clippings."[27] To McNeal, ALA deputy director Grace Stevenson wrote on March 28, 1961: "I understand that you are writing an article for *Library Journal* around the subject of ALA's civil rights activities. Would it be possible for us to see a copy of this article for our information? We have been a little concerned about LJ's treatment of ALA's activities in the field of civil rights over the past several months."[28]

In its May issue, the *Wilson Library Bulletin* opened its pages to several black librarians. All recommended more action in the form of programs, workshops, publicity, and resolutions to local library officials as well as the possibility of withholding federal funds provided by the Library Services Act to localities using them to support segregated library practices. "Conditions can not improve until ALA takes strong action to present itself as a model in democratic practices and until the leaders in the profession can do likewise," said Virginia Lacy Jones, who not only cited many of the details her students had uncovered in researching their master's theses but also noted that her request for membership in the Georgia Library Association had again been denied. "ALA needs to be less fearful of offending by making its influence felt at the local level," she wrote. She also called upon ALA headquarters to hire black people "above the clerical level." "Every profession at one time or another must endure the test of its convictions, and this will often involve grave social and moral issues," said Miles M. Jackson of the Hampton Institute Library. "Librarianship, up to this time, has managed to skirt many such issues by ignoring them. But the time has come for the profession to be tested on just how sincerely its members believe in the philosophy that supposedly guides them." Black children's librarian Spencer Shaw, of Hempstead, New York, noted only two months separated the ALA's modification of the Library Bill of Rights and the beating of black Americans at the Jackson, Mississippi, hearing for public library demonstrators. "Clearly, the gauntlet has been thrown down," he wrote. "Are we ready to pick it up?"[29]

The act of picking up the gauntlet brought different responses, however. Although former *ALA Bulletin* editor Beatrice Rossell thought "our northern communities are too far from being 'without sin' for us to indulge in self-righteous stone-throwing at anyone," she hoped "ALA leaders will not ignore the Jackson library situation, or take the easy path of considering it 'local.' It is of national and world-wide importance, as are all these racial incidents today."[30] But in his June editorial the current editor complained about "a small but vocal element of the membership" demanding "the ALA become a crusading agency." He supported modification of the Library Bill of Rights but, after citing previous ALA actions on the issue of race, quoted from the ALA charter and constitution (both documents crafted in the late 1870s) and concluded: "It is clear from the charter and the constitution that the Association exists to further the development of libraries, not to regulate the manner in which they are operated"[31]—a line of logic that, ironically, could also be applied to the Library Bill of Rights, an overt attempt to influence library collections, which librarians regarded as a professional imperative.

"After reading your editorial concerning ALA and the segregation issue in the June Bulletin, I have decided not to renew my membership," wrote University of Vermont cataloger Paul K. Swanson to ALA executive secretary David Clift on June 21, 1961. "I do not wish to belong to an organization which on the one hand affirms the rights of all to the use of libraries and with the other cooperates with those who deny those rights. . . . Someday the battle against segregation in libraries will be won. When that day comes ALA can claim very little credit for winning." In the ALA Archives a note is attached to a letter from Clift to Archie McNeal dated November 17, nearly five months later: "I am enclosing a copy of this letter that I received last June from Paul K. Swanson. I keep looking at it every other day or so to see what kind of a reply might be made and so far I haven't come up with anything that would be useful to say or helpful to him. Any ideas?" If McNeal answered, the archives do not contain his reply.[32]

Library Journal editor Eric Moon did complain publicly, however. "LJ, we have been told, has been unnecessarily harsh in its criticism" of ALA. "It is all too easy for a large organization to become so enmeshed in procedural and constitutional problems that it reaches the point where the rule book governs the association rather than the reverse." Moon also quoted Idaho State College librarian Eli Oboler: "If ALA 'was not designed to do and by its present nature and structure cannot do' those things which its membership want it to do as relates to segregation, then the major and urgent and vital task for the Association now is to change the nature and structure of ALA to conform to its membership's wishes."[33]

In September 1961, the U.S. Commission on Civil Rights called for congressional action to withhold federal funds, under the Library Services Act, from states using those funds to maintain segregated library services.[34] More and more, as public libraries in the South became routine targets of demonstrations and sit-ins, librarians became introspective and examined themselves on the issue. *Library Journal* published a survey of twenty-two national professional associations, comparing them with the ALA on attitudes toward segregation. "ALA seems to be well above the middle range of the professional associations in statements of policy," its author reassured readers, "as well as in some of the actions already taken and now under consideration."[35]

For decades, the ALA had hosted two conferences per year—one a midwinter meeting primarily for planning, the other the ALA's main summer conference, at which it hosted major programs. At its 1961 summer conference in Cleveland, the IFC refined two recommendations to the ALA Executive Board. The first called upon the board to make sure state chapters were meeting ALA requirements by admitting all applicants for membership. At the time, because the Alabama, Georgia, and Mississippi Library Associations openly refused to admit blacks, they were not ALA chapters. The second recommended that no library be given membership if it "discriminates among users on the grounds of race, religion, or personal beliefs." Thereafter, the committee polled fourteen chapters (twelve state, two regional) primarily from the South to see "whether Negroes are eligible for membership" and "whether any Negroes are members." All fourteen reported that they did not restrict membership on the basis of race, but because an unnamed three said they had "no Negro members at the present time," the IFC concluded: "It appears equally clear that some of the chapters involved are not providing their members with the fundamental rights of membership."

When the board took up the recommendations at its 1962 midwinter meeting in Chicago, members balked at the first recommendation because, they said, it "will surely force the withdrawal or expulsion of some chapters" that operated under laws over which they had no control and would bring a "concurrent loss of many personal members in the states affected." In addition, ALA members from the South were "making significant contributions to librarianship," despite social customs and legal constraints. Therefore, the board concluded: "Should the ALA, by drastic action, separate these chapters and personal members from

ALA, breaches in understanding and professional relations might be created that would require years to heal." The second recommendation was equally troublesome. "Such a provision would surely . . . cause a regrettable and on the part of the libraries affected an unwilling loss in ALA membership and support," stated the board. Rather than impose "presently impossible-to-meet conditions on all libraries," the board recommended that the ALA Council issue a "Declaration of Belief, Encouragement and Confident Expectation" that public libraries in the South would soon desegregate and, after the IFC also endorsed it, provided a draft for council consideration.

At the meeting at which the council considered the draft, one member complained about the "short notice" given and called for a stronger statement. "I am not asking for punitive action," she said, "but for leadership." Another argued the declaration "is a monstrously cynical statement, a confession of moral bankruptcy. I would feel tragically desolate if this confession were made by the association." Recently appointed New Orleans Public Library director Jerome Cushman countered that the statement "will put us squarely, in terms of philosophy, where I want to be," but at the same time he admitted that "it will not change one blamed thing anywhere." Another council member condemned the declaration's "weasel words." Virginia Lacy Jones, the only black librarian to speak at the meeting, called the statement weak. It reads as if "ALA is fearful of losing membership in the South and the financial support of the South," she argued. After what the *Library Journal* called "much parliamentary confusion and a vigorous though meandering discussion," the council voted three to one to "recommit" the declaration to the executive board for further study and possible revision at the summer conference. "A bouquet to the ALA Council for their refusal to rubber-stamp the highly dubious statement," Moon wrote. "Brave statements, unsupported by action, can only provoke those in the South who oppose integration and irritate those who are working towards it," said the *Wilson Library Bulletin*'s Wakeman.[36]

After the midwinter conference the executive board appointed a subcommittee to revise the statement, and the council ultimately approved the "Statement on Individual Membership, Chapter Status, and Institutional Membership" on June 19. "The statement calls on *individual members* of ALA to work for an end of discrimination in libraries and in ALA chapters," the *Wilson Library Bulletin* explained. "It lists the rights of members of *ALA chapters* to certify that these rights are guaranteed to their members, it urges *institutional members* (libraries) to end discrimination among library users, and states the Council's intention of pursuing 'with diligence' a proposed study of access to libraries." ALA members thought the document more "tightly organized and concise" than its predecessor. At the same conference the ALA announced it had gathered sufficient funds to engage a nationwide study on access to public libraries.[37] Just over a month later, five black teenagers were arrested at the Albany Public Library in Georgia, and while they were conducted down the library steps, CBS News filmed the activities and broadcast the story across the nation that evening.

In his April 1963 issue, *Bay State Librarian* editor John Berry III asked if the eleven southern libraries receiving ALA-administered library awards were "segregated." He said he had contacted the Southern Regional Council about these libraries and received the following response: "Our files show no record of desegregation at any of the libraries cited in your letter. We assume, therefore, that they are still segregated." With this statement in hand, Berry concluded: "We violently oppose any award to strengthen institutions which maintain a system of service that in any way separates one citizen from another in his use of books. We ask the question in the sincere hope that every library and system involved can and will truthfully answer with a resounding 'no!' to separation, segregation, and unequal library service. Can we expect a reply?"

Because Berry made no attempt to contact the eleven libraries prior to publishing the editorial, *Library Journal* did, supplying each with a copy of Berry's editorial and requesting a response. From the responses, *LJ* reported, two evaded the question, but "seven denied unequivocally that they were segregated," some in colorful language. "I'll be damned if I'll answer [Berry's] editorial question," said the Beaufort, South Carolina, County Library director. "The *principle* of 'assuming a fact without any evidence' is something I deplore," said the North Arkansas Regional Library director. "Unfortunately racial strife will continue so long as people, expecting the worst, act on someone's assumptions instead of fact," argued the Plant City, Florida, Public Library director. "As I write from a desk in our library," wrote her board chairman, "I see in the reading room almost as many Negro patrons as white ones, and they have been coming ever since the library first opened its doors for service, and without incident!" Of the respondents, only Jackson Parish Library in Jonesboro, Louisiana, admitted segregated services that, incredibly, the librarian wrote, were "designed for the use of all citizens. The same staff—trained bookmobile librarian and clerk-driver—operate two bookmobiles, one of which is devoted exclusively to the service for Negroes, with a collection selected to appear to their interest and informational needs."[38]

By the time *LJ* published the article, ALA had met in Chicago, where it eagerly awaited the results of the survey work the association had commissioned International Research Associates (INRA) to conduct. But the results of the study that surveyed 1,789 library systems nationally (22 percent of the total)—issued in the form of a seven-page digest to a packed room at the conference—were not what most librarians expected. "This research project is highly unusual insofar as it is a self-audit by a professional group in the very delicate area of civil rights," the study began. "The position of the American Library Association in this area has been emphasized by a revision of its Bill of Rights." Yes, INRA concluded, direct racial discrimination did exist in southern public libraries, in 1963 more in rural areas than urban. In twenty-one southern public libraries in cities of at least fifty thousand people, only five had fully segregated systems. At the same time, nineteen still had segregated school systems, thus demonstrating that public library integration greatly outpaced school integration, in most cases "with a minimum of disturbance." The study also charged that "the rate of library integration is also affected by the generally low priority accorded to it by the leaders of the Negro community, as compared to the fields of voting, housing, education and other public facilities."[39]

When analyzed through the physical location of branch libraries and resources allocated to neighborhood branches, however, it became obvious that public libraries across the country—South and North—engaged in "indirect" racial discrimination. "In Philadelphia, a white neighborhood is six times as likely to possess a branch library as is a predominantly nonwhite section," the report noted. "In Detroit, twice as many branches are located in white neighborhoods as in Negro neighborhoods, and these branches contain more than one and one-half times as many books as those in predominantly non-white areas."[40]

After hearing the word *indirect*, audience members scrambled for microphones located in the aisles to protest in a cacophony that followed. "It was notable," the *ALA Bulletin* later reported, "not one question was asked about any of the ten principal findings of the Access of Public Libraries study, and that only one criticism was made—of number three," the finding referencing "indirect discrimination." That the report highlighted Detroit and Philadelphia—two systems run by former ALA presidents—may have been a coincidence, but both directors protested. Philadelphia's Emerson Greenaway took issue with "assumptions" in the report. Detroit's Ralph Ulveling was more forthright. "You've made some very serious charges about this city," he told the study's director. "This is a most damaging kind of thing." He accused INRA of using "old statistics which don't show the true picture."[41]

The statistics could also be used to explain another form of indirect discrimination that had not been acknowledged: school segregation in northern cities had actually increased in the North after the *Brown* decision. In 1960, for example, 40 percent of New York City's black and Puerto Rican schoolchildren had no white classmates; seven years later, that number had jumped to 50 percent. Across the North, cultural historian Lizbeth Cohen notes, *Brown* "became increasingly meaningless as growing residential segregation kept whites and minorities apart and persistent localism, fortified by a stratified real estate market and substantial municipal property taxes, made remedying inequality difficult." Public library funding reflected similar patterns. Virginia Lacy Jones, who recognized the indirect discrimination, spoke in favor of the study. "No one should be surprised," she said, that branch libraries across the country discriminated against black people. All public institutions "had discrimination against Negroes built into them. This fact is well known in the South; it is time the North woke up to it."[42]

After the full report was published in August—several library directors had persuaded the ALA to include a disclaimer that "poor methodology" characterized the INRA research on northern library services[43]—*Library Journal* opened the pages of its December 15 issue to a forum on the study that consisted of eleven statements and an editorial. Several contributors groused about methodologies, while others were more forgiving. "Almost invariably, libraries reflect the neighborhood served rather than the ideals of librarianship," wrote one. "The report has exposed a ghost in our purpose. This ghost is known by many aliases: apathy, cowardice, conformity, weakness, lack of political imagination, expediency, ignorance, inability, security, and defeatism." The forum included three black library professionals. Virginia Lacy Jones noted that the master's theses her students had written "reveal that [black] branches not only have an insufficient quantity of books, but that the quality of the materials is often inferior in terms of scope of subjects included and recency of publications." "A monumental document," black librarian and civil rights activist E. J. Josey called it, "that stirred up a hornet's nest in Chicago," where, "strangely enough," he teased, "the most vehement denunciations . . . came from the North and not the South." He was most disappointed at the comments of the "timid lot" of southern librarians and board members, which reflected a "poverty of values" and convinced him "that the keepers of knowledge in these communities are not concerned about providing library service to all citizens which will strengthen democracy in America."[44]

The same issue carried an article by Bernice Lloyd Bell, whose research was based on her master's thesis at Atlanta University's School of Library Service. In her summary she reported the progress made, which was also evident in the "Access" study. She did not mention the fact that what little existed as a research base on library services to black Americans was little read and had been written almost entirely by blacks and that the vast majority of that literature came from master's degree students at a black university in the South. As a group, white library researchers at any level—student, library school faculty member, or professional librarian—were almost entirely absent, a telling example of the limits of a professional discourse in the middle of a civil rights revolution.[45]

Although several southern state library association chapters had been banished from ALA membership, not all communications between them ceased. When, for example, Virginia Steele organized a Community Center Freedom Library in Greenville, Mississippi, during the 1964 Freedom Summer, she wrote to Mississippi Library Commission director Lura G. Currier for help. When she received no response, she wrote to Grace Stevenson at the ALA, who forwarded publications designed to help start a library. In her response, however, Stevenson added: "I think you can understand why it is not possible for Mrs. Currier, who has labored valiantly for years to improve library service for all the people of Mississippi, to become involved with your program in any way." A day later Currier and Steele did have a phone conversation, after which Steele wrote Currier: "Just a note to thank you for the phone conversation yesterday, and the background of your struggle for library service. My impression is that you're doing an heroic and brave job."[46]

As more public libraries in the South integrated, the library press did finally take notice—*Library Literature* cited fifty-six articles under "Segregation and the Library" for 1961–63—but thereafter, as Jim Crow libraries rapidly diminished in numbers, the subject heading disappeared again in 1965. Most professional attention was instead redirected at denying segregated library institutions and segregated state library associations the privilege of ALA membership. But by 1966 all southern state library associations were integrated. In 1968 one librarian perceived a professional "consensus" on the issue of the integration of southern public libraries and concluded, "The American Library Association has probably done as much as it can to enforce non-discrimination among its members."[47]

Ultimately, little that the ALA, its members, or any other state and national library organization or association did or said about segregated public library practices in the South had significant impact at the local level. "For both black and white [Alabama] librarians, there were social, economic, and even physical dangers associated with open opposition to the prevailing racial order," writes library historian Toby Graham. White southern librarians who agreed with or supported the desegregation of public libraries ran the risk of being called "nigger lovers"— an epithet that threatened to separate them from friends and family. Precedent existed and was part of the grapevine. "The library organizations at the state and national levels had less to fear," according to Graham, "but they were also unprepared to forcefully address issues as complex and as emotionally charged as race relations. Librarians lacked a tradition of organized resistance and were wary of becoming entangled in social issues of 'local' concern." The ALA, Graham argues, "had little influence" on the desegregation of Alabama's public libraries, adding: "The support it provided for [anti-segregationist] librarians like Juliette Morgan, Emily Reed and Patricia Blalock was negligible." His conclusion that events in Alabama "demonstrated that the efforts of black protesters were ultimately more important to the cause of equal access to public libraries than the impulses of librarians on the state and national level to fulfill their professional values" is equally accurate for other Jim Crow states.[48]

In our research, we were unable to find any references that ALA actions directly or even marginally influenced decisions to desegregate local libraries. Although the ALA filed one amicus brief in an Alabama censorship case regarding Henry Miller's *Tropic of Cancer* in 1962, it failed to file similar briefs in any of the cases involving public library desegregation that we covered in previous chapters. And after 1965 the impact of race riots in northern cities captured most of the attention of the library press on race issues, perhaps in part because many of these riots occurred closer to editorial homes.

In the 1960s, librarians carped at each other about right moves and wrong moves, and many expressed righteous indignation about the manifestations of segregated libraries. Always, however, they spoke from the periphery of desegregation activities. Although *Library Journal* editor Eric Moon later recalled a few unpleasant encounters at ALA conferences with "three or four lady battle-ax state librarians, all from the South" who opposed his civil rights positions on public libraries, these encounters never left the conference hallways.[49] Few librarians were ready to put their lives on the line for the cause; few had suffered Jim Crow humiliations as a routine way of life, walked up public library steps through hostile white crowds carrying bats and clubs and shouting "Nigger," sat in libraries before the eyes of angry white librarians and their white patrons, or were arrested on site only to be walked back through (and occasionally beaten by) the same crowds, then carted off to jail, where, if the history they knew was any teacher, they were easy prey for lynch mobs.

EPILOGUE

By 1965, public libraries in the South were no longer primary targets of demonstrations, sit-ins, and read-ins. When, for example, civil rights activists announced a three-month campaign in Bessemer, Alabama, in June and targeted the public library as its first site, they met no opposition. As "demonstrators" approached the circulation desk, the librarian registered them for borrowers' cards without resistance and calmly explained library rules and regulations. One of them checked out his first library book, *The Negro Protest*.[1] Before the end of the decade, racially separate state library organizations no longer existed, and by 1972, 90 percent of people living in the South—black and white—lived in public library service areas.[2] The goal of integrating southern public libraries had been accomplished, but not without pain, anguish, and danger.

The history of desegregating southern public libraries shows mixed patterns. Some people in black communities across the South were repulsed by the concept of black branches from the beginning of the twentieth century; some welcomed black branches whenever they came. Although youthful 1950s and 1960s protesters were overwhelmingly local blacks and not "outside agitators," they were nonetheless minorities even among their peers (high school and college) because they dared to risk their futures—if not their lives—by participating in the demonstrations. In addition, they differed from previous generations of blacks in the South.

Young people did not tolerate segregation as well as older generations and were more willing to challenge it. The generation that grew up after *Brown* sensed that nothing would change unless they changed it. They wanted a better world than their parents, and they rejected not only the practices of the white world in which they existed but also those of the black world they had inherited. Jesse Jackson's relationship with his stepfather is a good example. "As the student movement grew throughout the South—the younger the potential volunteer, the more willing he or she was to take risks," notes David Halberstam, "while the converse was generally true—the older the students, the more they had a stake in terms of career and career expectations, and the less likely they were to join up."[3] "The scenario of the drama," Annie McPheeters later recalled, "was largely written and produced by our young people" not "willing to wait any longer. They wanted freedom NOW."[4]

Unlike the 1955 Montgomery bus boycott, the 1960 Greensboro lunch counter sit-ins, the 1961 Freedom Riders, and the 1963 March on Washington, public library protests seldom made front-page news, even in local papers. Generally they happened in the background of the larger civil rights movement, which by 1963 many Americans identified primarily with the activities of Martin Luther King Jr., who participated in very few public library protests. In some places public library protests increased racial polarization and civil disorder; in others they had the opposite effect. Except for CORE's work in rural Louisiana in 1964, none of the civil rights organizations—CORE, the NAACP, the SCLC, or SNCC—can claim primary credit for desegregating southern public libraries. Protests were spontaneous, often loosely organized, yet in their willingness to sacrifice by going to jail and subjecting themselves to harassment to integrate public libraries, protesters found unity.

White community reactions to pressures brought by young blacks to integrate public library systems were also mixed. Some followed the lead of white power establishments and resisted vehemently, sometimes violently. On the other hand, some fought Jim Crow public library practices in myriad ways (seldom publicly) and for a variety of reasons, including a sense of fairness, fear of negative publicity, and a desire not to see the local public library close. As a group, southern white librarians were hardly unified. "Most white librarians" in Alabama, Toby Graham concludes, "were moderates and largely apolitical on the subject of race; they were neither fervent segregationists nor vocal supporters of civil rights. . . . Librarians' attitudes toward blacks were as varied and as difficult to explain as the complex relationships between white moderates and blacks in the general population." His conclusion that "most" Alabama public library directors "led their institutions toward integration only after the libraries became the subject of sit-in protests or federal pressure" is just as true for the rest of the South.[5]

Brown v. Louisiana (1966) largely marked the end of Jim Crow practices in southern public libraries. Understandably, in many libraries forced to integrate, many of the new black patrons who showed up at the circulation desk initially met a very chilly reception. Only time tempered that response. But even with these newly acquired rights to use public libraries, southern blacks did not rush to use library services in great numbers. "Negroes are not taking advantage of this great opportunity of using library facilities," complained black Savannah State College librarian and civil rights activist E. J. Josey in 1962. "It is disheartening to note the many references made by directors of recently desegregated libraries that 'there has not been any substantial increase in the use of the library by Negroes.'"[6]

Nonetheless, during the 1950s and 1960s, southern public libraries played an important role by functioning as sites for trial-and-error desegregation efforts to see what worked, and what didn't. In most communities, desegregating public library systems worked faster than the desegregation of other public accommodations, especially in public education. In many cases, public libraries subsequently also became sites and symbols of reconciliation between the white and black races in the South, places where "the ghost of Jim Crow" seldom visited. In her analysis of 1950s and 1960s segregated recreational facilities in the United States, Victoria Walcott found that "whites no longer perceived" these facilities "as safe havens for families, and as a result most closed by the early 1970s. This fact demonstrates the limits of the 1964 Civil Rights Act. Because racial inequality is deeply spatial, legislation cannot change the association of black-dominated spaces with disorder."[7] Walcott's observations, however, do not apply to segregated public library systems, all of which are still open and now open to all.

Examples abound. Twenty years after the Birmingham Public Library desegregated, the city's first black mayor opened a new building that contained a large civil rights archive, including the papers of Eugene "Bull" Connor—"part of our history," the mayor commented at the dedication, "but one we're proud to have moved away from."[8] The black literature collection Annie McPheeters worked for years to build at the Atlanta Public Library's Sweet Auburn Branch eventually became the Auburn Avenue Research Library on African American Culture and History, "the first library in the Southeast to offer specialized reference and archival collections dedicated to the study and research of African American culture and history and of other peoples of African descent."[9] In 1996 the Broward County Public Library system in Florida began plans to build an African American Research Library and Cultural Center in the black community. "An exciting, ambitious concept," Fort Lauderdale's Sun Sentinel called it, to consist of seventy-five thousand books by and about African Americans housed in a "community cultural center" with a three hundred–seat auditorium and multiple exhibit spaces to host authors, artists, actors, dancers, and musicians.[10] It opened in 2002. In 1999 John

Lewis, a 1960s Freedom Rider, SNCC organizer, and since 1986 a Georgia congressman, returned to the Troy Public Library in Alabama, to which he had been denied access in the 1950s, to sign copies of his award-winning book, *Walking with the Wind: A Memoir of the Movement,* published the previous year.[11]

In 2006 the widow of Michael Schwerner—who, with fellow civil rights workers James Chaney and Andrew Goodman, was killed in 1964 by Ku Klux Klan members in Philadelphia, Mississippi—donated money to the Neshoba County Public Library's Collier-Mars Civil Rights Collection, established several years earlier by a multiracial Philadelphia coalition that led efforts to bring one of the killers to trial and convict him in 2005 for his part in the murders. The collection was named for the black minister who bravely delivered Chaney's graveyard eulogy and a white woman who had immediately denounced the murders and as a result lost her local business.[12] Whereas forty years earlier a Mississippi public library was often a place that divided races, now, in Philadelphia, it was a place to bring them together. Two years later the Jackson Public Library renamed its South Hills Branch after Richard Wright. As a child in Jim Crow Mississippi, Wright had been denied access to any public library.[13]

In Georgia in 2008 the Columbus Public Library hosted "381 Days: The Montgomery Bus Boycott Story," an exhibit circulating public libraries across the South and the rest of the country that marked the fiftieth anniversary of Rosa Parks's arrest. Fifty years earlier, the library had itself been segregated.[14] In 2015 a six-panel mural depicting the 1965 Selma to Montgomery, Alabama, march completed by George Washington Carver High School students in the mid-1990s found a home outside the Rufus Lewis Regional Library on Mobile Highway, which fifty years earlier marchers had passed.[15]

While the public library as a place in the South offered platforms for racial reconciliation after 1965, the library profession as a whole does not appear to have internalized into its collective memory the deeply painful experiences desegregating public libraries brought to black Americans. As part of the "Libraries and the Life of the Mind in America" series of lectures the ALA hosted for its centennial year, in 1975 eminent black historian John Hope Franklin—who in the 1950s had to turn down luncheon invitations from fellow researchers at the Library of Congress because nearby restaurants denied him service—delivered an address entitled "Libraries in a Pluralistic Society." American librarians "have many reasons to be pleased with their contributions to the life of the mind in the United States," he said, but Franklin also reminded his audience that Carnegie had been complicit with local southern whites who segregated their public library services. And "until the recent cases involving public education and the passage of the Civil Rights Act of 1964," he noted, "public libraries in the South and in the ghettos of the North were not serving in a manner to promote the healthy growth of a pluralistic society." He concluded by calling on the profession to recognize its flawed history as a way to help it live up to its high ideals.[16]

Yet less than two years later, the ALA's Office of Intellectual Freedom (OIF) released *The Speaker*, a film that depicted a high school group's contested decision to invite a controversial but fictitious eugenicist (based on the real-life Stanford University scientist William Shockley), who believed black people were genetically inferior to whites, to speak on their campus. When ALA executive board members previewed it in early 1977, "not a person moved," recalled Robert Wedgeworth, the ALA's first black executive director. Reaction was so intense that it "pitted friend against friend; colleague against colleague."[17]

On one side were members who argued the film represented a good way to generate discussion about the importance of defending intellectual freedom. They were led by Judith Krug, a Pittsburgh, Pennsylvania, native who had received a library science degree from the University of Chicago in 1962 and spent several years as a reference librarian in the Windy City before becoming the ALA's first director of the newly created Office of Intellectual Freedom in 1967. She held an absolutist position on people's right to free access to information—no matter how controversial—and a commitment to link that position with ALA policy and librarianship's professional practice. She did not, however, have any personal experience in southern Jim Crow practices as a librarian or patron nor any direct experiences with the way the ALA had addressed the issue of segregated public library services before 1960.

On the other side were members who said the subject of the film was probably racist, certainly highly insensitive. Among those leading this group was ALA Black Caucus organizer E. J. Josey, born and raised in Norfolk, Virginia, and from 1959 to 1966 chief librarian at the historically black Savannah State College. At the 1963 ALA conference, he had objected vehemently when the ALA sought to honor the Mississippi Library Association's journal and cited the fact that no black Mississippi librarians were allowed to be members of that association. Another was Clara Stanton Jones, Detroit Public Library director, who, as the association's first black president, presided over the 1977 conference. Jones had grown up in the 1920s in segregated St. Louis, in the 1930s was educated at historically black Spelman College in segregated Atlanta, and spent the early years of her professional career serving as an academic librarian at Dillard and Southern Universities, both historically black colleges, in segregated New Orleans.

Both Josey and Jones had directly experienced the humiliations Jim Crow forced on their lives, and both had witnessed the ALA's relative silence against segregated public library systems in the American South throughout the 1950s and 1960s. Perhaps it was these experiences that caused Josey to refer to *The Speaker* as "that goddamned film" and grounded Jones's thinking when she accused the OIF of being "insensitive." Together, they echoed the thoughts of many others who wondered why the OIF had chosen the subject, when other subjects would have served the purpose equally well. That Josey and Jones lived the history this book describes—and Krug did not—perhaps explains why. How else to explain Krug's historically ill-informed response to a *Chicago Daily News* reporter who covered an ALA debate about *The Speaker* at its January 1978 midwinter conference? The association, she said, had "been front and center since 1940 in support of the First Amendment."[18]

At its 2014 summer conference, thirty-seven years after the ALA showed *The Speaker*, the association hosted a program entitled "Speaking about 'The Speaker,'" cosponsored by its Intellectual Freedom Committee, the Black Caucus, and the Library History Round Table. The association had arranged for two conference screenings of the film before the program, then followed it with a moderated audience discussion. "OIF is aware of the hard feelings—and even pain—the film and its controversy brought to many members of the association," a preliminary program summary noted. "It's our belief that a thoughtful reflection of the film and the controversy by those who were there, as well as those who have studied and otherwise considered the issues, can help ALA members, particularly those who are newer members, as we continue to discuss often difficult issues within the association." Yet one member—who was also a member of the Intellectual Freedom Round Table, the Social Responsibilities Round Table, and its Feminist Task Force—would have none of it. "There is no way having this program can help but open old wounds," she argued. "It was a very painful time for ALA and I, for one, see no reason to rehash this experience. It might be different if this would lead us to a better understanding of intellectual freedom and racism, but I doubt that it will do either of these things."[19]

The stories we tell in previous pages are an undeniable part of southern, civil rights, and library history. We hope we've done an adequate job of filling a knowledge gap in southern and civil rights historical literature. As for library history, our purpose is broader. Several years ago, when we told a couple of colleagues from other institutions in the South that we were working on this book, one asked, "You mean southern public libraries were segregated at one time?" Another wanted us to lecture to his Intellectual Freedom class about the heroic defense he assumed that public librarians had put up against segregated services. Both had absorbed professional myths and assumed that librarianship's twenty-first-century rhetoric about opposing censorship, defending intellectual freedom, and offering neutral service to all people characterized its entire history.

Although librarianship has moved away from the 1960s chronologically, the story we tell here directly challenges the profession's collective memory of this subject and time period and provides essential information heretofore absent from our professional discourse. In 1995 Todd Honma addressed what he saw as "the invisibility of race in library and information studies" and concluded that over the years librarianship has by its silence been complicit in the formation and to some extent the perpetuation of systemic racism.[20] John Hope Franklin's admonition to develop "better understanding of intellectual freedom and racism" as subjects in contemporary professional practice is as relevant today as when he delivered it in 1975. Without coming to grips with a history that portrays both halos and warts, the library profession will always have difficulty seeing the limits of its ability to provide services, books, and other materials "presenting all points of view concerning the problems and issues of our times."[21]

On July 11, 2010, four members of South Carolina's "Greenville Eight," who had conducted a sit-in at the Greenville Public Library fifty years earlier, met to celebrate and reminisce. "In this place of hope, 50 years ago we found rejection and degradation," said Jesse Jackson, one of the protesters present. "We persevered—and now America is better off for it." Margaree Crosby, another of the protesters, told a reporter: "Everybody asks me, 'Well, were you afraid?' I say, 'No, I was not afraid.'" "I still stand for justice. I still stand for the right thing," added Elaine Means, a third protester. When it was brought to their attention that the public library had no permanent marker to commemorate their act, Jackson expressed regret; he hoped that would be corrected.[22]

Over previous decades, members of the media (national, state, and local), local and state governments, business leaders, professional associations, and civic organizations of all kinds have apologized either for previous racist behavior or for doing little or nothing while black people were beaten, jailed, and sometimes killed for standing up for their civil rights. Library associations, including the American Library Association, have never done that—in large part, we suspect, because most librarians living today do not know the history recorded in these pages. It's long past time that library organizations and individual libraries do something to recognize the kids—now senior citizens for those who are still alive—who literally risked their lives to integrate libraries. Perhaps libraries can start by posting a commendation on the wall next to a copy of a Library Bill of Rights that provided these young activists no support in the 1960s.

APPENDIX

SELECTED LIST OF PUBLIC LIBRARY PROTESTERS

NAME	RACE	SEX	AGE	RESIDENCE	OCCUPATION/STATUS

Alexandria, Va., August 21, 1939

NAME	RACE	SEX	AGE	RESIDENCE	OCCUPATION/STATUS
William "Buddy" Evans	B	M	19	Alexandria	
Edward Gaddis	B	M	21	Alexandria	
Morris M. Murray	B	M	22	Alexandria	
Bobby Strange	B	M	14	Alexandria	
Clarence "Buck" Strange	B	M	20	Alexandria	
Otto Lee Tucker	B	M	22	Alexandria	

Petersburg, Va., February 28, 1960
140 protesters, mostly students from Peabody High School
and Virginia State College, including

NAME	RACE	SEX	AGE	RESIDENCE	OCCUPATION/STATUS
Betty Johnson	B	F	19		College student
C. J. Malloy	B	M	20		College student
E. J. McLaughlin	B	M	20		College student

March 7, 1960
Those Arrested

NAME	RACE	SEX	AGE	RESIDENCE	OCCUPATION/STATUS
Horace Brooks	B	M	17	Petersburg	High school student
Edwin Jordan	B	M	19	Petersburg	College student
Foster Miles Jr.	B	M	20	Charles City	College student
Lillian E. Pride	B	F	20	Hampton	College student
Virginius B. Thornton	B	M	25	West Point	College student
Cassie L. Walker	B	F	30	Petersburg	Beautician
Leon R. Walker	B	M	17	Petersburg	High school student
Sandra Walker	B	F	19	Petersburg	College student
Wyatt T. Walker	B	M	31	Petersburg	Minister

NAME	RACE	SEX	AGE	RESIDENCE	OCCUPATION/STATUS
R. G. Williams	B	M		Petersburg	Minister
Robert W. Williams	B	M	24	Front Royal	College student

Those Not Arrested

Patrice Walker	B	F	8	Petersburg	Grade school
Mrs. Wyatt T. Walker	B	F		Petersburg	Housewife
Wyatt T. Walker Jr.	B	M	6	Petersburg	Grade school
R. Gilmore Williams	B	M	11	Petersburg	Grade school

Memphis, Tenn. March 20, 1960

Marion S. Barry	B	M	24	Memphis	College student
Aminda Battles	B	F			
Clyde Battles	B	M	19	Memphis	College student
Horace John Bell	B	M			
Aaron Booker	B	F			
Laverda Bradford	B	F			
Roosevelt Brassel	B	M			
Willie Brown	B	M			
Chester B. Cade Jr.	B	M			
Josephine Bonita Cashel	B	F			
Arthur Eberhardt	B	M			
Jevita Lois Edwards	B	F			
Evander Ford	B	M			
Gwen Glover	B	F			
Willie F. Granderson	B	M			
Ray F. Grimes	B	M			
Emilyn Harris	B	F			
Hardin Jones Jr.	B	M			
Ernestine Lee	B	F			
Martha Ellis Little	B	F			
Eddie Charles Meacham	B	M			
Elmer Moore Jr.	B	M			
Henry Moses	B	M			
Curtis R. Murphy	B	M			
Olly Neal Jr.	B	M			
Mary Ellis Perry	B	M			
Marvin L. Plunkett	B	M			
Coy Sanders	B	M			

NAME	RACE	SEX	AGE	RESIDENCE	OCCUPATION/STATUS
Willie Lee Shotwell Jr.	B	M			
Doris Jean Townsend	B	F			
Gwendolyn Y. Townsend	B	F			
Benjamin Ward Jr.	B	M			
Joan Louise Wiggins	B	F			
Walter Wilson	B	M			
Edgar M. Young	B	M			
George E. Hardin	B	M			*Memphis Tri-State Defender* photographer
Burleigh Himes	B	M			*Memphis Tri-State Defender* city editor
Robert Morris	B	M			*Memphis World* photographer
Lutrelle F. Palmer	B	F			*Memphis Tri-State Defender* editor
Thaddeus T. Stokes	B	M			*Memphis World* editor

Memphis, Tenn., March 22, 1960

NAME	RACE	SEX	AGE	RESIDENCE	OCCUPATION/STATUS
Ronald B. Anderson	B	M			
Rosetta Jean Bonds	B	F			
Mattie M. Daniels	B	F			
Jo Iris	B	F			
Virginia Owens	B	F			
Darnell L. Thomas	B	M			

Danville, Va. April 2, 1960

NAME	RACE	SEX	AGE	RESIDENCE	OCCUPATION/STATUS
Inez Coleman	B	F	17	Danville	High school student
Wayne L. Dallas	B	M	18	Danville	High school student
James Dixon Jr.	B	M	24	Danville	
Gladys Giles	B	F	16	Danville	High school student
Virginia G. Gunner	B	F	16	Danville	High school student
Dennis Harris	B	M	16	Danville	High school student
William Love	B	M	17	Danville	High school student
Joe B. McNoir	B	M	17	Danville	High school student
Chalmas W. Mebane	B	M	23	Danville	High school student
William E. Redd Jr.	B	M	17	Danville	High school student
Fred H. Vann Jr.	B	M	16	Danville	High school student
Sylvester Walton	B	M	16	Danville	High school student
Barbara Watkins	B	F	16	Danville	High school student

NAME	RACE	SEX	AGE	RESIDENCE	OCCUPATION/STATUS
Jerry Williams	B	M	13	Danville	High school student
Robert Williams	B	M	15	Danville	High school student
Carolyn L. Young	B	F	18	Danville	High school student

Greenville, S.C., July 16, 1960
"Greenville 8"

NAME	RACE	SEX	AGE	RESIDENCE	OCCUPATION/STATUS
Margaree S. Crosby	B	F	16	Greenville	High school student
Joan Mattison Daniel	B	F	16	Greenville	High school student
Benjamin Downs	B	M	16	Greenville	High school student
Jesse Jackson	B	M	19	Greenville	College student
Elaine Means	B	F	17	Greenville	High school student
Dorris Wright	B	M	17	Greenville	High school student
Hattie Smith Wright	B	F	15	Greenville	High school student
Willie Joe Wright	B	M	16	Greenville	High school student

Jackson, Miss., March 27, 1961
"Tougaloo Nine"

NAME	RACE	SEX	AGE	RESIDENCE	OCCUPATION/STATUS
Meredith Anding	B	M		Jackson	College student
James Cleo Bradford	B	M		Memphis	College student
Alfred Cook	B	M		Flint, Mich.	College student
Geraldine Edwards	B	F		Natchez	College student
Janice Jackson	B	F		Clarksdale	College student
Joseph Jackson Jr.	B	M		Memphis	College student
Albert Lassiter	B	F		Vicksburg	College student
Evelyn Pierce	B	F		Buffalo, N.Y.	College student
Ethel Sawyer	B	F		Memphis	College student

Montgomery, Ala., March 15, 1962
Five Montgomery high school students, four boys, one girl, including

NAME	RACE	SEX	AGE	RESIDENCE	OCCUPATION/STATUS
Robert L. Cobb	B	M	18	Montgomery	High school student

Albany, Ga., March, 1963

NAME	RACE	SEX	AGE	RESIDENCE	OCCUPATION/STATUS
Bernice Johnson Reagon	B	F			College student

NAME	RACE	SEX	AGE	RESIDENCE	OCCUPATION/STATUS

Birmingham, Ala., April 10, 1963
Eight Mills College students, including

NAME	RACE	SEX	AGE	RESIDENCE	OCCUPATION/STATUS
U. W. Clemon	B	M			College student
Addine "Deenie" Drew	B	F			College student
Sandra Edwards	B	F			College student
Catherine Jones	B	F			College student
Shelley Millender	B	M			College student

Columbus, Ga., July 5, 1963
Seven high school students, ages 13–17, six girls, one boy, including

NAME	RACE	SEX	AGE	RESIDENCE	OCCUPATION/STATUS
Gwendolyn Smyre	B	F	15	Columbus	High school student
Cleophas Tyson	B	M	17	Columbus	High school student

July 9, 1963

NAME	RACE	SEX	AGE	RESIDENCE	OCCUPATION/STATUS
William T. Crawford	B	M	19	Columbus	
Forge M. McGruder	B	M	17	Columbus	High school student
Jake D. Porter Jr.	B	M	17	Columbus	High school student
Charles Henry Wright	B	M	18	Columbus	High school student

July 10, 1963

NAME	RACE	SEX	AGE	RESIDENCE	OCCUPATION/STATUS
Gene Lewis	B	M	20	Columbus	
James Mitchell	B	M	17	Columbus	High school student
Mary Moss	B	F	20	Columbus	"NAACP employee"
Cleophas Tyson	B	M	17	Columbus	High school student
Charles Willis	B	M	18	Columbus	High school student

Hattiesburg, Miss., August 14, 1964

NAME	RACE	SEX	AGE	RESIDENCE	OCCUPATION/STATUS
Sandra Adickes	W	F	29	New York	Schoolteacher
Curtis Duckworth	B	M	15	Hattiesburg	High school student
Gwen Merritt	B	F	13	Hattiesburg	High school student
Carolyn Moncure	B	F	14	Hattiesburg	High school student
Diane Moncure	B	F	17	Hattiesburg	High school student
Lavon Reed	B	M	15	Hattiesburg	High school student
Jimella Stokes	B	F	16	Hattiesburg	High school student

NAME	RACE	SEX	AGE	RESIDENCE	OCCUPATION/STATUS

August 17, 1964

NAME	RACE	SEX	AGE	RESIDENCE	OCCUPATION/STATUS
Lee Pollard Abrams	B	M	16	Hattiesburg	High school student
Ben Achtenberg	W	M	20	Kansas City	COFO volunteer
Thomas L. Edwards	W	M	33	Illinois	COFO volunteer
William D. Jones	B	M	38	New York	COFO volunteer
Cynthia McCarty	B	F	9	Hattiesburg	Grade school student
Dorothy Jean Patterson	B	F	12	Hattiesburg	Grade school student
Susan Patterson	W	F	26	New York	COFO volunteer
Janice Walton	B	F	16	Hattiesburg	High school student
Shirley White	B	F	15	Hattiesburg	High school student
Jerry Wilson	B	M	17	Hattiesburg	High school student

Audubon Regional Library, Clinton (La.) Branch, March 7, 1964

NAME	RACE	SEX	AGE	RESIDENCE	OCCUPATION/STATUS
L. C. Bibbins	B	M	17	St. Francisville	Student
Henry Brown	B	M	26	Jackson	
Willie Kelly	B	M	17	St. Francisville	Student
Cleveland McKinzie	B	M	17	St. Francisville	Student
Robert Smith	B	M	19	St. Francisville	

St. Helena Branch, March 11, 1964
"A group of Negro youths"

NAME	RACE	SEX	AGE	RESIDENCE	OCCUPATION/STATUS
Alton Crier	B	M			
Sterling Hall	B	M			
David Howard	B	M			

Jackson Parish Library, Jonesboro, La., July 22, 1964

NAME	RACE	SEX	AGE	RESIDENCE	OCCUPATION/STATUS
Fred Beard	B	M		Jonesboro	
Fred Brooks	B	M		Jonesboro	
Charles Crow	B	M		Jonesboro	
Earlene Knox	B	F		Jonesboro	
Mary Potts	B	F		Jonesboro	
Shirley Potts	B	M		Jonesboro	
Larry Robinson	B	M	13	Jonesboro	High school student

NAME	RACE	SEX	AGE	RESIDENCE	OCCUPATION/STATUS

Ouachita Parish Public Library, Anna Meyer Branch, July 9, 1964

NAME	RACE	SEX	AGE	RESIDENCE	OCCUPATION/STATUS
Jimmy Andrews	B	M	16	Monroe	High school student
Bennie Roy Brass	B	M	18	Monroe	High school student
Etta Faye Carter	B	F	16	Monroe	High school student
Dorothy Higgins	B	F	18	Monroe	High school student
Betty Jo Johnson	B	F	17	Monroe	High school student
Robert Earl Peevey	B	M	15	Monroe	High school student
Ronnie Lee Taylor	B	M	13	Monroe	High school student

July 20, 1964

NAME	RACE	SEX	AGE	RESIDENCE	OCCUPATION/STATUS
Bessie Dill	B	F	20	Monroe	
Larry Edwards	B	F	16	Monroe	High school student
Diane Gordon	B	F	17	Monroe	High school student
Vera Stewart	B	F	15	Monroe	High school student
William Thomas	B	M	19	Monroe	

July 22, 1964

NAME	RACE	SEX	AGE	RESIDENCE	OCCUPATION/STATUS
Robert Garner	B	M	16	Monroe	High school student
George Padio	B	M	15	Monroe	High school student
Tommy Robinson	B	M	16	Monroe	High school student
Donnell Wyatt	B	M	16	Monroe	High school student

Ouachita Parish Public Library, Main Library, July 20, 1964

NAME	RACE	SEX	AGE	RESIDENCE	OCCUPATION/STATUS
Charles Pressley	B	M	26	Monroe	
Tommie Robinson	B	M	16	Monroe	High school student
Alice Smith	B	F	16	Monroe	High school student
Jackie Smith	B	F	14	Monroe	High school student
Marjorie Smith	B	F	22	Monroe	
Belva Stewart	B	F	13	Monroe	High school student

July 22, 1964

NAME	RACE	SEX	AGE	RESIDENCE	OCCUPATION/STATUS
Lettie Bess	B	F	13	Monroe	High school student
Betty Carter	B	F	19	Monroe	
Alma Henderson	B	F	18	Monroe	High school student
Robert Peevey	B	M	15	Monroe	High school student

NAME	RACE	SEX	AGE	RESIDENCE	OCCUPATION/STATUS
Ouachita Parish Public Library, West Monroe Branch, July 20, 1964					
Willie Mellion	B	M	17	Monroe	High school student
Robert Saulsberry	B	M	17	Monroe	High school student
David Tribble	B	M	19	Monroe	
Joe Tribble	B	M	17	Monroe	High school student
July 22, 1964					
James Johnson	B	M	16	Monroe	High school student
Eddie Myles	B	M	18	Monroe	High school student
Joseph Profit	B	M	15	Monroe	High school student
Henry Steele	B	M	14	Monroe	High school student

SOURCE: Taxonomy adapted from Arsenault, *Freedom Riders*, 533–87.

NOTES

INTRODUCTION

1. Quoted in Fred Powledge, *Free at Last? The Civil Rights Movement and the People Who Made It* (Boston: Little, Brown, 1991), 98–99.

2. Sec. 2 of the Fourteenth Amendment reads in part: "Representatives shall be apportioned among the several states according to their respective numbers. . . . But when the right to vote at any election for the choice of electors for President and Vice President . . . Representatives in Congress, the executive and judicial officers of a state, or the members of the legislature thereof, is denied to any of the *male* inhabitants of such state, . . . or in any way abridged, . . . the basis of representation therein shall be reduced in the proportion which the number of such male citizens shall bear to the whole number of male citizens twenty-one years of age in such state" (emphasis added).

3. Eugene Gressman, "The Unhappy History of Civil Rights Legislation," *Michigan Law Review* 50 (June 1952): 1323, 1326, 1336.

4. See, e.g., Slaughterhouse Cases, 83 U.S. 36 (1873); United States v. Cruikshank, 92 U.S. 542 (1876); Virginia v. Rives, 100 U.S. 313 (1879). For a general discussion of this development, see Gressman, "Unhappy History," 1337–40.

5. See United States v. Stanley, 109 U.S. 3 (1883).

6. Gressman, "Unhappy History," 1342.

7. Plessy v. Ferguson, 163 U.S. 537, 544, 548–49, 551 (1896).

8. Joseph William Singer, "No Right to Exclude: Public Accommodations and Private Property," *Northwestern University Law Review* 90 (Summer 1996): 1283, 1388.

9. Isabel Wilkerson, *The Warmth of Other Suns: The Epic Story of America's Great Migration* (New York: Random House, 2010), 44–45.

10. Ira Berlin, *The Making of African America: The Four Great Migrations* (New York: Viking, 2010), 184.

11. Constance Webb, *Richard Wright: A Biography* (New York: G. P. Putnam's Sons, 1968), 227–28.

12. PBS Newshour Transcript, Brown v. Board of Education, www.pbs.org/newshour/bb/law/jan -june04/brown_05–12.html.

13. Brown v. Board of Education, 347 U.S. 483, 495 (1954).

14. PBS Newshour Transcript, Brown v. Board of Education.

15. See Timothy B. Tyson, *The Blood of Emmett Till* (New York: Simon & Schuster, 2017).

16. Quoted in Powledge, *Free at Last*, 71–72.

17. Powledge, *Free at Last*, 107.

18. See Raymond Arsenault, *Freedom Riders: 1961 and the Struggle for Racial Justice* (New York: Oxford University Press, 2006), 511–12. See also James Laue, *Action and Desegregation, 1960–1962: Toward a Theory of the Rationalization of Protest* (Brooklyn: Carlson Publishing, 1989), 107–8; and Diane McWhorter, *Carry Me Home: Birmingham, Alabama: The Climactic Battle of the Civil Rights Revolution* (New York: Simon & Schuster, 2001), 236.

19. Powledge, *Free at Last,* 523, 542.

20. Quoted in Nick Kotz, *Lyndon Baines Johnson, Martin Luther King Jr., and the Laws That Changed America* (Boston: Houghton Mifflin, 2005), 33.

21. Civil Rights Act of 1964, 42 U.S.C. 2000a.

22. Bruce Ackerman, *We the People,* vol. 3: *The Civil Rights Revolution* (Cambridge: Belknap Press of Harvard University Press, 2014), 133.

23. "Civil Rights: And the Walls Came Tumbling," *Time,* July 17, 1964, 25–26.

24. Benjamin Muse, *The American Negro Revolution* (Bloomington: Indiana University Press, 1968), 97.

25. Stephen Tuck, *We Ain't What We Ought to Be: The Black Freedom Struggle from Emancipation to Obama* (Cambridge: Belknap Press of Harvard University Press, 2010), 276.

26. We have benefited from a rich scholarly literature on the effect of public space on human agency. See, e.g., Sharon Zukin, *Landscapes of Power: From Detroit to Disney World* (Berkeley: University of California Press, 1991); Don Mitchell, *The Right to the City: Social Justice and the Fight for Public Space* (New York: Guilford Press, 2003); Edward W. Soja, *Seeking Spatial Justice* (Minneapolis: University of Minnesota Press, 2010); and George Lipsitz, *How Racism Takes Place* (Philadelphia: Temple University Press, 2011).

27. Quoted in Powledge, *Free at Last,* 223–24.

28. See, e.g., Taylor Branch, *Parting the Waters: America in the King Years, 1954–63* (New York: Simon & Schuster, 1988); *Pillar of Fire: America in the King Years, 1963–65* (New York: Simon & Schuster, 1998); and *At Canaan's Edge: America in the King Years, 1965–68* (New York: Simon & Schuster, 2006); David Halberstam, *The Children* (New York: Random House, 1999); Bruce Watson, *Freedom Summer: The Savage Season That Made Mississippi Burn and Made America a Democracy* (New York: Viking, 2010); Arsenault, *Freedom Riders;* and Tuck, *We Ain't What We Ought to Be.*

29. For an analysis of the desegregation of other public accommodations during this period, see Victoria W. Wolcott, *Race, Riots, and Roller Coasters: The Struggle over Segregated Recreation in America* (Philadelphia: University of Pennsylvania Press, 2012).

30. See Jeanne Theoharis, "Hidden in Plain Sight: The Civil Rights Movement Outside the South," in *The Myth of Southern Exceptionalism,* ed. Matthew D. Lassiter and Joseph Crespino (New York: Oxford University Press, 2010), 49–73.

31. Patterson Toby Graham, *A Right to Read: Segregation and Civil Rights in Alabama's Public Libraries, 1900–1965* (Tuscaloosa: University of Alabama Press, 2002).

32. Cheryl Knott, *Not Free, Not for All: Public Libraries in the Age of Jim Crow* (Amherst: University of Massachusetts Press, 2015). See also *Untold Stories: Civil Rights, Libraries, and Black Librarianship,* ed. John Mark Tucker (Champaign: Graduate School of Library and Information Science, University of Illinois, 1998); and David M. Battles, *The History of Public Library Access to African Americans in the South, or Leaving the Plow Behind* (Lanham, Md.: Scarecrow Press, 2009).

33. Gavin Wright, *Sharing the Prize: The Economics of the Civil Rights Revolution in the American South* (Cambridge: Belknap Press of Harvard University Press, 2013), 1.

34. Catherine A. Barnes, *Journey from Jim Crow: The Desegregation of Southern Transit* (New York: Columbia University Press, 1983), 16.

1. JIM CROW PUBLIC LIBRARIES BEFORE 1954

1. Leon F. Litwack, *Trouble in Mind: Black Southerners in the Age of Jim Crow* (New York: Vintage Books, 1998), xvi.

2. Dorothy B. Parker, "The Organized Educational Activities of Negro Literary Societies, 1828–1846," *Journal of Negro Education* 5 (October 1936): 555–76, quotation on 561. See also William Henry Johnson, *Autobiography of Dr. William Henry Johnson* (New York: Haskell House, 1900), 159–61. Elizabeth McHenry's *Forgotten Readers: Recovering the Lost History of African American Literary Societies* (Durham, N.C.: Duke University Press, 2002) is the definitive work on the subject.

3. "City News," *Cincinnati Daily Gazette,* April 15, 1868; "The Public Library," *Cincinnati Daily Gazette,* December 9, 1870.

4. Bliss Perry later told this story as a keynote speaker for the dedication of the public library building in Brookline, Mass. See *Dedication of the Brookline Public Library Building, November 17, 1910* (Cambridge, Mass.: Riverside Press, 1911), 19–20.

5. "Colored National Liberal Convention," *Cincinnati Daily Gazette,* September 26, 1872.

6. "A Negro Denied a Seat among Whites," *New York Times,* March 6, 1875; "Negro Rights in Theatres," *New York Times,* March 8, 1875.

7. Litwack, *Trouble in Mind,* 102, 234, 363, 415.

8. James A. Atkins, *The Age of Jim Crow* (New York: Vantage Press, 1964), 112.

9. "A Public Library for the Colored People," *Macon (Ga.) Weekly Telegraph,* January 23, 1881.

10. Paula J. Giddings, *Ida: A Sword among Lions: Ida B. Wells and the Campaign against Lynching* (New York: Amistad, 2008), 74–76.

11. Eventually, the city gave the library thirty dollars per month. See Beverly Washington Jones, *Stanford L. Warren Branch Library, 77 Years of Public Service: A Phoenix in the Durham Community* (Durham, N.C.: Durham County Library, 1990).

12. Flyer found in Joan C. Browning Papers, box 1, Emory University, Manuscripts and Rare Book Library, Atlanta, Ga.

13. "Storytellers Set Dates for Summer," *New York Amsterdam News,* June 17, 1950.

14. "Libraries for Colored Children," *Boston Globe,* November 13, 1910. See also G. S. Dickerson, "The Marblehead Libraries," *Southern Workman* 40 (August–September 1910): 491–500.

15. See Dan R. Lee, "Faith Cabin Libraries: A Study of an Alternative Library Service in the Segregated South, 1932–1960," *Libraries & Culture* 26 (January 1991): 169–82.

16. "Seek Public Library," *Norfolk New Journal and Guide,* January 22, 1938.

17. Pennie Williams Dickey, "A History of Public Library Service for Negroes in Jackson, Mississippi, 1950–1957" (Master's thesis, Clark Atlanta University, 1960), 12–17.

18. Dickey, "History of Public Library Service for Negroes in Jackson," 13–14.

19. Library History Committee, *Gadsden Public Library; 100 Years of Service* (Charleston, S.C.: Arcadia Publishing Co., 2008), 19, 43. In 1923 the library opened a branch in the high school serving Gadsden's black people.

20. William T. Miller, "Library Service for Negroes in the New South: Birmingham, Alabama,

1871–1918," *Alabama Librarian* 27 (November–December 1975): 6–8. See also Graham, *Right to Read,* 11–17.

21. Angela Davis, *Angela Davis: An Autobiography* (New York: Random House, 1974), 97.

22. Annie L. McPheeters, *Library Service in Black and White: Some Personal Recollections, 1921–1980* (Metuchen, N.J.: Scarecrow Press, 1988), 102, 103.

23. Two more African American branches opened within a decade. See "In the Libraries," *Christian Science Monitor,* January 24, 1917.

24. "Library Growth in the South," *Charlotte Observer,* May 14, 1907. The library remained independent until 1929, when it became part of the Charlotte Public Library. "It continued as a branch library and the cultural center for the Black community until it was closed and demolished" in 1961. See William Gattis, "Branch Manager's Statement," in Jones, *Stanford L. Warren Branch Library,* 3.

25. Pamela R. Bleisch, "Spoilsmen and Daughters of the Republic: Political Interference in the Texas State Library during the Tenure of Elizabeth Howard West, 1911–1925," *Libraries & the Cultural Record* 45, no. 4 (2010): 396.

26. "Public Library Is Opened in School," *Philadelphia Tribune,* October 31, 1929.

27. See Graham, *Right to Read,* 17–25. See also Susan Purdy, "Mobile and the Black Experience," *Florida Times Union* (Jacksonville), February 15, 1998.

28. "Library with Actor's Name Serves Negroes of Raleigh," *Christian Science Monitor,* November 12, 1936.

29. Anne Robinson, "Never Too Late," *Bulletin of the American Library Association* 47 (February 1953): 57, 74.

30. Edith Foster, *Yonder She Comes! A Once Told Li'bry Tale* (Bremen, Ga.: Gateway Printing Co., 1985), 219–26.

31. "Colored Children in Library," *Baltimore Sun,* January 16, 1910; "Defends Pratt Library," *Baltimore Sun,* February 3, 1910; "Pratt Library Stoops to Jim Crow," *Baltimore Afro-American,* May 19, 1934; "Mississippi Whines," *Baltimore Afro-American,* April 25, 1936. See also Stanley Rubinstein and Judith Farley, "Enoch Pratt Free Library and Black Patrons: Equality in Library Services, 1882–1915," *Journal of Library History* 15 (Fall 1980): 445–53.

32. Annual Report (hereafter AR) (1911), District of Columbia Public Library, 44.

33. "Segregation at Branch Libraries," *Washington Times,* March 18, 1922.

34. W. E. Burghardt Du Bois, "The Opening of the Library," *Independent* 54, April 3, 1902, 809. On April 7, 1902, the *Chicago Tribune* editorialized on this article: "Perhaps Mr. Carnegie, whose income is continually gaining upon him, if approached in the right manner might give the negroes of Atlanta a library of equal importance with that he has given to the white people of the city." "The Color Line in a Library," *Chicago Tribune,* April 7, 1902. The definitive biography of Du Bois is David Levering Lewis, *W. E. B. Du Bois, 1868–1919: Biography of a Race* (New York: Henry Holt, 1994); and Lewis, *W. E. B. Du Bois, 1919–1963: The Fight for Equality and the American Century* (New York: Henry Holt, 2001).

35. For quotation on being taxed, see "In Aid of the Negroes," *Springfield Republican,* June 1, 1909. Quotation from *Waterbury American* in "A 'Public' Library in Atlanta," *Springfield Republican,* July 6, 1909.

36. W. E. B. Du Bois, *Efforts for Social Betterment among Negro Americans* (Atlanta: Atlanta University Press, 1909), 117–18; Booker T. Washington, *Up from Slavery* (New York: Norton, 1901), 38–39.

37. Julia Collier Harris, "A Library for Negroes," *New York Evening Post,* quoted in *Kansas City Star,* July 7, 1921.

38. Ron Blazek, "Florida's First Public Library," *Southeastern Librarian* 27 (Fall 1978): 171; John Lee Curry, "A History of Public Library Service to Negroes in Jacksonville, Florida" (Master's thesis, Clark Atlanta University, 1957), 38.

39. "'Jim Crow' Law for Public Libraries?" *Daily Oklahoman*, September 3, 1910; Editorial, *Daily Oklahoman*, October 25, 1910.

40. Story in Virginia Porter, "America's Black Holocaust," *Pittsburgh Courier*, September 18, 1999.

41. William Beer to George F. Bowerman, December 4, 1909, New Orleans Public Library Archives.

42. Quoted in "Carnegie Is Generous," *Savannah Tribune*, June 29, 1912.

43. Quotations from Pamela Tyler, *Silk Stockings and Ballot Boxes: Women and Politics in New Orleans, 1920–1963* (Athens: University of Georgia Press, 1996), 211.

44. Elaine Hardy, "A Timeline of Important Events in Georgia Public Library History," *Georgia Library Quarterly* 45 (Summer 2008): 13; "The Colored Public Library," *Savannah Tribune*, July 20, 1907; "Liberal Response for the Library," *Savannah Tribune*, November 19, 1911; "Carnegie Library Concert," *Savannah Tribune*, June 8, 1912; "An Immense Crowd to Attend," *Savannah Tribune*, June 22, 1912; "Colored Public Library," *Savannah Tribune*, August 31, 1912; "Have You One?" *Savannah Tribune*, December 6, 1913; "Carnegie Library's Many Readers," *Savannah Tribune*, November 28, 1914. See also "Savannah" file of Carnegie Corporation Records, Columbia University, New York.

45. From "Going Up to Atlanta," in *The Norton Book of American Autobiography*, ed. Jay Parini (New York: Norton, 1999), 560.

46. Clarence Thomas, *My Grandfather's Son: A Memoir* (New York: HarperCollins, 2007), 17.

47. Abigail A. Van Slyck, *Free to All: Carnegie Libraries & American Culture, 1890–1920* (Chicago: University of Chicago Press, 1995), 158.

48. Paul M. Culp Jr., "Carnegie Libraries of Texas: The Past Still Present," *Texas Libraries* 43 (Summer 1981): 91; Culp, "Carnegie Libraries: The Past No Longer Present," *Texas Libraries* (Fall 1981): 136; and Margaret I. Nichols, "Lillian Gunter: County Librarian," *Texas Libraries* 39 (Fall 1977): 138. See also Cheryl Knott Malone, "Unannounced and Unexpected: The Desegregation of Houston Public Library in the Early 1950s," *Library Trends* 55 (Fall 2007): 665–74. The Houston branch was razed in 1961 to make way for a street extension.

49. Battles, *History of Public Library Access for African Americans*, 44.

50. "Pittman's Success as an Architect," *Pittsburgh Courier*, July 26, 1912.

51. Quoted in Larry Grove, *Dallas Public Library: The First 75 Years* (Dallas: Dallas Public Library, 1977), 51, 52.

52. See "Mound Bayou Improvements," *Savannah Tribune*, May 25, 1912. Correspondence between Mound Bayou and Carnegie Corporation in "Mound Bayou" file, Carnegie Corporation Records. See especially, Charles Banks to R. R. Moton, January 20, 1917; and Mrs. Mary C. Booze (club president) to Carnegie Foundation, July 11, 1925. See also Booker T. Washington, "A Town Owned by Negroes," *World's Work* 14 (July 1907): 9125–34.

53. Shirley Schutte and Nathania Sawyer, *From Carnegie to Cyberspace: 100 Years at the Central Arkansas Library System* (Little Rock, Ark.: Butler Center Books, 2010), 28–29, 36–37.

54. Blyden Jackson, *The Waiting Years: Essays on American Negro Literature* (Baton Rouge: Louisiana State University Press, 1976), 3–4.

55. Washington to Bertram, August 28, 1909, copy found in "Savannah" file, Carnegie Corporation Records. That Washington provided Savannah with a copy of this letter strongly suggests he regularly advocated for separate Carnegie-funded "colored branches."

56. Battles, *History of Public Library Access for African Americans*, 33–34.

57. Berlin, *Making of African America*, 25, 30.

58. AR (1906), Louisville Free Public Library, 61–64; AR (1907), 53. Racist humor followed the opening of the library. In 1905 the *Duluth News Tribune* claimed the *Washington Post* "as authority for the statement that the first book taken out of the public library for negroes at Louisville was on chicken culture." See "The Washington Post Is Authority," *Duluth News Tribune*, December 7, 1905. See also Benjamin Mays, *Born to Rebel: An Autobiography* (New York: Scribners, 1971), 2.

59. Lillian Taylor Wright, "Thomas Fountain Blue, Pioneer Librarian, 1865–1935" (Master's thesis, Clark Atlanta University, 1955), 32–37.

60. AR (1910), Louisville Free Public Library, 37.

61. See Joseph S. Cotter Sr., "The Story Hour," *Library Journal* 35 (October 1910): 466.

62. Pamphlet for "Dedication Ceremony of the Eastern Colored Branch, January 28–30, 1914," in Library of Congress collections. See also "Colored Department, Louisville Free Public Library" (1927), Library of Congress collections.

63. Quoted in "Negro Libraries as Social Centers," *Savannah Tribune*, July 17, 1915.

64. Thomas F. Blue, "The Library as a Community Center," paper read at the Library Conference, Hampton Institute, Hampton, Va., March 1927, quoted in Wright, "Thomas Fountain Blue, Pioneer Librarian," 27.

65. *Southern Workman*, quoted in "Louisville Negroes and the Public Library System," *Philadelphia Tribune*, August 4, 1927. In *The Political Worlds of Slavery and Freedom* (Cambridge: Harvard University Press, 2009) Steven Hahn critiques the "integrationist framework" in black history that he says privileges and legitimizes black struggles for "inclusion and assimilation" but treats separatist efforts as "somehow lacking in integrity" (160). The loyalty many black public library patrons showed for their branches, and in some cases their subsequent resistance to integrating because they did not want to share these spaces with whites, lends some credence to Hahn's critique.

66. "Negro Branch of Louisville Library Novel," *Philadelphia Tribune*, April 4, 1929.

67. Julia A. Hersberger, Lou Sua, and Adam L. Murray, "The Fruit and Root of the Community: The Greensboro Carnegie Negro Library, 1904–1964," in *The Library as Place: History, Community, and Culture,* ed. John E. Buschman and Gloria J. Leckie (Westport, Conn.: Libraries Unlimited, 2007), 79–99, quotations on 87, 88, 95, and 97.

68. Ella Carruth and Isabel Monro, "Hannibal Square Library," *Wilson Library Bulletin* 26 (February 1952): 463–65.

69. "Books in Dixie," *Christian Science Monitor*, April 22, 1933. See also Rosemary Ruhig Du Mont, "Race in American Librarianship: Attitudes of the Library Profession," *Journal of Library History* 21 (Summer 1986): 494.

70. "Library Bias in South, Says FDR Committee," *Philadelphia Tribune*, April 4, 1940.

71. Tommie Dora Barker, *Libraries of the South: A Report on Developments, 1930–1935* (Chicago: American Library Association, 1936), 35–36, 199–201. See also Eliza Atkins Gleason, *The Southern Negro and the Public Library: A Study of the Government and Administration of Public Library Services to Negroes in the South* (Chicago: University of Chicago Press, 1941), 89–109.

72. Barker, *Libraries of the South*, 35–36, 50–57, 199–201. See also Edwin R. Embree and Julia Waxman, *Investment in People: The Story of the Julius Rosenwald Fund* (New York: Harper & Brothers, 1949), 5–28, 37–51.

73. "Free Library," *New York Amsterdam News*, September 3, 1938.

74. Louisiana Library Commission, *Report on the Louisiana Library Demonstration, 1925–1930* (New York: League of Library Commissions, 1931), 47–49.

75. Quoted in Lillie S. Walker, "Black Librarians in South Carolina," in *The Black Librarian in the Southeast: Reminiscences, Activities, Challenges,* ed. Annette L. Phinazee (Durham: North Carolina Central University School of Library Science, 1980), 92.

76. Graham, *Right to Read*, 27–30, 31–32.

77. Jones, *Stanford L. Warren Branch Library,* 17.

78. Hardy, "Timeline of Important Events in George Public Library History," 14. By 1939 the WPA funded 140 bookmobiles nationwide. See "The Library Takes to the Trail," *Christian Science Monitor,* November 14, 1939.

79. Quoted from Edward Barrett Stanford, "Library Extension under the WPA: An Appraisal of an Experiment in Federal Aid" (Ph.D. diss., University of Chicago, 1944), 182–83.

80. McPheeters, *Library Service in Black and White,* 105.

81. Graham, *Right to Read,* 34, 35–36.

82. Graham, *Right to Read,* 36–43.

83. Graham, *Right to Read,* 49–56, quotation on 49.

84. Dorothy M. Broderick, *Image of the Black in Popular and Recommended American Juvenile Fiction, 1927–1967* (New York: R. R. Bowker, 1973), 177–78.

85. Litwack, *Trouble in Mind,* 91, 108, 187, 429.

86. "Fond of Good Books," *Washington Post,* April 6, 1902.

87. George B. Utley, "What the Negro Reads," *Critic* 49 (July 1906): 28; "Negro Reads; Jacksonville," *Macon (Ga.) Daily Telegraph,* August 5, 1906.

88. AR (1906), Louisville Free Public Library, 61–64; AR (1907), 53.

89. "Negro Branch Library," *Biloxi (Miss.) Daily Herald,* April 18, 1920.

90. *Report on the Louisiana Library Demonstration, 1925–1930,* 47–49.

91. "Selecting Suitable Books for Public Libraries," *Dallas Morning News,* October 13, 1903.

92. Sam W. Small, "Looking and Listening," *Atlanta Constitution,* December 9, 1928.

93. "Library Lacks 'Uncle Tom's Cabin,'" *New York Times,* March 15, 1931.

94. Halberstam, *Children,* 72–73.

95. Transcript, Oral History Interview with Annie McPheeters, Collection No. aarlohe 92-001, Archives Division, Auburn Avenue Research Library on African American Culture and History, Atlanta-Fulton Public Library System, quotations on 54–56. There is some disagreement among historians concerning how much King knew about Gandhi before the Montgomery bus boycott. Glenn Smiley, a student of Gandhian thinking and field secretary for a civil rights organization in Montgomery, remembers King saying he knew "very little about the man" at the time. See Arsenault, *Freedom Riders,* 72.

96. McPheeters Transcript, 57–58.

97. Erik Larson, *In the Garden of Beasts: Love, Terror, and an American Family in Hitler's Berlin* (New York: Broadway Books, 2011), 12; Marion Humble, *Rural America Reads: A Study of Rural Library Service* (New York: American Association for Adult Education, 1938), 68.

98. Joseph Moreau, *Schoolbook Nation: Conflicts over American History Textbooks from the Civil War to the Present* (Ann Arbor: University of Michigan Press, 2003), 272, 277; Hillel Black, *The American Schoolbook* (New York: William Morrow, 1967), 121.

99. See Catherine A. Barnes, *Journey from Jim Crow: The Desegregation of Southern Transit* (New York: Columbia University Press, 1983).

2. RUMBLES OF DISCONTENT BEFORE 1960

1. Gleason, *Southern Negro and the Public Library*, 74–85, 90–96. See also Knott, *Not Free, Not for All*.

2. Anna Holden, "The Color Line in Southern Libraries," *New South* 9 (January 1954): 1.

3. C. D. Halliburton, "Inadequate Library Facilities," *Philadelphia Tribune*, May 29, 1951.

4. L. D. Reddick, "Where Can a Negro Read a Book?" *New South* 9 (January 1954): 5.

5. Quoted in *Access to Public Libraries* (Chicago: American Library Association, 1963), 37, 38, and 39.

6. James R. Wright, "The Public Library and the Black Experience," quoted in Peter Booth Wiley, *A Free Library in This City: The Illustrated History of the San Francisco Public Library* (San Francisco: Weldon Owen, 1996), 82.

7. Evelyn C. White, *Alice Walker: A Life* (New York: Norton, 2004), 58.

8. Richard Wright, *Black Boy: A Record of Childhood and Youth* (New York: Harper & Brothers, 1937), 214–17, 224. See also Constance Webb, *Richard Wright: A Biography* (New York: Putnam, 1968), 56, 78–79, 96.

9. Quotations can be found in Charles S. Johnson, *Patterns of Negro Segregation* (New York: Harper & Brothers, 1943), 27. See also Gunnar Myrdal, *An American Dilemma: The Negro Problem and Modern Democracy*, 2 vols. (New York: Transaction Publishers, 1944); and Richard Kluger, *Simple Justice* (New York: Random House, 1975), 256. Gavin Wright believes "the growing regional isolation noted by Myrdal is what made the southern Civil Rights revolution both necessary and possible." See Wright, *Sharing the Prize*, 6.

10. See "Suit Filed to Secure Use of City Library," *Norfolk New Journal and Guide*, May 13, 1939; "Va. Library War in Court Again," *Baltimore Afro-American*, September 2, 1939.

11. "Boys Wanted to Read, but Librarians Had Them Jailed," *Norfolk New Journal and Guide*, September 2, 1939; "5 Youths Face Strike Charge," *New York Amsterdam News*, September 9, 1939.

12. "Smash Va. Library Color Bar," *Baltimore Afro-American*, January 20, 1940. See also "Find No Legal Bars to Virginia Library," *Atlanta Daily World*, January 21, 1940.

13. For a complete account of the Alexandria sit-ins, see Brenda Mitchell-Powell, "A Seat at the Reading Table: The 1939 Alexandria, Virginia, Public Library Sit-In Demonstration—A Study in Library History, 1937–1941" (Ph.D. diss., Simmons College, Boston, 2015). See also "Alexandria Library to Be Named for Minister," *Baltimore Afro-American*, March 30, 1940; and Gleason, *Southern Negro and the Public Library*, 64–66. In 1959 black Alexandrian adults and high school students were allowed to check books out of the main library. Not until 1962 was the library fully integrated.

14. Louise S. Robbins, *The Dismissal of Miss Ruth Brown: Civil Rights, Censorship and the American Library* (Norman: University of Oklahoma Press, 2000).

15. "Speaks Up for Negro Plea, Ga. Newscaster Resigns Post," *Pittsburgh Courier*, February 16, 1952.

16. Richard Morris, "Calvert Foes Threaten to Burn Bookmobile," *Washington Post*, April 20, 1952.

17. Graham, *Right to Read*, 56–62. See also Battles, *History of Public Library Access to African Americans*, 94.

18. Rosa Parks, *Rosa Parks: My Story* (New York: Dial Books, 1992), 94. See also Montgomery Branch, National Association for the Advancement of Colored People, Minutes, May 22, 1955, Schomburg Center for Research in Black Culture, New York Public Library.

19. Ackerman, *We the People*, 135.

20. All quotations in P. L. Prattis, "Plain Murder," *Pittsburgh Courier*, January 18, 1958. See also

"Miss Juliette Hampton Morgan," *Alabama Librarian* 8 (October 1957): 91–92 (commemorations by Margaret L. McClurkin and Dixie Lou Fisher); and Graham, *Right to Read,* 102.

21. Robert S. Alvarez, *Library Log: The Diary of a Public Library Director* (Foster City, Calif.: Administrator's Digest Press, 1991), 280–83, 305–8. See also Mary Ellen McCrary, "A History of Public Library Service to Negroes in Nashville, Tennessee, 1916–1958" (Master's thesis, Clark Atlanta University, 1959).

22. Halberstam, *Children,* 100, 101.

23. "Richmond Branch Library Inviting," *Norfolk New Journal and Guide,* August 22, 1925; "Richmond Branch Library Rapidly nears Completion," *Norfolk New Journal and Guide,* October 17, 1931; "EMR Dresses Up Bowser Library," *Norfolk New Journal and Guide,* August 25, 1934.

24. "Richmonders Request Use of Public Library," *Norfolk New Journal and Guide,* April 19, 1947; "Board Defers Action on White Library Rule," *Richmond Afro-American,* April 19, 1947.

25. "Race Bar Is Removed at Central Library," *Richmond Times-Dispatch,* May 28, 1947; "City Library Opens Its Doors to All Citizens," *Richmond Afro-American,* May 31, 1947; "Richmond Opens Main Library to Negroes," *Atlanta Daily World,* June 7, 1947; "White Boycott Hits Library in Richmond," *Pittsburgh Courier,* February 21, 1948.

26. "Louisville Drops Ban on Libraries," *Philadelphia Tribune,* April 19, 1952; William R. Bryer, comp., *Libraries and Lotteries: A History of the Louisville Free Public Library* (Cynthiana, Ky.: Hobson Book Press, 1944), 199. See also George C. Wright, "Desegregation of Public Accommodations in Louisville," in *Southern Businessmen and Desegregation,* ed. Elizabeth Jacoway and David R. Colburn (Baton Rouge: Louisiana State University, 1982), 191–210.

27. Quotations from Kim Lacy Rogers, *Righteous Lives: Narratives of the New Orleans Civil Rights Movement* (New York: New York University Press, 1993), 43.

28. Robert Franklin Williams, *Negroes with Guns* (New York: Marzani & Munsell, 1962), 14–15.

29. Email, Patricia Poland (Dickerson Genealogy and Local History Room, Union County Public Library, N.C.), to Wayne A. Wiegand, May 7, 2014. For a discussion of Williams's role in the larger civil rights movement, see Arsenault, *Freedom Riders,* 404–18.

30. McPheeters Transcript, 24–25; Howard Zinn, "A Quiet Case of Social Change," in *The Zinn Reader: Writings on Disobedience and Democracy,* ed. Howard Zinn (New York: Seven Stories Press, 1997), 31–39, quotation on 31–32. See also McPheeters, *Library Service in Black and White,* 75–89, quotations on 78, 87.

31. These events are described in greater length in Graham, *Right to Read,* 81–82.

32. "File Suit against Library Practices," *Philadelphia Tribune,* August 12, 1950; "Newport News Library Target of Litigation," *Philadelphia Tribune,* July 19, 1952; "Newport News Opens Library to Negroes," *New York Amsterdam News,* July 19, 1952.

33. Graham's statement quoted in Isaac R. Barfield, "A History of the Miami Public Library, Miami, Florida" (Master's thesis, Clark Atlanta University, 1958), 31.

34. "Library Threatened with Legal Action for Denying Service to Negro Reader," *Washington Post–Times Herald,* February 23, 1957; "Library Is Told to Lend to All," *Washington Post–Times Herald,* March 5, 1957; "Supervisors Say Library Should Obey Virginia Law," *Blue Ridge Herald* (Purcellville, Va.), March 7, 1957; "Library Must Obey Law to Get Money from Town," *Blue Ridge Herald* (Purcellville, Va.), March 14, 1957; "Pays Taxes, He May Sue to Use Library," *Baltimore Afro-American,* March 2, 1957; "Upholsterer Acts to Wipe Out Discrimination in Va. Library," *Baltimore Afro-American,* March 16, 1957; "Negro Makes News as Va. Library Lends a Book," *Philadelphia Tribune,*

March 30, 1957. Those Austrian shades stayed in the Eisenhower family. When President Eisenhower and his wife saw them, "they asked the Murrays to fashion and refurbish the drapes . . . at the Eisenhower farm near Gettysburg. There, millions have admired [them]." Eugene Scheel, "Couple Wrote the First Chapter of County's Civil Rights Movement," *Washington Post*, April 8, 2001.

35. "Countians Speak Up on Tax Hike, Library at Hearing; Dog Control Extended," *Blue Ridge Herald* (Purcellville, Va.), April 4, 1957; "Supervisors Set $2.10 Tax Rate, Appropriate $6,000 for Library," *Blue Ridge Herald* (Purcellville, Va.), April 11, 1957.

36. "Plans Shaping at Portsmouth Public Library," *Norfolk New Journal and Guide*, August 18, 1945. See also "Judge Tells Portsmouth Library to Open to All," *Norfolk New Journal and Guide*, February 20, 1960.

37. "Ministers Endorse Stand Taken by Two Dentists," *Norfolk New Journal and Guide*, April 19, 1958; Johnnie Moore, "Conference on Library Practices Is Postponed," *Norfolk New Journal and Guide*, October 25, 1958; Norman Regner, "Library Integration Asked," *Virginian-Pilot* (Norfolk), November 26, 1959. See also Owens v. Portsmouth Library, Civil Action No. 3100, Records of the District Court for the Eastern District of Virginia, Norfolk Division (1960), RG 21, box 277, National Archives and Record Administration at Philadelphia. The quoted language became standard in future federal suits arguing against segregated public library services.

38. "Desegregation Pledge Given," *Virginian-Pilot* (Norfolk), December 23, 1959; "The Law and Reason at a Library Door," *Virginian-Pilot* (Norfolk), December 24, 1959.

39. William L. Tazewell, "Negroes Win at Library," *Virginian-Pilot* (Norfolk), February 18, 1960; "Library Integration to Stay on Docket," *Virginian-Pilot* (Norfolk), February 19, 1960; "Civil Rights Roundup," *Philadelphia Tribune*, February 27, 1960.

40. "Portsmouth Library Open; Petersburg Arrests Group," *Norfolk New Journal and Guide*, March 12, 1960; John Jordan, "This Is Portsmouth," *Norfolk New Journal and Guide*, March 12, 1960 and March 16, 1963.

41. Quoted in Ellen Levine, *Freedom's Children: Young Civil Rights Activists Tell Their Own Stories* (New York: Puffin Books, 1993), 42. At Green's Central High School graduation ceremony he had empty chairs on either side "because nobody wanted to sit next to me."

42. See John Dittmer, *Local People: The Struggle for Civil Rights in Mississippi* (Urbana: University of Illinois Press, 1994), 60–61. See also Tom Brady, *Black Monday* (Winona, Ala.: Association of Citizens' Council of Mississippi, 1955), 12; and Karen Cook "Struggles Within: Lura G. Currier, the Mississippi Library Commission and Library Services to African Americans," *Information & Culture* 48, no. 1 (2013): 143.

43. Graham, *Right to Read*, 102–12. Reed's story was reproduced in a play that premiered in 2015 entitled *Alabama Story*. See www.sltrib.com/home/1965509-155/newly-mounted-utah-play-tells-an.

3. MEMPHIS, TENNESSEE, AND GREENVILLE, SOUTH CAROLINA

1. Quotations in Powledge, *Free at Last*, 104–5, 116.

2. For more complete coverage of these incidents and the desegregation of Memphis public libraries, see Steven Anthony Knowlton, "Memphis Public Library Service to African Americans, 1903–1961: A History of Its Inauguration, Progress, and Desegregation" (Master's thesis, University of Memphis, 2015), esp. 61–95.

3. See U.S. Census, https://www.census.gov/prod/www/decennial.html. The population of blacks in Memphis would remain at approximately 40 percent throughout the 1940s and 1950s.

4. Rheba Palmer Hoffman, "A History of Public Library Service to Negroes in Memphis, Tennessee" (Master's thesis, Clark Atlanta University, August 1955).

5. Allegra W. Turner with Jini M. Kilgore, *Except by Grace: The Life of Jesse H. Turner* (Jonesboro, Ark.: Four-G Publishers, 2003), viii, 110.

6. "Farewell Salute to Allegra W. Turner," *Tri-State Defender: A Quiet Engine for Desegregation,* February 21–27, 2008. Louisiana State University enrolled its first black student in 1953.

7. Ed Frank, "Tri-State Bank," *The Tennessee Encyclopedia of History and Culture,* http://tennessee encyclopedia.net/entry.php?rec=1403.

8. Turner, *Except by Grace,* 111, 112; Turner v. Randolph, Civil Action 3525 (W.D. Tenn. 1958), Deposition of Wassell Randolph.

9. Unsigned letter, Dig Memphis—The Digital Archive of the Memphis Public Library & Information Center, http://memphislibrary.contentdm.oclc.org/cdm/search/searchterm/desegregation%20 library/order/nosort.

10. Randolph to Lockard, October 2, 1957, Dig Memphis, https://memphislibrary.contentdm.oclc .org/digital/collection/p15342coll4/id/91/rec/14.

11. Lockard to Randolph, January 3, 1958, Dig Memphis, https://memphislibrary.contentdm.oclc .org/digital/collection/p15342coll4/id/95/rec/25.

12. "A Petition by Employees of Memphis State University in Support of the Integration of Library Facilities," Dig Memphis, http://memphislibrary.contentdm.oclc.org/cdm/search/searchterm/desegre gation%20library/mode/all/order/nosort/page/2; "Library Board Revises Rules on Segregation," newspaper article, n.d., A-16 (listing the specific numbers).

13. Randolph to Lockard, letter, n.d., Dig Memphis, https://memphislibrary.contentdm.oclc.org /digital/collection/p15342coll4/id/96/rec/7.

14. Turner v. Randolph et al., Turner v. Randolph, Civil Action 3525 (W.D. Tenn. 1958), Complaint.

15. Brown v. Board of Education (Brown II), 349 U.S. 294 (1955).

16. Daniel Kiel, "Exploded Dream: Desegregation in the Memphis Public Schools," *Law & Inequality* 26 (Summer 2008): 261, 270.

17. "Nashville and Memphis Close, but Still Far Apart," *Baltimore Afro-American,* October 15, 1960.

18. "Nashville and Memphis Close, but Still Far Apart."

19. Letter from E. M. Hall, a broker of fruits, vegetables, and produce, to head librarian Jesse Cunningham, Dig Memphis, http://memphislibrary.contentdm.oclc.org/cdm/search/searchterm/ desegregation%20library/mode/all/order/nosort/page/1.

20. "Handwritten Letter from an Unknown Author to Mr. and Mrs. C. Lamar Wallis" and "Letter from Lamar Wallis to Mr. Edward P. Russell, Sr. of Canada," Dig Memphis, http://memphislibrary.con tentdm.oclc.org/cdm/search/searchterm/desegregation%20library/mode/all/order/nosort/page/1.

21. "Negroes Stage Sitdowns in 2 Libraries," *Chicago Daily Tribune,* March 20, 1960; "41 Arrested in Memphis Libraries," *Atlanta Daily World,* March 20, 1960; "40 Arrested in Memphis," *New York Times,* March 20, 1960.

22. "37 Negroes Fined in Memphis Case," *New York Times,* March 22, 1960; "37 Fined in Sitdown at Library," *Washington Post–Times Herald,* March 22, 1960; "Negroes Fined for Sitdowns in Libraries," *Chicago Daily Tribune,* March 22, 1960.

23. "Memphis Stops 2 New Sitdowns," *New York Times*, May 23, 1960.

24. "2 Week 'Cooling Off Period' in Memphis Protest," *Atlanta Daily World*, March 24, 1960.

25. "Sitdowns Successful in Galveston, San Antonio," *Philadelphia Tribune*, April 9, 1960.

26. "Judge Denies Order Opening Memphis Libraries," *Philadelphia Tribune*, July 12, 1960; "A Copy of a Letter Sent from Lamar Wallis to Frank Gianotti," Dig Memphis, http://memphislibrary.content dm.oclc.org/cdm/search/searchterm/desegregation%20library/mode/all/order/nosort/page/1; Turner, *Except by Grace*, 116.

27. "A Letter from Memphis Resident Malcolm McAlpin to the Board of Trustees of the Memphis Public Library," Dig Memphis, http://memphislibrary.contentdm.oclc.org/cdm/search/search term/desegregation%20library!McAlpin/field/all!all/mode/all!all/conn/and!and/order/nosort/ad/asc; "Integration: An Interim Report," *Wilson Library Bulletin* 35 (April 1961): 632.

28. Dawley v. City of Norfolk, 159 F. Supp. 642 (E.D. Va. 1958).

29. Turner v. Randolph, Civil Action 3525 (W.D. Tenn.), Memorandum Brief on Behalf of the Defendants, n.d., 7.

30. Turner v. Randolph, 195 F. Supp. 677, 679, 680 (W.D. Tenn. 1961).

31. Turner, *Except by Grace*, 70–71.

32. See Turner v. City of Memphis, 199 F. Supp. 585 (W.D. Tenn. 1961).

33. Turner v. City of Memphis, 369 U.S. 350, 353 (1962) (citing Burton v. Wilmington Parking Authority, 365 U.S. 715 (1961).

34. Turner, *Except by Grace*, 122–23.

35. See "Time for Level Heads to Take Over," *Greenville News*, July 23, 1960.

36. Calverta Elnora Davis, "A Survey of Public Library Service Offered to Negroes in Greenville County, South Carolina" (Master's thesis, Clark Atlanta University, 1958), 53.

37. Quoted in Eugene Griffin, "The South Has Its Own Version of U.S. History," *Chicago Daily Tribune*, April 11, 1947.

38. "Group of Young Negroes Enters Greenville Library," *Greenville News*, March 2, 1960; "Close Library after 20 S.C. Pupils Use It," *Chicago Defender*, March 12, 1960; "7 Arrested in Greenville," *New York Times*, March 17, 1960.

39. "7 Negroes Leave Library Quietly When Greenville Police Show Up," *Charleston News and Courier*, July 17, 1960. See also "Sitdown in a Library," *New York Times*, July 17, 1960.

40. Leslie Timms, "8 Negros Sit-In at Library Here," *Greenville News*, July 17, 1960. See also "8 Arrested in Sit-In at Greenville," *Columbia (S.C.) State*, July 17, 1960.

41. Marshall Frady, *Jesse: The Life and Pilgrimage of Jesse Jackson* (New York: Random House, 1996), 130–35. Quotations taken from Frady's interviews with Jackson.

42. "Time for Level Heads to Take Over," *Greenville News*, July 23, 1960; Frady, *Jesse*, 130–35. See also columns in *Greenville News* that summer reporting the incidents. Joan Mattison Daniel quotation in Rodney L. Hurst Sr., *Unless WE Tell It . . . It Never Gets Told!* (Jacksonville, Fla.: KiJas Press, 2015), 172.

43. "White Youth Leads Negroes in Protest," *New York Times*, July 19, 1960; "Spectators Rough Up Leader of Sitdown," *Washington Post–Times Herald*, July 19, 1960; "White Man Hurt in S. Carolina Sit-In Attempt," *Philadelphia Tribune*, July 19, 1960.

44. Gil Rowland, "Federal Litigation in Library Case Promised," *Greenville News*, July 21, 1960. See also "Atlantan Leads Demonstration in Greenville," *Atlanta Daily World*, July 19, 1960; "NAACP Pledges Litigation Soon," *Columbia State*, July 21, 1960.

45. "Greenville Has Mixed Street Fight," *Columbia State,* July 22, 1960; "Mixed Fight Breaks Out at Greenville," *Columbia State,* July 26, 1960.

46. "Races Clash in Greenville," *Greenville News,* July 26, 1960; "NAACP Leader for Race Group," *Greenville News,* July 27, 1960; "Curfew Imposed in Race Clashes," *New York Times,* July 27, 1960.

47. "Greenville Library Segregation Suit Filed," *Columbia State,* July 29, 1960; "Integration in Local Library Is Sought," *Greenville News,* July 29, 1960.

48. "Chain Stores Desegregate in 69 Dixie Communities," *Columbia State,* August 11, 1960; "The Curfew Is Lifted," *Greenville News,* August 25, 1960. See also Gavin Wright, *Old South, New South: Revolutions in the Southern Economy since the Civil War* (New York: Basic Books, 1986), 84.

49. "Dismissal of Library Mixing Suit Is Asked," *Greenville News,* August 27, 1960; "White and Negro Libraries Closed," *Greenville News,* September 3, 1960; "City Library Closes at Greenville," *News and Courier,* September 3, 1960; "Greenville Library Closes in Face of Mixing Suit," *Columbia State,* September 3, 1960; "Library Integration Suit Voided," *Columbia State,* September 14, 1960.

50. "Mayor to Hold Meeting on Status of Library," *Greenville News,* September 17, 1960; "Inadequacies at Libraries Cited," *Greenville News,* September 18, 1960.

51. "Library Is Open for 'Any Citizen,'" and "Library Needs Help, Not Criticism, *Greenville News,* September 19, 1960. See also "Library Opens at Greenville as Integrated," *Columbia State,* September 20, 1960.

52. J. Hunter Stokes, "City Library Reopens on Integrated Basis," *Greenville News,* September 20, 1960. See also "Greenville Library Admits Negroes," *News and Courier,* September 20, 1960.

53. Charles E. Stowe, Reply to Editorial, *Wilson Library Bulletin* 35 (November 1960): 210.

54. "Sex and Library," *Richmond Afro American,* October 1, 1960.

4. PETERSBURG AND DANVILLE, VIRGINIA

1. Susan McBee, "Negro Relates Objectives of Sitdown," *Washington Post–Times Herald,* June 12, 1960. See also "Petersburg Students in Library Protest," *Richmond Afro-American,* February 28, 1960; "Council to Consider Future of the Library," *Petersburg Progress-Index,* March 1, 1960; and Robert Gordon, "Integrated, Library May Revert to Estate," *Richmond Times-Dispatch,* March 1, 1960.

2. Arsenault, *Freedom Riders,* 115. See Douglas Southall Freeman, *Robert E. Lee: A Biography* (New York: C. Scribner's Sons, 1934).

3. See John Lewis, *Walking with the Wind: A Memoir of the Movement* (New York: Simon & Schuster, 1998), 135–36. See also Jimmy Ezzell, "Negroes Here Protest Segregation at Library," *Petersburg Progress-Index,* February 28, 1960; letter of Mrs. Robert W. Claiborne (McKenney's daughter) in "Library Desegregation Asked by Kin of Donor," *Washington Post–Times Herald,* April 5, 1960. Wyatt T. Walker later became the Southern Christian Leadership Conference's "chief logistician and strategist" and a major player in the desegregation of Birmingham's public library in 1963. See also Powledge, *Free at Last,* 108.

4. Jimmy Ezzell, "Negroes Here Protest Segregation at Library," *Petersburg Progress-Index,* February 28, 1960; "From the Right Way to the Wrong," *Petersburg Progress-Index,* February 29, 1960. See also "Petersburg Students in Library Protest," *Richmond Afro-American,* February 28, 1960; "NAACP Branch Leaders Stand In for Pickets," *Richmond Times-Dispatch,* February 28, 1960; and Robert Gordon, "If Integrated, Library May Revert to Estate," *Richmond Times-Dispatch,* March 1, 1960.

5. Robert Gordon, "Segregation to Continue at Library," *Richmond Times-Dispatch*, March 2, 1960; Mary Cherry Allen, "Library to Be Reopened on Segregated Basis" and "Law and Order Will Be Served," *Petersburg Progress-Index*, March 2, 1960; "No Demonstrations as Library Reopens," *Petersburg Progress-Index*, March 3, 1960; "No More Incidents Reported at Library," *Petersburg Progress-Index*, March 4, 1960; and Ernest Shaw, "Student's Say Petersburg, Va. Is 'Police State,'" *Baltimore Afro-American*, March 12, 1960.

6. Mary Cherry Allen, "Trials Set Monday in Trespass Case," *Petersburg Progress-Index*, March 8, 1960. See also Robert Gordon, "11 Negroes Are Arrested at Petersburg Library," *Richmond Times-Dispatch*, March 8, 1960; "11 Arrested in Library," *Richmond Afro- American*, March 12, 1960.

7. Mary Cherry Allen, "5 Arrested in Trespass Case Freed on Bond," *Petersburg Progress-Index*, March 9, 1960; Robert Gordon, "Negro Group Scores Petersburg Arrests," *Richmond Times-Dispatch*, March 9, 1960; Ruth Jenkins, "2,000 Sing, Pray at Library Trial," *Richmond Afro-American*, March 19, 1960.

8. Robert Gordon, "Petersburg Library Case Injunction to Be Asked," *Richmond Times-Dispatch*, March 10, 1960; Thacher Lascelle, "2 Negro Ministers Draw Fines, Terms," *Petersburg Progress-Index*, March 14, 1960.

9. Civil Action No. 3072, Plaintiffs Rev. Wyatt T. Walker, Rev. R. G. Williams et al. v. Petersburg Public Library et al., in Civil Action No. 3072, Records of the District Court for the Eastern Division of Virginia, Richmond Division, RG 21, box 19, NARS Philadelphia. See also Lascelle, "2 Negro Ministers Draw Fines"; "Negroes Given Fines, Terms," *Los Angeles Times*, March 15, 1960.

10. "Library to Stay Open Pending Injunction Petition Outcome," *Petersburg Progress-Index*, March 15, 1960. See also "Virginia's Library Folly," *Richmond Afro-American*, March 15, 1960; "13 Negroes File U.S. Suit in Library Case," *Richmond Times-Dispatch*, March 15, 1960.

11. Mary Cherry Allen, "New Negro Group Pledges Wave of Counter Sitdowns," *Petersburg Progress-Index*, March 17, 1960; "Segregation Protests Produce More Arrests," *Richmond Times-Dispatch*, March 20, 1960.

12. Elsie Carper, "White Leaders Unruffled by Petersburg Sitdowns," *Washington Post–Times Herald*, April 4, 1960.

13. "Klan Note Is Hurled at Window," *Richmond Afro-American*, March 26, 1960. See also "Negroes Open Major Fight against Segregation," *Washington Post–Times Herald*, April 14, 1960.

14. "Library Desegregation Asked by Kin of Donor," *Washington Post–Times Herald*, April 5, 1960; "Dismissal of Suit Filed by Negroes Asked," *Danville Bee*, April 5, 1960. Claiborne quoted in "Parents Would Want Library J-C Halted," *Richmond Afro-American*, April 9, 1960; "Daughter of Library Donor Wants Facility Integrated," *Atlanta Daily World*, April 17, 1960; Ernest Shaw, "Inside—Petersburg, Va.," *Baltimore Afro-American*, May 21, 1960.

15. "Negroes Open Major Fight against Segregation"; Chester M. Hampton, "'Lid Is Off' in Petersburg as Sitdowns Imperil All Jim Crow," *Baltimore Afro-American*, April 23, 1960. "Anti-Trespass Law Ruled Constitutional," *Washington Post–Times Herald*, April 16, 1960. See also O. L. Edwards, letter to the editor, *Petersburg Progress-Index*, May 22, 1960.

16. "Closing of Library Here Held Possible," *Petersburg Progress-Index*, May 21, 1960; "Library Racial Suit Being Studied by Judge," *Richmond Times-Dispatch*, May 21, 1960; "Petersburg Library Suit in U.S. Court," *Baltimore Afro-American*, May 28, 1960; "Court Pictures Seized," *New York Times*, May 21, 1960.

17. Thacher Lascelle, "Integration of Library Here Is Backed," *Petersburg Progress-Index*, June 19, 1960.

18. "Negro Student's Appeal Upheld at Petersburg," *Richmond Times-Dispatch*, June 17, 1960; "Council Says Decision on Library Up to Court," *Petersburg Progress-Index*, June 22, 1960; "While the Lecturing Goes On," *Petersburg Progress-Index*, June 23, 1960.

19. "Library Closes after Negroes Ask for Service in White Section," *Petersburg Progress-Index*, July 7, 1960; "Harassment for Its Own Sake?" *Petersburg Progress-Index*, July 8, 1960; "Librarian Is Named, Starts Next Month," *Petersburg Progress-Index*, July 9, 1960; "Public Library Closing Here Is Indefinite," *Petersburg Progress-Index*, July 12, 1960; "Library at Petersburg Is Closed Indefinitely," *Richmond Times-Dispatch*, July 7, 1960. See also "Town Closes Library to Keep Negroes Out," *Washington Post–Times Herald*, July 8, 1960.

20. "Ten Negroes Freed in City Library Case," *Washington Post–Times Herald*, July 23, 1960; "300 Negroes Demonstrate for 11 Jailed in Petersburg," *Washington Post–Times Herald*, August 1, 1960. See also "Petersburg Library Sit-Down Charges Are Dropped," *Norfolk New Journal and Guide*, July 30, 1960.

21. "Ruling on Library Declined by Judge," *Petersburg Progress-Index*, October 7, 1960; "Court Declines Library Ruling," *Washington Post–Times Herald*, October 8, 1960.

22. "Public Library to Open Doors Here Tomorrow," *Petersburg Progress-Index*, November 6, 1960; "Library to Reopen," *New York Times*, November 6, 1960; Ernest Shaw, "Petersburg, Va. Council Integrates Public Library," *Richmond Afro-American*, November 12, 1960; "Petersburg Opens Library on Integrated Basis," *Library Journal* 85, December 15, 1960, 4440.

23. Arsenault, *Freedom Riders*, 115.

24. Interview with Robert A. Williams, "Danville, Virginia, 1945–1975," *Mapping Local Knowledge* online exhibit, www.vcdh.virginia.edu/cslk/danville; "Negroes Given Fines, Terms," *Los Angeles Times*, March 15, 1960.

25. Evans D. Hopkins, *Life after Life: A Story of Rage and Redemption* (New York: Free Press, 2005), 12.

26. See "Summer 1963: Danville's Racial Unrest," *Memphis Commercial Appeal*, September 16, 1963. See also "First Library Opens in Danville Soon," *Atlanta Daily World*, January 13, 1950; "Danville, Va.," *Baltimore Afro-American*, January 30, 1954. See also Hopkins, *Life after Life*, 12.

27. Williams Interview, "Danville, Virginia, 1945–1975."

28. "Young Negroes Invade Library, Bringing about Early Closing," *Danville Bee*, April 2, 1960; "Council Limits Use of Main Library and Parks to Head Off Further Negro Demonstrations," *Danville Bee*, April 3, 1960; "An Invasion of Community Quiet," *Danville Bee*, April 3, 1960.

29. Williams Interview, "Danville, Virginia, 1945–1975." See also "Library Callers Rarely Use Own Facilities," *Danville Bee*, April 6, 1960; "Negroes Seek Court Order on Library," *Danville Bee*, April 11, 1960; "Burning Crosses Does No Good," *Danville Bee*, April 11, 1960.

30. "Committee to Be Named on Library," *Danville Bee*, April 12, 1960

31. "31 Petition to Keep Open City Library," *Danville Bee*, April 20, 1960; "Library Petition Signed by 300," *Danville Bee*, April 26, 1960.

32. "Defendants in Library Suit File Reply in Federal Court," *Danville Bee*, May 4, 1960.

33. "Judge Says Library Cannot Be Closed to Negroes Solely Because of Race," *Danville Bee*, May 6, 1960; "Library Suit Topic before Rotary Club," *Danville Bee*, May 31, 1960.

34. "Count-Down on the Library," *Danville Bee*, May 10, 1960.

35. "Library Referendum Set June 14, Same Day of Council Election," *Danville Bee*, May 14, 1962;

"Libraries, Industry, Education, Taxes Discussed during Forum," *Danville Bee*, May 28, 1960; "Library Suit Topic before Rotary Club," *Danville Bee*, May 31, 1960.

36. "Danville Ordered to Let Negroes in City Library," *Washington Post–Times Herald*, May 7, 1960; "Danville Closes Public Libraries," *Washington Post–Times Herald*, May 20, 1960; "Council Faces Library Decisions after City Loses Round in Court," *Danville Bee*, May 7, 1960; "Two Moves to Foil Library Integration," *Danville Bee*, May 17, 1960; "Library Staff Not Affected by Closing," *Danville Bee*, May 19, 1960; "Sign Placed on Library on Weekend," *Danville Bee*, May 23, 1960.

37. "Danville Plans Private Library after Closing of Public Libraries," *Library Journal* 85, September 1, 1960, 2902; "Library Group Gets Charter, Details Plans," *Danville Bee*, June 1, 1960.

38. "New Danville Library Will Be 'Private,'" *Norfolk New Journal and Guide*, June 4, 1960; "Virginians Plan Private Library," *New York Times*, June 19, 1960.

39. Gerald Tetley, "A Library Closes in Danville," *Wilson Library Bulletin* 35 (September 1960): 52–54.

40. "Closing Libraries Silly, Says Author," *Richmond Afro-American*, June 4, 1960.

41. "Keep the Libraries Open!" *Richmond Times-Dispatch*, June 13, 1960.

42. "Library Group Mails Appeal," *Danville Bee*, June 8, 1960; "Library Debate Reaches Climax; Letter Draws Replies from Private Group," *Danville Bee*, June 13, 1960.

43. "Election Activity Erupts," *Danville Bee*, June 14, 1960.

44. "Danville Votes to Close Library," *Washington Post–Times Herald*, June 15, 1960.

45. "Council Backs Up Library Vote; Facilities Will Remain Closed," *Danville Bee*, June 15, 1960; "Vox Populi," *Danville Bee*, June 15, 1960.

46. "Bid Renewed to Re-Open City Library," *Danville Bee*, June 21, 1960; "Site Is Leased for Library: Officers Named," *Danville Bee*, June 25, 1960; "Group Plans to Try Again on Library," *Danville Bee*, June 25, 1960.

47. Tetley, "Library Closes in Danville," 54.

48. "The Danville Story, Open Again, but Not an Open Library," *Library Journal* 85, November 1, 1960, 3942.

49. Tetley, "Library Closes in Danville," 52.

50. Harry Golden, *Only in America* (Cleveland, Ohio: World Publishing, 1958), 122.

51. "Klansman Assails 'Judas' Preachers," *New York Times*, September 5, 1960.

52. "Danville Story, Open Again, but Not an Open Library," 3942–43. See also "City's Libraries Re-Open Today after 5–4 Vote by City Council," *Danville Bee*, September 13, 1960.

53. "Letters: Danville and Russia," *Wilson Library Bulletin* 36 (November 1961): 218.

54. "In the Face of Public Sentiment," *Danville Bee*, September 13, 1960; "Library Catechism," *Danville Bee*, September 15, 1960.

55. "Danville Library Injunction Ends," *Washington Post–Times Herald*, September 15, 1960; Ruth Jenkins, "A Library Where You Can't Read," *Baltimore Afro-American*, October 8, 1960; "Judge Dalton Dismisses Library Suit," *Danville Bee*, September 15, 1960.

56. "Danville Reopens Public Library under Stiff Rules for Borrowing," *New York Times*, September 18, 1960.

57. Hopkins, *Life after Life*, 14–15.

58. "Danville Story, Open Again, but Not an Open Library," 3942–43.

59. "Library Sets Up Formal Sit-Down," *Washington Post–Times Herald*, November 30, 1960; "Virginia Library Shift," *New York Times*, December 2, 1960; "The Danville, Virginia, Public Library," *Wilson Library Bulletin* 36 (June 1962): 798.

5. ALABAMA

1. Much of chapter 5 relies on information in Graham, *Right to Read*. For a more comprehensive account of civil rights activities in the state of Alabama, see Frye Gaillard, *Cradle of Freedom: Alabama and the Movement That Changed the World* (Tuscaloosa: University of Alabama Press, 2004).

2. These events are described in greater length in Graham, *Right to Read*, 71–75. See also "Alabama Library Serves Negroes," *Wilson Library Bulletin* 36 (March 1962): 504, 506.

3. Summarized in Graham, *Right to Read*, 62–66.

4. Foster Hailey, "Negroes Uniting in Birmingham," *New York Times*, April 11, 1963.

5. Hailey, "Negroes Uniting in Birmingham"; "More Racial Moves," *Birmingham News*, April 11, 1963.

6. These events described in greater length in Graham, *Right to Read*, 82–91. See also "Nine Years After: How Desegregation Stands in Dixie," *Chicago Defender*, May 18, 1963.

7. Graham, *Right to Read*, 75–76.

8. Arsenault, *Freedom Riders*, 211–21.

9. Cobb v. Montgomery Library Board, Civil Action 1807-N (M.D. Ala.1962), Deposition of Robert L. Cobb, June 15, 1962. See also Graham, *Right to Read*, 76.

10. "Negroes Stage Library Test but Leave without Incident," *Montgomery Advertiser*, March 16, 1962. See also Bessie Rivers Grayson, "The History of Public Library Service for Negroes in Montgomery, Alabama" (Master's thesis, Clark Atlanta University, 1965); "City on 'Bottom' in Library Funds," *Alabama Journal*, April 12, 1962.

11. "Charles Conley (1921–2010)," *NYU Law Magazine* online, http://blogs.law.nyu.edu/magazine/2011/charles-conley-1921–2010/.

12. Quoted in Graham, *Right to Read*, 77.

13. "Suit Demands Library End Segregation," *Montgomery Advertiser*, April 28, 1962. See also Dan T. Carter, *The Politics of Rage: George Wallace, the Origins of New Conservatism, and the Transformation of American Politics* (Baton Rouge: Louisiana State University Press, 2000), 105. Because he was a minor, Robert Cobb's father had to serve as plaintiff on behalf of his son. Cobb v. Montgomery Library Board, 207 F. Supp. 880 (M.D. Ala. 1962).

14. "Frank M. Johnson Jr., Judge Whose Rulings Helped Desegregate the South, Dies at 80," *New York Times*, July 24, 1999.

15. "Frank M. Johnson Jr."

16. Cobb, 207 F. Supp. at 883.

17. *Museum News, Montgomery Museum of Fine Arts*, April–May 1962 (emphasis added).

18. Cobb, 207 F. Supp. at 881–82.

19. Id. at 882, citing Giles v. Library Advisory Committee of the City of Danville, Civil Action No. 452, W.D. Va., September 1960. See also "Judge Rules Integration of Library," *Montgomery Advertiser*, August 8, 1962.

20. "'Vertical Integration' Installed at Montgomery Public Library," *Library Journal* 87, September 1, 1962, 2856.

21. "Birmingham Will Have Stand-Up Integration," *Norfolk New Journal and Guide*, August 11, 1962. (The article discusses Montgomery but erroneously names Birmingham in its title.)

22. "Library 'Stand Up' Follows Court Order," *Baltimore Afro-American*, August 18, 1962.

23. "New Jim Crow Law May Wipe Out 'Slouching' in Alabama Libraries," *Philadelphia Tribune*, August 25, 1962; "The World Today," *Pittsburgh Courier*, August 25, 1962; "Library Patrons Find 'Stand-

ing Room Only,'" *Montgomery Advertiser*, August 10, 1962; "Library Still Unvisited by Negroes," *Montgomery Advertiser*, August 11, 1962; "Negro Youth Gets Library Card, Checks Out One Book," *Montgomery Advertiser*, August 12, 1962. See also Graham, *Right to Read*, 78–79.

24. See the following letters to the editor in the *Montgomery Advertiser*: Helen M. Chance, August 18, 1962; Mrs. E. M., August 19, 1962; Harold Anderson, August 13, 1962; Mrs. John Moffiet, August 14, 1962; John T. Parker, August 19, 1962; J. Mills Thornton III, August 19, 1962; Stephen Saltzman, August 19, 1962; Fred D. Terry, August 21, 1962; Marion Marsh, August 2, 1962; Nell Jordan, August 16, 1962; Mrs. J. M. Parker, August 16, 1962; J. C. Kendrick, August 17, 1962; Richard Harris, August 17, 1962; Mrs. D. G. Hallmark, August 22, 1962; Bill Rogers, August 22, 1962; Jesse Hodges, August 23, 1962.

25. "Take the Library," *Montgomery Advertiser*, August 21, 1962.

26. Graham, *Right to Read*, 79, 81; "Negroes Served at Library under Careful Police Watch," *Montgomery Advertiser*, August 14, 1962.

27. Graham, *Right to Read*, 79–80; "Only Few Negroes Seen Using Branch Library on Cleveland," *Montgomery Advertiser*, August 14, 1962.

28. See Arsenault, *Freedom Riders*, 140–49.

29. These events described in Graham, *Right to Read*, 91–98.

30. Summarized from Graham, *Right to Read*, 112–20.

6. GEORGIA

1. For a comprehensive account of the history of civil rights activities in Georgia, see Stephen G. N. Tuck, *Beyond Atlanta: The Struggle for Racial Equality in Georgia, 1940–1980* (Athens: University of Georgia Press, 2003).

2. "Mayor Says Library Open to All Races," *Savannah Morning News*, July 21, 1961.

3. Kevin Merida and Michael A. Fletcher, *Supreme Discomfort: The Divided Soul of Clarence Thomas* (New York: Doubleday, 2007), 1.

4. Arsenault, *Freedom Riders*, 477.

5. W. E. B. Du Bois, *The Souls of Black Folk* (New York: Norton, 1903), 82, 85.

6. Bernice Johnson Reagon, "Since I Laid My Burden Down," in *Hands on the Freedom Plow: Personal Accounts by Women in SNCC*, ed. Faith S. Holsart et al. (Urbana: University of Illinois Press, 2010), 147–48. Among SNCC leaders several "grew up" in Atlanta's black libraries. Some—including Julian Bond, well-known civil rights activist who later became a long-serving Georgia legislator, NAACP chairman, and first president of the Southern Poverty Law Center—used the branches for meetings and "as a place where they could rest in between activities," Annie McPheeters later recalled. See McPheeters Transcript, 27–28, 34–35.

7. Norma L. Anderson and William G. Anderson, D.O., *Autobiographies of a Black Couple of the Greatest Generation* (Lansing, Mich.: Norma L. and William G. Anderson, 2004), 177–78, 179.

8. See Arsenault, *Freedom Riders*, 468–75.

9. "Ten Suspended Albany Students Try Libraries," *Atlanta Daily World*, January 1, 1962; "Integrating Carnegie Library," *Freedom on Film* website, University of Georgia, www.uga.edu/civilrights/cities/albany/library.htm.

10. "Young Negroes Again Invade Albany Library," *Albany Herald*, January 11, 1962; Jimmy Robinson, "Hearing Completed on Race Suits Here," *Albany Herald*, September 26, 1962.

11. "Library Arrests—A 'Sad Picture,'" *Baltimore Afro-American*, August 11, 1962.

12. Martin Luther King Jr., *The Autobiography of Martin Luther King, Jr.* (New York: Warner Books, 1998), 159.

13. "Negroes Pushing Tests in Georgia: Albany Masses Police Units—F.B.I. Reinforced," *New York Times*, July 18, 1962.

14. "Negroes Pushing Tests in Georgia."

15. "Library Arrests—'A Sad Picture.'"

16. Jim Houston, "Judge Elliott Reflects on Career," *Columbus (Ga.) Ledger-Enquirer*, July 4, 2006.

17. Judge Elliott remained on the bench for thirty-eight years and is perhaps best remembered as the judge who overturned the conviction of army lieutenant William Calley in the 1968 My Lai massacre of civilians in Vietnam.

18. Hedrick Smith, "Leader Disavows Georgia Violence," *New York Times*, August 2, 1961.

19. Kelley v. Page, Civil Action No. 727 (U.S. Dist. Ct., M.D. Ga., Albany Division), Hearing, August 7, 1962.

20. Frank Hunt, "'We'll Keep on Marching until Victory Is Ours,'" *Baltimore Afro-American*, August 18, 1962.

21. Hedrick Smith, "Albany, Ga., Closes Parks and Libraries to Balk Integration," *New York Times*, August 12, 1962.

22. Hunt, "'We'll Keep on Marching until Victory Is Ours.'"

23. Powledge, *Free at Last*, 406.

24. Anderson v. City of Albany, 321 F.2d 649 (5th Cir. 1963).

25. Anderson v. City of Albany, 321 F. 2d 649.

26. Jackie Robinson, "Home Plate: The Right to Hate," *New York Amsterdam News*, August 25, 1962; Hunt, "'We'll Keep on Marching until Victory Is Ours.'"

27. "Library Involved in Incidents in Albany, Ga., Demonstrations," *Library Journal* 87, September 1, 1962, 2856; Anderson and Anderson, *Autobiographies of a Black Couple*, 220–21.

28. "Albany Trustees Chairman Protests CBS Documentary," *Library Journal* 87, September 15, 1962, 3006; Everett T. Moore, "Still No Decision in Albany," *ALA Bulletin* 57 (February 1963): 111–16.

29. "Judicial Filibuster," *Baltimore Afro-American*, December 15, 1962; Jim Houston, "Judge Elliott Reflects on Career," *Columbus Ledger-Enquirer*, July 4, 2006.

30. Moore, "Still No Decision in Albany," 111–16.

31. "Albany Wipes Out Segregation Statutes in Maneuver to Block Court Action to Knock Down Laws," *Atlanta Daily World*, March 8, 1963; "City Cancels Out Segregation Laws," *Albany Herald*, March 7, 1963.

32. "Albany Desegregates 'Chairless' Library," *Atlanta Daily World*, March 12, 1963; "Three 'Mixing' Preachers Slated for Albany Trials," *Albany Herald*, March 12, 1963.

33. Martin Luther King Jr., "The Solid Wall Cracks," *New York Amsterdam News*, April 13, 1963; Claude Sitton, "Negro 'Victory' Fades in Georgia," *New York Times*, March 14, 1963; "Albany, Ga., Public Library Reopens on 'Vertical Integration' Basis," *Library Journal* 88, April 15, 1963, 1638.

34. "Integration Comes—but Slyly," *Albany Herald*, March 9, 1963.

35. Sitton, "Negro 'Victory' Fades in Georgia."

36. "Appeal Filed in Albany Dismissal," *Atlanta Daily World*, March 15, 1963.

37. See Peterson v. Greenville, 373 U.S. 244 (May 20, 1963); Shuttlesworth v. Birmingham, 373 U.S. 262 (May 20, 1963); Lombard v. Louisiana, 373 U.S. 267 (May 20, 1963). The Court had reached a similar decision the previous year in Turner v. Memphis, 369 U.S. 350 (1962).

38. Anderson v. City of Albany, 321 F.2d 649 (5th Cir. 1963).

39. Anderson v. City of Albany, 321 F.2d 649.

40. Anderson and Anderson, *Autobiographies of a Black Couple*, 179–80, 188, 191, 192, 193–94.

41. Powledge, *Free at Last*, 352, 418–19. See also Anderson and Anderson, *Autobiographies of a Black Couple*, 222.

42. "Negroes Use Library Here," *Columbus Ledger*, July 6, 1963.

43. "Group Tries to Integrate Library Here," *Columbus Ledger*, July 9, 1963; "Four Negroes Bound Over in 'Read-In,'" *Columbus Ledger*, July 10, 1963; "Five Bound Over in Library Case," *Columbus Ledger*, July 11, 1963. See also "Eleven Negroes Arrested in Georgia at Horizontally Integrated Library," *Library Journal* 88 (August 1963): 2854.

44. "Negro Leaders Say Demonstrations Unnecessary," *Columbus Ledger*, July 11, 1963; "19 Negroes Halt Read-In after Plea," *Columbus Ledger*, July 12, 1963.

45. "39 State 'Read-In'; No Arrests Made," *Columbus Ledger*, July 14, 1963.

46. "2 Arrested at Library 'Read-In' Tiff," *Columbus Ledger*, July 15, 1963; "Read-Ins Continue at Library Here," *Columbus Ledger*, July 16, 1963; "Negro Fined in 'Scuffle' at Library," *Columbus Ledger*, July 17, 1963.

47. "Community Can Continue to Be City of Peace and Orderliness," *Columbus Ledger*, July 18, 1963.

48. "Muscogee County to Integrate Public Libraries," *Atlanta Daily World*, August 22, 1963; "Negroes 'Apply through Channels' at Latest 'Integrated' Library," *Library Journal* 88, October 15, 1963, 3566.

7. MISSISSIPPI

1. "Dawn of Freedom in Darkest Dixie? Plans for 'Operation Mississippi' Made during High-Level Meeting," *New Journal and Guide*, April 22, 1961. See also Medgar Wiley Evers, *The Autobiography of Medgar Evers: A Hero's Life and Legacy Revealed through His Writings, Letters, and Speeches* (New York: Basic Civitas Books, 2005), 60–61. For a comprehensive account of civil rights activities in Mississippi, see John Dittmer, *Local People: The Struggle for Civil Rights in Mississippi* (Urbana: University of Illinois Press, 1995).

2. Quoted in Cook, "Freedom Libraries," 264.

3. Wright, *Sharing the Prize*, 85.

4. Virginia Steele, "'Freedom Libraries' of the Mississippi Summer Project," *Southeastern Librarian* 15 (Summer 1965): 77.

5. See Jeanne Broach, *The Meridian Public Libraries: An Informal History, 1913–1974* (Meridian, Miss.: Meridian Public Library, 1974), 45; and Cook, "Freedom Libraries," 210.

6. Gabriel San Román, "Joseph Jackson Jr. Made Civil Rights History as a Member of Mississippi's Tougaloo Nine," *OC Weekly* (Orange County, Calif.), June 25, 2015; "9 Seized at Sit-In at Jackson,

Miss.," *New York Times,* March 28, 1961. This article also reported that the only other anti-segregation demonstration in the state had occurred the previous year, when a group of black youths tried to swim at an all-white beach. They were chased off by whites armed with clubs, chains, and sticks.

7. Clark v. Thompson, Civil Action No. 3235 (S.D. Miss. 1962), Transcript of Evidence, Direct Examination of Miss Frances French, 72–73, 28.

8. Elise Chenier interview with Ethel Sawyer, "Neither Sin nor Civil Rights: Ethel Sawyer's Study of a Lesbian Community," *Elise Chenier* blog, elisechenier.com/2016/02/10/neither-sin-nor-civil-rights. Sawyer, herself a heterosexual, conducted a 1965 academic study of a black lesbian community.

9. Román, "Joseph Jackson, Jr."

10. Quoted in "Library Segregation at Work," *America* 195, April 15, 1961, 139.

11. Clark v. Thompson, Transcript of Evidence, Direct Examination of Miss Frances French, 70–73, and Direct Examination of Ethel Sawyer, 28.

12. Clark v. Thompson, Transcript of Evidence, Direct Examination of Ethel Sawyer; "'Read-In' Demonstration at Jackson (Miss.) Public Library," *Library Journal* 85, May 1, 1961, 1750, 1751.

13. Román, "Joseph Jackson, Jr."

14. "Dogs, Clubs Used on Negroes; Ask Whites to Leave," *Atlanta Daily World,* March 30, 1961; Clark v. Thompson, Transcript of Evidence, Plaintiff's Exhibit no. 3, Deposition of W. R. Wren, 294; "'Concerned Department of Justice Asks: Were Savage Dogs Really Necessary?" *Baltimore Afro-American,* April 8, 1961.

15. Evers, *Autobiography of Medgar Evers,* 228–29.

16. "Call Off Dogs—Slavery Is Over," *Philadelphia Tribune,* April 4, 1961; "SNCC Sends Miss. Protest on Beatings," *Pittsburgh Courier,* April 8, 1961; "Arrests Unjustified; Convictions Illegal," *Baltimore Afro-American,* April 8, 1961; "'Concerned' Department of Justice Asks: Were Savage Dogs Really Necessary," *Baltimore Afro-American,* April 18, 1961; "Dawn of Freedom in Darkest Dixie? Plans for 'Operation Mississippi' Made during High-Level Meeting," *New Journal and Guide,* May 22, 1961.

17. Everett T. Moore, "The 'Study-In' as Reported in Jackson, Mississippi," *ALA Bulletin* 55 (June 1961): 497–99, quoting the *Clarion-Ledger* article.

18. See David M. Oshinsky, *"Worse than Slavery": Parchman Farm and the Ordeal of Jim Crow Justice* (New York: Free Press, 1996).

19. For a description of the 1961 Freedom Rider "visits" to Jackson, see Arsenault, *Freedom Riders,* 269–98. Martin Luther King quotation on 371.

20. "Jack Young," Mississippi Civil Rights Project website, http://mscivilrightsproject.org/hinds /person-hinds/jack-young/.

21. State Senate Concurrent Resolution No. 125 (1956); Mississippi Code sections 4065.3, 2056 (7) (emphasis added).

22. Clark v. Thompson, Transcript of Evidence, Direct Examination of Leon F. Hendrick, 128–32.

23. Clark v. Thompson, Transcript of Evidence, Plaintiff's Exhibit 2, Deposition of Mayor Allen C. Thompson, 160–62 (emphasis added).

24. Clark v. Thompson, Transcript of Evidence, Plaintiff's Exhibit 3, Deposition of Rev. L. A. Clark Sr.; Clark v. Thompson, Transcript of Evidence, Plaintiff's Exhibit 3, Deposition of Mary Cox; Clark v. Thompson, Transcript of Evidence, Plaintiff's Exhibit 3, Deposition of W. R. Wren. A Mississippi Sovereignty Commission investigator later identified Cox as a "homosexual," then apparently thought he needed to explain the term to superiors as a "lesbian, or one that prefers to have sex relations with

other women instead of men." See a report on Mary Cox to the Mississippi Sovereignty Commission at www.mdah.ms.gov/arrec/digital_archives/sovcom/result.php?image=images/png/cd03/019665 .png&otherstuff=2|55|7|47|1|1|1|19273|.

25. Clark v. Thompson, Transcript of Evidence, Testimony of W. D. Rayfield; Clark v. Thompson, Transcript of Evidence, Defendant's Exhibit 3, Affidavit of A. L. Grey, executive secretary of the Mississippi State Board of Health.

26. Clark v. Thompson, 204 F. Supp. 30 (S.D. Miss.), April 19, 1962.

27. Clark v. Thompson, 206 F. Supp. 539, 541 (S.D. Miss. 1962), *affd*, 313 F.2d 637 (5th Cir. 1963).

28. Clark v. Thompson, 206 F. Supp. 539, 541.

29. Clark v. Thompson, 206 F. Supp. 543 (S.D. Miss. 1962), *affd*, 313 F.2d 637 (5th Cir. 1963).

30. See Cook, "Freedom Libraries"; story of the Schwerners on 98–101. See also Sandra E. Adickes, "The Legacy of the Mississippi Freedom Schools," *Radical Teacher* 44 (Winter 1993): 177, quoted in Cook, "Freedom Libraries," 346.

31. Donald G Davis Jr. and Cheryl Knott Malone, "Reading for Liberation: The Role of Libraries in the 1964 Mississippi Summer Project," in Tucker, *Untold Stories*, 110–25, quotation on 121.

32. Essay by Sandra Adickes, Civil Rights Movement Veterans website, www.crmvet.org/vet /adickes.htm.

33. Interview with Sandra Adickes, October 26, 2011, New Brunswick, N.J.

34. All quotations in Cook, "Freedom Libraries," 377. Rochell was not alone. Evidence suggests, Cook argues, that Walter Wicker, Jackson Public Library director from 1955 to 1957, resigned "because he refused to allow the Citizens' Council to dictate who could use the library and what books he could put in the collection" (377). For an analysis of the dilemma in which Currier found herself, see Karen Cook, "Struggles Within: Lura G. Currier, the Mississippi Library Commission and Library Services to African Americans," *Information & Culture* 48, no. 1 (2013): 134–56.

35. "Woman Recalls Library Card Denial," *Hattiesburg American*, November 26, 2006.

36. Quoted in Cook, "Freedom Libraries," 263.

37. "Woman Recalls Library Card Denial". See also Cook, "Freedom Libraries," 260–63.

38. "Library Closed after Integration Attempt," *Hattiesburg American*, August 14, 1964.

39. Adickes went on to successfully challenge that conviction, and when she returned to New York, she filed a Civil Rights action against the Kress store, ultimately winning a settlement. She donated her portion to the Southern Conference Education Fund. See Adickes essay, Civil Rights Movement Veterans website. See also Adickes v. S. H. Kress and Company, 39 U.S. 144 (1970), Brief for the Petitioner (July 28, 1969).

40. Achtenberg v. Mississippi, 393 F.2d 468 (5th Cir. 1968), at 470.

41. Affidavit of William D. Jones, Achtenberg v. Mississippi, 393 F.2d 468 (5th Cir. 1968), at 471.

42. Jones Affidavit, Achtenberg v. Mississippi, at 471–72.

43. "Library Shut Again," *Jackson Clarion Ledger*, August 18, 1964. See also "Public Library Is Closed Again," *Hattiesburg American*, August 17, 1964.

44. "One Tough Case," *Berkeley Law* blog, https://www.law.berkeley.edu/article/one-tough-case/.

45. "Judge William Harold Cox," *Famous Trials* blog, University of Missouri–Kansas City School of Law, www.famous-trials.com/mississippi-burningtrial/145-keyfiguresmissi/1965-cox.

46. "William Harold Cox, Outspoken Judge," *New York Times*, February 27, 1988.

47. "Elbert Parr Tuttle, 1897–1996," International Civil Rights Walk of Fame, National Park Service website, www.nps.gov/features/malu/feat0002/wof/Elbert_Tuttle.htm. For an excellent biogra-

phy of Judge Tuttle, see Anne Emanuel, *Elbert Parr Tuttle: Chief Jurist of the Civil Rights Revolution* (Athens: University of Georgia Press, 2011).

48. Nina Totenberg, "Elbert Tuttle, Quiet Civil Rights Revolutionary," www.npr.org/2011/10/05 /140948689/elbert-tuttle-quiet-civil-rights-revolutionary.

49. "Elbert Parr Tuttle, 1897–1996"; Totenberg, "Elbert Tuttle"; and Emanuel, *Elbert Parr Tuttle,* xv–xvi.

50. Achtenberg v. Mississippi, 393 F.2d 468, 474 (5th Cir. 1968).

51. "Hattiesburg Public Library Reopened on Integrated (but Not Really) Basis," *Library Journal* 89, November 15, 1964, 4490.

52. "Will Mississippi Library Integrate?" *Baltimore Afro-American,* October 3, 1964.

53. Cook, "Freedom Libraries," 307–8.

54. Quotations in Cook, "Freedom Libraries," 367. See also Miriam Braverman, "Mississippi Summer," *Library Journal* 90, November 15, 1965, 5046.

55. Braverman, "Mississippi Summer," 5046.

56. *Vicksburg Project Newsletter,* February 17, 1965, folder 1, box 3, Bryan Dunlap Papers, 1964–66, Wisconsin Historical Society (WHS) Archives, Madison; "Negroes at Library," *Vicksburg Citizens' Appeal,* March 15, 1965; Braverman, "Mississippi Summer," 5047.

57. Quoted in Cook, "Freedom Libraries," 398–99.

8. BLACK YOUTH IN RURAL LOUISIANA

1. Benjamin Muse, *The American Negro Revolution* (Bloomington: Indiana University Press, 1968), 97.

2. For a deeper analysis of the civil rights era in Louisiana history, see Adam Fairclough, *Race and Democracy: The Civil Rights Struggle in Louisiana, 1915–1972* (Athens: University of Georgia Press, 1999). See also Adam Fairclough, "Race and Democracy: The Civil Rights Struggle in Louisiana," *Southern Changes* 17, no. 1 (1995): 16.

3. "Weekly Field Report, August 19–24, 1963," folder 18, box 1, Mss 516, CORE Papers, WHS.

4. See Field Report, Pointe Coupee Parish, January 1964, found in folder 12, box 1, Mss 516, "District CORE Records, Field Reports—Miscellaneous Parishes, 1964," CORE Papers.

5. "CORE Meets Resistance Testing Civil Rights Bill," *New York Amsterdam News,* August 1, 1964.

6. See "Negroes Charged after Attempts at Integration," *Monroe (La.) News-Star,* July 10, 1964; and "Church Announcement," July 12, 1964 (circular prepared by the Monroe CORE Chapter), box 3, Mss 119, Monroe Branch, La., CORE Papers.

7. Etta Faye Baker, "Affidavit," July 11, 1964, Dorothy Higgins, "Affidavit," July 12, 1964, both in box 3, Mss 119, Monroe Branch, La., CORE Papers.

8. Bonnie Ray Brass, "Affidavit," copy found in box 3, Mss 119, Monroe Branch, La., CORE Papers.

9. Bennie Ray Brass, "Affidavit," copy found in box 3, Mss 119, Monroe Branch, La., CORE Papers.

10. Brass, "Affidavit."

11. Dorothy Higgins, "Affidavit," copy found in box 3, Mss 119, Monroe Branch, La., CORE Papers.

12. Brass, "Affidavit."

13. David Paul Kramer, "Affidavit," July 19, 1964, box 3, Mss 119, Monroe Branch, La., CORE Papers.

14. Brass, "Affidavit."

15. Form in box 3, Mss 119, Monroe Branch, La., CORE Papers.

16. Report dated July 20, 1964, and authored by Mike Lesser, CORE Task Force worker, in box 3, Mss 119, Monroe Branch, La., CORE Papers.

17. Joint Statement, Mr. and Mrs. Oliver Smith, July 22, 1964, document in box 3, Mss 119, Monroe Branch, La., CORE Papers. See also Gretha Castle (director of CORE's North Louisiana Committee on Registration Education) to L. L. Mitchell (U.S. Commission on Civil Rights), December 9, 1964, box 1, Mss 119, Monroe Branch, La., CORE Papers.

18. Descriptions of these incidents in individual documents signed by protesters Robert Garner, George Padio, Donnell Wyatt, and Tommy Robinson, dated July 22, 1964, in box 3, Mss 119, CORE Papers. See also Michael Lesser's description, same date.

19. See descriptions of these events in documents signed by testers dated July 22, 1964, in box 3, Mss. 119, CORE Papers. It was no surprise that police were at the West Monroe Branch because a CORE Task Force worker had not only contacted the FBI before testers approached the library, but he had also called the local police. It is likely CORE believed that giving advance notice to police would minimize the chances of violence. See undated notes, box 3, Mss 119, Monroe Branch, La., CORE Papers.

20. Lettie Bess's description of these incidents in document she signed, dated July 22, 1964, box 3, Mss 119, Monroe Branch, La., CORE Papers. See also Michael Lesser's description, same date.

21. Notes found in box 3, Mss 119, Monroe Branch, La., CORE Papers.

22. "Court Asked to End Ban at Libraries," *Monroe (La.) Morning World*, July 29, 1964; "Negroes Ask for Federal Jurisdiction," *Monroe Morning World*, August 4, 1964.

23. CORE complained about this practice—"as pernicious as it is out-of-date"—on January 6, 1965. See *CORE Freedom News* (CORE Monroe office newsletter), February 6, 1965, copy found in box 4, Mss. 119, Monroe Branch, La., CORE Papers.

24. "Carver-McDonald Branch Public Library," Monroe Black History, *Wikispaces.com*, http://monroe blackhistory.wikispaces.com/Carver-McDonald+Branch+Public+Library.

25. Statement, Earlene Knox, July 22, 1964, CORE Testing Form, found in box 1, Mss 537, Jackson Parish Records, 1961–65, CORE Papers.

26. W. C. Flanagan and E. N Francis to C. E. Thompson, Frank Dunbaugh, and L. L. Mitchell, July 23, 1964, box 1, Mss 537, Jackson Parish Records 1961–65, CORE Papers.

27. Statement, Larry Robinson, age thirteen, July 27, 1964; Statement, Will Farmer Jr., August 3, 1964, both in box 1, Mss 537, Jackson Parish Records, 1961–65, CORE Papers. When asked by the *New York Times*, the sheriff said he had "some 25 to 30 Negroes in jail, but that's not unusual after a weekend." He declined to comment on whether any were library picketers. See "Jonesboro, La.," *New York Times*, July 28, 1964.

28. Robinson Statement, July 27, 1964; Farmer Statement, August 3, 1964.

29. "5 Integrate Library at Jonesboro," *Louisiana Weekly* (New Orleans), January 2, 1965. See also CORE Press Release, December 17, 1964, box 1, Mss 119, Monroe (La.) Office, CORE Papers.

30. Brief for Petitioners, Brown v. State of Louisiana, 383 U.S. 131 (1966).

31. See "Library Sit-In," *East Feliciana Watchman*, April 24, 1964.

32. Report titled "Louisiana in Brief," "New Orleans CORE Research Office, Memos and Reports, 1963, 1965," folder 4 (p. 11), box 1, Mss 516, CORE Papers; "Negro Students Arrested in Attempt to Use Library in Louisiana," *Library Journal* 89, April 15, 1964, 1702.

33. See Ellis Howard, Report, "Refused Public Library Service," n.d.; Loria Davis, "Field Report—St. Helena's Parish, March 1–Mar. 31, 1964"; Mimi Feingold, "Field Report—St. Helena, Apr. 14–30, 1964"; Report, "Negroes Again Refused Public Library Service," March 13, 1964; Report, "St. Helena Youths Refused Public Library Service, March 16, 1964; all in folder 13, box 1, Mss 516, Louisiana, Sixth Congressional District Records, 1963–65, CORE Papers.

34. "Negro Students Arrested in Attempt to Use Library in Louisiana," Library Journal 89, April 15, 1964, 1702.

35. "Field Report, West Feliciana Parish, Feb. 10–Feb. 29, 1964," in folder 13, box 1, Mss 516, CORE Papers.

36. "Field Report, West Feliciana Parish, Feb. 10–Feb. 29, 1964."

37. Neither the librarian nor the sheriff had ever seen African Americans in the library. Brief for Petitioner, Brown v. Louisiana, 383 U.S. 131 (1966).

38. Brown v. Louisiana, 383 U.S. 131, 135.

39. Actually, Brown handed the librarian a slip of paper that read, "Wandell Arna, the Story of the Negro, Bontems." The librarian was apparently able to decipher the request. Brown v. Louisiana, Brief for the Respondent, 1965 WL 115711 (August 25, 1965).

40. La. Rev. Stat. sec. 14:103.1.

41. See Loria Davis, "Field Report—East Feliciana Parish, Mar. 1–Mar. 31, 1964," folder 13, box 1, Mss 516, CORE Papers. See also "Six Arrested in Library 'Sit-In' Scheduled for Trial March 25," East Feliciana Watchman, March 13, 1964.

42. Copy of cable in folder 14, box 1, Mss 85, CORE Papers.

43. "Branch Libraries in Louisiana Shut Down to 'Improve' Service," Library Journal 89, June 15, 1964, 2566. See also East Feliciana Watchman, April 17 and 24, 1964.

44. "Lockouts and Arrests—Repeat Performance," Wilson Library Bulletin 39 (September 1964): 22.

45. Oral Argument, Brown v. Louisiana (USSC 1966), www.oyez.cases/1960–1969/1965/1965_41.

46. See "At the Library," East Feliciana Watchman, April 2, 1964; and "KKK Beats Newsman," East Feliciana Watchman, April 24, 1964.

47. Obituaries, "Carl Rachlin, 82, a Lawyer for Civil Rights Demonstrators," New York Times, March 3, 2000.

48. Robert Morris, "Southern Politics: Judge Robert Collins Speaks," Southern Changes: The Journal of the Southern Regional Council 1 no. 7 (1979). Unfortunately, less than fifteen years later he also became the first judge in the federal judiciary's two hundred–year history to be convicted of taking a bribe. He was sentenced to six years and ten months in prison and resigned his position under threat of impeachment. "Judge Is First Federal Jurist Convicted of Taking a Bribe," Los Angeles Times, June 30, 1991; John McQuaid, "Collins Resigns Federal Judgeship; Resignation Letter Is Given to Clinton," New Orleans Times-Picayune, August 7, 1993.

49. Brief for the Respondent, Brown v. Louisiana, 383 U.S. at 131.

50. Oral Argument, Brown v. Louisiana (USSC 1966), www.oyez.cases/1960–1969/1965/1965, 41.

51. Brown v. Louisiana, 393 U.S. 131, 142, 159.

52. Brown v. Louisiana, 383 U.S., 159–60.

53. Brown v. Louisiana, 383 U.S., 160–61, 165, 167–68 (J. Black, dissenting).

54. Brown v. Louisiana, 383 U.S. 131, 133, 139, 142, 143. Only two other justices joined Justice Fortas's entire opinion. Justices William J. Brennan and Byron White concurred in the result—i.e.,

reversing the convictions—but neither thought it necessary to determine whether the protesters' actions were constitutionally protected. It was enough to find that their actions did not violate the Louisiana statute.

55. "Editorial: Access and the Supreme Court," *Library Journal* 91, April 1, 1966, 1788.

9. THE AMERICAN LIBRARY ASSOCIATION

1. See William Henry Beer to Anne Wallace, February 6, 1899, New Orleans Public Library Archives; Anne Wallace to Henry J. Carr, March 7, 1899; William Coolidge Lane to Carr, March 30, 1899; Carr to Lane, March 30, 1899; Wallace to Carr, April 1, 1899; Carr to Wallace, April 4, 1899; and Lane to Carr, April 15, 1899, all in Henry J. Carr Mss, American Library Association Archives (hereafter cited as ALA Archives). See also Litwack, *Trouble in Mind*, 404–6. We have been unable to determine if Du Bois knew he was being considered for a lecture slot at the conference.

2. Stated in a letter to the editor, *Columbia State,* June 22, 1919.

3. "The Library: New Developments in Training for Librarianship," *Christian Science Monitor,* February 3, 1926.

4. "Memorandum on Efforts to Establish Segregated Training School for Librarians," August 25, 1925; Walter F. White (NAACP assistant secretary) to ALA president Charles F. D. Beldon, August 28, 1925; White to Frederick Keppel (Carnegie Corp. president), August 29, 1925, all in box C-204, NAACP Papers, Manuscripts Reading Room, Library of Congress. See also S. L. Smith, "The Passing of the Hampton Library School," *Journal of Negro Education* 9 (January 1940): 51–58.

5. Barker, *Libraries of the South,* 50–57, quotation on 51.

6. Wallace Van Jackson, "Negro Segregation," *Library Journal* 61 (June 1936): 467–68; editorial, *New Republic* 87, May 20, 1936, 30; Jesse Cunningham, letter to the editor, *Library Journal* 61 (May 1936): 515.

7. Cunningham, letter to the editor, 515.

8. E. J. Josey, "Race Issues in Library History," in *Encyclopedia of Library History,* ed. Wayne A. Wiegand and Donald G. Davis (New York: Garland Publishing, 1994), 534.

9. "U.S. Libraries Demand Freedom of Choice of Books," *Christian Science Monitor,* May 31, 1940.

10. See *Intellectual Freedom Manual,* 5th ed. (Chicago: American Library Association, 1996), 6–7.

11. See Carrie C. Robinson, "First by Circumstance," in *The Black Librarian in America,* ed. E. J. Josey (Metuchen, N.J.: Scarecrow Press, 1970), 282; S. R. Harris, "Civil Rights and the Louisiana Library Association: Stumbling toward Integration," *Libraries & Culture* 38 (Fall 2003): 322–50; and K. Barrett and B. A. Bishop, "Integration and the Alabama Library Association: Not So Black and White," *Libraries & Culture* 33 (Spring 1998): 141–61.

12. Susan Lee Scott, "Integration of Public Library Facilities in the South: Attitudes and Actions of the Library Profession," *Southeastern Librarian* 18 (Fall 1968): 162.

13. "No Segregation Here," *Library Journal* 80, November 15, 1955, 2633–34. The council, founded in 1919, has for nearly one hundred years monitored and produced influential reports on racial conditions in the South and advocated for racial justice.

14. These letters are quoted in Archie McNeal, "Integrated Service in Southern Public Libraries," *Library Journal* 86, June 1, 1961, 2045–46.

15. Excerpt from ALA Executive Board Minutes, March 27, 1960, box 1, ser. 69/2/6, ALA Archives.

16. "ALA Adopts Integration Statement," *Wilson Library Bulletin* 35 (March 1961): 486.

17. John Wakeman, "Segregation and Censorship," *Wilson Library Bulletin* 35 (September 1960): 63–64.

18. Eric Moon, "The Silent Subject," *Library Journal* 85, December 15, 1960, 4436–37; Rice Estes, "Segregated Libraries," *Library Journal* 85, December 15, 1960, 4418–21. See also Kenneth F. Kister, *Eric Moon: The Life and Library Times* (Jefferson, N.C.: McFarland & Co., 2002), 154–76.

19. W. R. Eshelman, Editorial, *California Librarian* 22 (January 1961): 23–24. See also William R. Eshelman, *No Silence! A Library Life* (Lanham, Md.: Scarecrow Press, 1997), 145–47.

20. "Readers' Voices," *Library Journal* 86, February 15, 1961, 730–33.

21. See "Readers' Voices," *Library Journal* 86, February 15, 1961, 733–35.

22. "Pratt Library Stoops to Jim Crow," *Baltimore Afro-American*, May 19, 1934. Baker quotation in Braverman, *Youth, Society, and the Public Library,* 227.

23. Eshelman, *No Silence,* 147.

. 24. See, e.g., "Jerry" of the New Orleans Public Library to David Clift, March 11, 1963, regarding efforts to ban *The Last Temptation of Christ,* box 1, ser. 69/2/6, ALA Archives. Quotation from McNeal in Archie McNeal, "A New Statement and Its Significance," *ALA Bulletin* 56 (July 1962): 623+.

25. Eric Moon, "A Survey of Segregation," *Library Journal* 86 (March 1961): 1110.

26. Harold C. Gardiner, "National Library Week—for All?" *America* 105, April 15, 1961, 139+.

27. Everett T. Moore to McNeal, January 12, 1961, box 1, ser. 69/2/6, ALA Archives.

28. Grace Stevenson to Archie McNeal, March 28, 1961, box 1, ser. 69/2/6, ALA Archives; Kister, *Eric Moon,* 161.

29. "Segregation in Libraries: Negro Librarians Give Their Views," *Wilson Library Bulletin* 35 (May 1961): 707–10. "When the dean of a library school is refused membership in her own state library association it is hard to believe that there can be any other reason than racial discrimination within the profession," Eric Moon wrote. "Perhaps even before we can hope to be very effective in removing discriminatory practices from our libraries, we shall have to set our own internal house in order." See Moon, "Internal Integration," *Library Journal* 86 (June 1961): 2060.

30. Beatrice Rossell, "Have We Sufficient Vision?" *ALA Bulletin* 55 (June 1961): 477–78.

31. "ALA and the Segregation Issue," *ALA Bulletin* 55 (June 1961): 485–67. See also "ALA Adopts Integration Statement," *Wilson Library Bulletin* 35 (March 1961): 486–88.

32. Paul K. Swanson to American Library Association, June 21, 1961, box 2, ser. 69/2/6, ALA Archives.

33. Eric Moon, "On Editorials," *Library Journal* 86 (August 1961): 2618–19.

34. "Legislation Urged against Segregated Libraries," *Wilson Library Bulletin* 36 (November 1961): 202.

35. Eli M. Oboler, "Attitudes on Segregation: How ALA Compares with Other Professional Associations," *Library Journal* 86, December 15, 1961, 4233–39.

36. Eric Moon, "Who's Out of Step?" *Library Journal* 87, March 1, 1962, 936–37; John Wakeman, "Time to Act," *Wilson Library Bulletin* 36 (April 1962): 677. All council quotations taken from "Integration and Censorship," *Library Journal* 87, March 1, 1962, 904–7. See also "Segregation and ALA Membership," *Wilson Library Bulletin* 36 (March 1962): 558–61.

37. "Segregation and ALA," *Wilson Library Bulletin* 37 (September 1962): 12.

38. All quotations taken from "Questioning a Question—and Some of the Answers," *Library Journal* 88 (July 1963): 2644–47.

39. "Library Bias Report Draws Angry Denials," *Chicago Tribune,* July 16, 1963.

40. "Library Bias Report Draws Angry Denials."

41. "Library Bias Report Draws Angry Denials."

42. "The Access to Public Libraries Study," *ALA Bulletin* 57 (September 1963): 745; "The Access Study: An Lj Forum," *Library Journal* 88, December 15, 1963, 4685–4712; and Austin C. Wehrwein, "Integration of South's Libraries Outpaces That of Its Schools," *New York Times,* July 16, 1963. For evidence of discrimination in urban housing practices in the North in the 1950s that gave rise to International Research Associates observations and left urban public library systems vulnerable to these kinds of criticisms, see Tuck, *We Ain't What We Ought to Be,* 247–56. See also Lizbeth Cohen, *A Consumer's Republic: The Politics of Mass Consumption in Postwar America* (New York: Knopf, 2003), 251.

43. *Access to Public Libraries: A Research Project Prepared for the Library Administration Division, American Library Association by International Research Associates, Inc.* (Chicago: American Library Association, 1963).

44. "Access Study," 4685–4712, quotations on 4690, 4693, 4702–3, 4704–5, 4706, and 4711. See also E. J. Josey, "The Civil Rights Movement and American Librarianship: The Opening Round," in *Activism in American Librarianship, 1962–1973,* ed. Mary Lee Bundy and Frederick J. Stielow (Westport, Conn.: Greenwood Press, 1987), 13–20.

45. Bernice Lloyd Bell, "Public Library Integration in Thirteen Southern States," *Library Journal* 88, December 15, 1963, 4713–15.

46. Quotations taken from Cook, "Freedom Libraries in the 1964 Mississippi Freedom Summer Project," 189–90. Three years earlier Currier had offered to help African American Frankie Bethea set up a black library in McComb but only privately as "an individual librarian," not officially as Mississippi Library Commission director. See chap. 7.

47. Scott, "Integration of Public Library Facilities in the South," 162–69.

48. Graham, *Right to Read,* 99, 120, 130.

49. Kister, *Eric Moon,* 175.

EPILOGUE

1. "Ala. Civil Rights Campaigners Start with Public Library," *Library Journal* 90 (July 1965): 2992; "Bessemer, Ala. Negroes Integrate Public Library," *New York Times,* June 3, 1965.

2. Mary Edna Anders, *Libraries and Library Services in the Southeast: A Report of the Southeastern States Cooperative Library Survey, 1972–1975* (University: University of Alabama Press, 1976), 145.

3. Halberstam, *Children,* 92–93.

4. McPheeters Transcript, 27–28.

5. Graham, *Right to Read,* 129, 133.

6. E. J. Josey, "Use of Libraries: Key to Negro Progress," *Negro History Bulletin* 26 (April 1963): 219–21, quotations on 220 and 221.

7. Wolcott, *Race Riots, and Roller Coasters,* 225.

8. See Dale Russakoff, "Relations Changing Rapidly in Segregation's Old Citadel," *Washington Post,* September 16, 1984.

9. "Auburn Avenue Research Library on African American Culture and History," *Wikipedia*, http://en.wikipedia.org/wiki/Auburn_Avenue_Research_Library_on_African_American_Culture_and_History.

10. "African American Center, Library Worthy Goal for Entire Community," *Sun Sentinel* (Fort Lauderdale), May 6, 1996.

11. Lewis, *Walking with the Wind*.

12. "Schwerner's Widow Donates to Phila. Library," *Deep South Jewish Voice* 16 (February 2006): 20.

13. "Branch Library Will Be Named for Mississippi Author Richard Wright," *Mississippi Link* (Jackson) 15, April 5–11, 2007.

14. Petra Gertjegerdes, "Travelling Civil Rights Exhibit Arrives at Columbus Public Library," *Columbus (Ga.) Times*, December 10–16, 2008.

15. Drew Taylor, "Mural Depicting Selma March Unveiled after 20 Years Inside Library," *Montgomery Advertiser*, March 19, 2015.

16. John Hope Franklin, "Libraries in a Pluralistic Society," in *Libraries and the Life of the Mind in America: Addresses Delivered at the Centennial Celebration of the American Library Association* (Chicago: American Library Association, 1977), 11–14.

17. Phil Morehart and George M. Eberhart, "Resurrecting the Speaker," *American Libraries*, July 1, 2014, 21:21, https://americanlibrariesmagazine.org/blogs/the-scoop/resurrecting-the-speaker/.

18. Quoted in "Plowing through Chicago," *School Library Journal* 24 (March 1978): 87.

19. See "Viewing and Speaking about 'The Speaker' at ALA Annual Conference," *Intellectual Freedom blog*, May 22, 2014, www.oif.ala.org/oif/?p=4985.

20. Todd Honma, "Trippin' over the Color Line': The Invisibility of Race in Library and Information Studies," *InterActions: UCLA Journal of Education and Information Studies* 1, no. 2 (1995): 1–28.

21. Principle 2, Library Bill of Rights. See *Intellectual Freedom Manual*, 5th ed. (Chicago: American Library Association, 1996), 13–14.

22. John Eby, "'Greenville 8' Together 50 Years after Segregation," WYFF.com, July 12, 2010, www.wyff4.com/-Greenville-8-Together-50-Years-After-Segregation/6161420.

NOTE ON PRIMARY SOURCES

Besides standard sources such as autobiographies and quotations taken from relevant secondary sources and published primary sources such as contemporary periodicals (all cited in the endnotes), this study relied heavily on primary sources that fit into several large categories.

NEWSPAPERS

Much of the story of the desegregation of public libraries in the American South can be found in black newspapers across the country. In many cases, editors of these newspapers phoned or wrote to participants in public library demonstrations in the South to get their observations of events that white local newspapers ignored or reported in ways that reflected "the southern way of life." Most valuable was the Historical Black Newspapers database in ProQuest Historical Newspapers (www.proquest.com/products-services/hist news-bn.html). By using *public library* as a search term, we found hundreds of accounts of events involving black libraries throughout the twentieth century that we could not find addressed or covered in local, state, and national white periodicals and newspapers or in the national, regional, and state library press. Black newspapers in the database (and years of coverage) include: *Atlanta Daily World* (1931–2003), *Baltimore Afro-American* (1893–1975), *Chicago Defender* (1910–75), *Cleveland Call and Post* (1934–91), *Los Angeles Sentinel* (1934–2005), *New York Amsterdam News* (1922–93), *Norfolk (Va.) Journal and Guide* (1921–2003), *Philadelphia Tribune* (1912–2001), and *Pittsburgh Courier* (1911–2002). No one doing research in twentieth-century black library history can ignore this rich resource.

Some local white papers did cover protests at local public libraries and in that coverage demonstrated that the local white community was often split in its reaction to integrating public libraries. By using dates of events we found first reported in black newspapers, we were able to target specific dates of unindexed local white newspapers. Especially helpful were microfilmed local newspapers at the Alabama Department of Archives and History in Montgomery, the Louisiana State University Library in Baton Rouge, the Mississippi Department of Archives and History in Jackson, the University of Georgia in Athens, the

University of South Carolina in Columbia, and the Virginia State Library in Richmond. Also helpful were local newspaper clipping files at the Albany Civil Rights Institute in Georgia.

National newspapers and periodicals occasionally covered library protests, especially after 1960. The ProQuest Historical Newspaper and Periodicals, 1850–2000 database was especially helpful here. Other databases that had some information include: America's Historical Newspapers, 1690–1922, ser. 1–5; Alexander Street Press databases (including Oral History Online, Manuscript Women's Letters and Diaries, 1750–1950, and Oral Histories: Black Thought and Culture); HarpWeek (1857–1912); and the Library of Congress's Online Accessible Archives: American Periodical Series Online, 1740–1940.

MANUSCRIPT COLLECTIONS

No archival depository has developed a focused interest in collecting materials that document the desegregation of public libraries in the American South. The American Library Association Archives at the University of Illinois at Urbana-Champaign were disappointing in the amount of information they contained on the subject. Correspondence concerning plans to invite W. E. B. Du Bois to speak at the 1899 Atlanta ALA conference can be found in the papers of Henry J. Carr, who was the ALA's treasurer at the time. Other evidence of ALA discussion and action involving civil rights activities in southern public libraries can be found in boxes 1 and 2, ser. 69/2/6.

The Louisiana District Congress on Racial Equality (CORE) Papers, located in the Wisconsin Historical Society (WHS) Archives in Madison, provided much of the evidence for chapter 8. Series numbers in the WHS CORE Papers that held the most information for this project are 119, containing the Pointe Coupee Parish field reports and the Monroe Branch papers, including the affidavits in which "testers" describe what happened to them; and 537, containing the Jackson Parish Papers, including field reports and affidavits.

Other manuscript collections that provided bits and pieces of information (several of which Wayne found while researching other projects) include:

Browning, Joan C. Papers. Emory University, Manuscripts and Rare Book Library, Atlanta (box 1).
Carnegie Corporation. Records. Columbia University, New York (microfilmed records for Mound Bayou, Miss., and Savannah, Ga.).
Dunlap, Bryan. Papers. 1964–66, WHS.
McPheeters, Annie W. Papers. Transcript, Oral History Interview no. aarlohe 92-001, Archives Division, Auburn Avenue Research Library on African American Culture and History, Atlanta-Fulton Public Library System, Atlanta.

Mississippi State Sovereignty Commission. Papers. Mississippi Department of Archives and History, available online at http://mdah.state.ms.us/digital_archives/sovcom.

Montgomery Branch, National Association for the Advancement of Colored People. Minutes, May 22, 1955. Schomburg Center, New York Public Library, New York.

National Association for the Advancement of Colored People. Box C-204, Manuscripts Reading Room, Library of Congress, Washington, D.C.

New Orleans Public Library Archives. Letter, William Beer (library director) to George F. Bowerman (director, District of Columbia Public Library), December 4, 1909, New Orleans.

Schein, Ruth. Papers. Schomburg Center, New York Public Library, New York.

PUBLIC LIBRARY ANNUAL REPORTS

While researching *Part of Our Lives: A People's History of the American Public Library* (2015), Wayne analyzed thousands of public library annual reports. Listed here are the libraries whose annual reports contained information on race issues in library services before 1968. Most are in the collections of the University of Wisconsin–Madison's School of Information Library. Annual reports are referenced in notes as "AR (year), library name, page numbers."

Atlanta Carnegie Library, Atlanta, 1899–1916.

District of Columbia Public Library, 1901–70.

Galveston (Tex.) Rosenberg Library, 1910–19.

Lexington (Ky.) Public Library, 1905–31.

Louisville Free Public Library, 1905–31.

New Orleans Public Library, 1905–21.

St. Louis Public Library, 1873–1938.

ATLANTA UNIVERSITY MASTER'S THESES BEFORE 1967

That students at the School of Library Service at the historically black Atlanta University heeded the mid-twentieth-century advice of Virginia Lacy Jones, dean of the university's library program, to write master's theses on black libraries in the South—especially from their hometowns—is evident from this list. In many of these theses we came across statements we found useful that student authors had quoted from local black librarians and patrons whom they had interviewed. Not only does this body of materials constitute a rich resource for understanding black libraries before 1967, but it also represents almost the entirety of the library profession's research literature on the subject. Master's theses we read include:

Adkins, Barbara Mamie. "A History of Public Library Service to Negroes in Atlanta, Georgia" (1951).

Aldrich, Willie Lee Banks. "The History of Public Library Service to Negroes in Salisbury, North Carolina, 1937–1963" (1964).

Barfield, Isaac R. "A History of the Miami Public Library, Miami, Florida" (1958).

Barnes, Glynell Shakelford. "A History of Public Library Service to Negroes in Galveston, Texas, 1904–1955" (1957).

Bell, Bernice Lloyd. "Integration in Public Library Service in Thirteen Southern States, 1954–1962" (1963).

Cantey, Evelyn Elizabeth. "A Study of Fiction and Non-Fiction Borrowed by Adult Patrons of the West Hunter Branch Library, Atlanta, Georgia" (1956).

Cogswell, Talullah King. "A Study of the Fiction and Non-Fiction Borrowed by the Adult Patrons of the Carnegie Public Library, Savannah, Georgia" (1958).

Cooper, Neloweze Williams. "The History of Public Library Service to Negroes in Savannah, Georgia" (1960).

Crittenden, Juanita Louisa Jones. "A History of Public Library Service to Negroes in Columbus, Georgia, 1931–1957" (1961).

Curry, John Lee. "A History of Public Library Service to Negroes in Jacksonville, Florida" (1957).

Davis, Calverta Elnora. "A Survey of the Public Library Service Offered to Negroes in Greenville County, South Carolina" (1958).

Dickey, Pennie Williams. "A History of Public Library Service for Negroes in Jackson, Mississippi, 1950–1957" (1963).

Fonville, Emma Ruth. "A History of Public Library Service to Negroes in Bessemer, Alabama" (1962).

Grayson, Bessie Rivers. "The History of Public Library Service for Negroes in Montgomery, Alabama" (1965).

Hansborough, Irene Cross. "Public Library Service to Negroes in Knoxville, Tennessee" (1959).

Hoffman, Rheba Palmer. "A History of Public Library Services to Negroes in Memphis, Tennessee" (1955).

James, Berdie Eichold Turner. "History and Development of Public Library Service to Negroes in Mobile, Alabama, 1931–1957" (1961).

Mays, Fayrene Neuman. "A History of Public Library Service to Negroes in Houston, Texas, 1907–1962" (1964).

McCrary, Mary Ellen. "A History of Public Library Service to Negroes in Nashville, Tennessee, 1916–1958" (1959).

Moore, Bennie Lee. "A History of Public Library Service to Negroes in Winston-Salem, North Carolina, 1927–1951" (1962).

Perres, Myrtle Janice. "History and Development of Public Library Service for Negroes in Pensacola, Florida, 1947–1961" (1963).

Redd, Gwendolyn Lewis. "A History of Public Library Service to Negroes in Macon, Georgia" (1961).

Rush, Shirley C. "History of Public Library Service to Negroes in Ouachita Parish, Monroe, Louisiana, 1949–1965" (1967).

Sturgis, Gladys Marie. "A Study of Master's Theses Submitted by Students of the Atlanta University School of Library Service in Partial Fulfillment of the Requirements for the Degree of Master in Science in Library Service, 1955 through 1959" (1963).

Tillman, Rosebud Harris. "The History of Public Library Service to Negroes in Little Rock, Arkansas, 1917–1951" (1953).

Walker, Margaret Louise. "Types of Juvenile Patrons of Two Branches of the Atlanta Public Library" (1952).

Wright, Lillian Taylor. "Thomas Fountain Blue, Pioneer Librarian, 1866–1925" (1955).

FEDERAL LITIGATION

Federal litigation can be confusing. The formal opinions of the federal courts are found in various federal reporters, but these are just the courts' decisions. Additional materials generated for federal cases (e.g., depositions, transcripts of hearings, transcripts of evidence, and the actual trial record) may be found in courthouses across the nation or, for older cases, in the collections of regional offices of the National Archives and Records Administration. Repositories, however, are not consistent in what they choose to save or discard. Some of these materials are also online. Materials relevant to cases discussed in this book are cited, and their locations identified, in the endnotes.

REPORTED CASES

Achtenberg v. Mississippi, 393 F.2d 468 (5th Cir. 1968).
Adickes v. S. H. Kress and Company, 39 U.S. 144 (1970).
Anderson v. City of Albany, 321 F.2d 649 (5th Cir. 1963).
Brown v. Louisiana, 383 U.S. 131 (1966).
Clark v. Thompson, 206 F. Supp. 539 (S.D. Miss. 1962).
Cobb v. Montgomery Library Board, 207 F. Supp. 880 (M.D. Ala. 1962).
Kelley v. Page, Civil Action No. 727 (U.S. Dist. Ct., M.D. Albany Division 1962).
Turner v. Randolph, 195 F. Supp. 677 (W.D. Tenn. 1961).

Owens v. Portsmouth Public Library, Civil Action 3100, Records of the District Court for the Eastern District of Virginia, Norfolk Division, RG 21, box 277, National Archives and Record Administration at Philadelphia.

Rev. Wyatt T. Walker v. Petersburg Public Library, in Civil Action 3072, Records of the District Court for the Eastern Division of Virginia, Richmond Division, RG 21, box 19, National Archives and Records Administration at Philadelphia.

INDEX

Aberdeen, MS, 35–36

Abernathy, Ralph, 120, 133, 134–35

academic libraries, public services of, 20

Achtenberg, Ben, 160, 165

Ackerman, Bruce, 12

Adickes, Sandra, 158, 159–60, 162, 240n39

adult education programs, 38, 41–42

African American library branches. *See* black library branches

African American newspapers and magazines. *See* black newspapers and magazines

African American reading interests. *See* black reading interests

African American veterans. *See* black veterans

African Americans in children's fiction. *See* blacks in children's fiction

ALA Bulletin. See Bulletin of the American Library Association

Alabama Christian Movement for Human Rights, 11

Alabama Library Association, 188, 196

Alabama State College, 118

Albany, GA, 10, 131–42, 164

Albany State College, 132, 133, 134, 138

Alexandria (VA) Public Library, 48–50

Alvarez, Robert, 53–54

American Library Association (ALA), 13, 24, 33, 40, 64, 184–202, 206–8; Intellectual Freedom Committee (IFC), 64, 189, 193, 196, 197, 208; Office of Intellectual Freedom (OIF), 207, 208

Anderson, Harold, 123

Anderson, William G., 132, 142

Andrews, Jimmie, 169, 171

Anniston, AL, 9, 55, 125–27

anticommunism, 50, 65, 97

anti-Semitism, 97, 162

Arey, D. Lurton, 97

Arsenault, Raymond, 9

assassinations, 1, 11, 12, 146

assaults, 118–19, 125–27, 166, 179; by police, 150, 152

Atkins, James A., 20

Atlanta, GA, 65, 130, 164, 185–86

Atlanta Council on Human Relations (ACHR), 58

Atlanta Public Library, 26–27, 41–42, 58–59, 205

Atlanta University, 21, 26, 52, 189, 191, 200

attacks. *See* assaults; bombings; murder of civil rights activists

Auburn Avenue Research Library on African American Culture and History, 205

Audubon Regional Library System, Louisiana, 177–84

Baker, Augusta, 193

Baker, Constance. *See* Motley, Constance Baker

Baltimore, MD, 25

Banks, Charles, 29

Barker, Tommie Dora, 27; *Libraries of the South,* 186

Barnes, Catherine, 16, 43

Bartlesville, OK, 50, 192

basement libraries, 23, 38, 44, 74, 82–83, 88, 89

bathrooms. *See* restrooms

Baton Rouge, LA, 66, 67, 168
Beaufort, SC, 198
Beaumont, TX, 24
Becker, Norma, 158
Bell, Bernice Lloyd, 200
Berlin, Ira, 4, 31
Bess, Lettie, 174
Bessemer, AL, 11, 203
Bethea, Frankie, 147
Bevel, Jim, 54
Birmingham, AL, 9, 10–11, 66, 115–18, 160;
    public library, 22–23, 24, 186, 205
Black, Hugo, 183–84
Black Boy (Wright), 191–92
Black Codes, 2
black librarians' education, 31, 41, 52, 186
black library branches, 15, 21–25, 29, 44–45, 62,
    203; Albany, GA, 134, 135, 137, 138–39; Alex-
    andria, VA, 50; Atlanta, GA, 27, 41–42, 205,
    236n6; Birmingham, AL, 22–23, 115, 116–17;
    Charleston, SC, 36; Columbus, GA, 143; Dan-
    ville, VA, 91; Gainesville, TX, 29; Greenville,
    SC, 76; Huntsville, AL, 39; Indianola, MS,
    165–66; Jackson, MS, 21–22, 148, 149; and
    librarians' training, 186; Little Rock, AR, 30;
    Louisiana, 170, 172, 173, 174, 175; Louisville,
    KY, 30–35; Memphis, TN, 23, 66; Meridian,
    MS, 148; Mobile, AL, 24, 113; Montgomery,
    AL, 52, 118, 119, 122, 125; Richmond, VA, 55,
    56; Savannah, GA, 28–29; statistics (Depres-
    sion era) on, 35; Vicksburg, MS, 166
black newspapers and magazines, 25, 34, 39,
    40, 47, 190
black reading interests, 39–43, 157, 191
black veterans, 5, 49, 57, 67, 90, 160
blacks in children's fiction, 39
Blalock, Patricia, 128, 202
Blue, Thomas Fountain, 31, 33–34, 40, 157
bombings, 121; Albany, GA, 138; Birmingham,
    AL, 7, 9, 11, 117; Nashville, TN, 70, 73
Bond, Julian, 164, 236n6
Bontemps, Arna, 72, 180
bookmobiles, 36–37, 46, 51, 52; Alabama, 37,
    38, 39, 52; Georgia, 20–21, 36, 134; Louisi-

ana, 169, 175, 177–78, 181; Memphis, TN,
    66; North Carolina, 24, 36; South Carolina,
    36–37, 76; Virginia, 60, 94
Boston Public Library, 18–19
Bostwick, Arthur E., 24
boycotts, 132, 165–66, 179. *See also* bus boycotts
Boynton v. Virginia, 9
Brady, Tom: *Black Monday,* 63
Brass, Bennie, 169–70, 171–72
Bridges, Ruby, 168
Broderick, Dorothy, 39
Broward County Public Library, 205
Brown, Henry, 180, 181. See also *Brown v.
    Louisiana*
Brown, Leola, 6
Brown, Linda, 6
Brown, Oliver, 6
Brown, Ruth, 50, 147, 192
Brown v. Board of Education, 1, 6–7, 12, 14, 43,
    57, 71, 100, 115; resistance to, 6–7, 12, 130,
    152–53
Brown v. Board of Education II, 6–7
Brown v. Louisiana, 181–84, 204
Brownlow, Louis, 88
Bryan, Albert V., 87, 88, 89
Bulletin of the American Library Association, 192,
    193, 195
Burnett, McKinley, 6
bus boycotts, 63; Baton Rouge, 168; Albany, GA,
    134; Montgomery, AL, 1, 7, 14, 52–53, 118,
    119, 206
bus desegregation, 7–8, 9, 52–53, 75, 121, 132,
    139, 151
bus stations, 89, 118, 124, 142, 182; sit-ins,
    132–33
Byrd, Harry F., Sr., 6–7

Calvert County, MD, 51
Campbell, Will B., 1–2
card catalog access, 28, 83, 88, 94, 119, 120, 139
Carnegie, Andrew, 21, 206–7
Carnegie Corporation grants, 23, 26–30, 34, 37,
    41, 185, 186
Carnegie libraries, 21, 27, 29, 30, 34, 131, 186

Carrollton, GA, 24–25

Carter, Jimmy, 182

Carter, John, 96, 98

Carter, Robert L., 152

Cary, Alice, 27

catalog access. *See* card catalog access

Catlin, James, 98

censorship, 189, 192, 202

chairs and tables, removal of: Albany, GA, 140; Danville, VA, 97, 98, 99, 100; Indianola, MS, 166; Jonesboro, LA, 177; Montgomery, AL, 122–23, 124, 125; Selma, AL, 128

Chaney, James, 13, 157, 159, 162, 163, 206

Charles, Ray, 131

Charleston County Free Library, SC, 36, 130

Charlotte, NC, 23, 44, 65

Chattanooga, TN, 70, 72

Chesnutt, Charles, 40

Chicago Defender, 39, 47

children's books, 39, 63–64, 161, 180

children's library services, 42, 47, 56, 83, 84–85, 161. *See also* story hours for children

churches: Albany, GA, 133, 138; Atlanta, GA, 130; bombing and burning of, 11, 117, 125, 133, 138, 157; Danville, VA, 91, 92; Durham, NC, 20; and library services, 20, 23, 24, 38; Louisiana, 36; Mississippi, 158; Montgomery, AL, 119, 120; Petersburg, VA, 85. *See also* Sixteenth Street Baptist Church, Birmingham, AL

Cincinnati, OH, 19

Citizens' Councils. *See* White Citizens' Councils

city bus desegregation. *See* bus desegregation

civil disobedience, 85, 119, 142. *See also* library sit-ins; lunch-counter sit-ins; read-ins; sit-ins

Civil Rights Act of 1957, 73, 146

Civil Rights Act of 1964, 12, 100, 142, 148, 163; Supreme Court cases and, 182; testing of, 158, 160, 169, 172; Title II, 15

Civil Rights Acts of 1866 and 1870, 2

civil rights legislation, 2–3, 7, 12, 62, 73, 158. *See also* Civil Rights Act of 1957; Civil Rights Act of 1964; Civil Rights Acts of 1866 and 1870

Civil War, 90; monuments, 76; textbook treat-ment of, 42, 43; and Winston County, AL, 121

Claiborne, VA, 83, 87–88

Clark, L. A., 152, 154

Clift, David, 195

Clinton, LA, 177–84

closure of government offices, 132

closure of libraries. *See* library closures

closure of parks, 118, 123

clubs and community organizations, 27, 29, 31, 33, 34. *See also* women's clubs

Cobb, Robert L., 119–22, 123, 125

Coleman, Henry, 166

colleges and universities, desegregation of, 10, 11, 155, 164, 168

Collins, Robert F., 182

Colored National Liberal Convention, 19

Columbus, GA, 143–45, 206

Commission on Civil Rights. *See* U.S. Commis-sion on Civil Rights

community center, library as, 27, 33–35, 38, 44

community organizations. *See* clubs and com-munity organizations

community referenda. *See* referenda

Confederate flag, 97, 130, 141, 150

Congress. *See* U.S. Congress

Conley, Charles, 120

Conley, Ellen, 120

Connor, Eugene "Bull," 10, 11, 115, 117, 205

Congress of Racial Equality (CORE), 5, 182, 204; and Freedom Rides, 9, 10, 118; and Free-dom Summer, 13; in Louisiana, 169, 170–71, 172, 174, 176, 178–81, 204; in Virginia, 83

constitutional amendments, 1–2. *See also* Four-teenth Amendment

Cook, Karen J., 148

Cotter, Joseph S.: "Story Hour," 32–33

Council of Federated Organizations (COFO), 157

Council on Library Resources (CLR), 193

Covington, KY, 44

Cox, Mary A., 152, 154

Cox, William Harold, 162, 164

Crosby, Margaree, 209

cross burning, 92, 97, 121

Mississippi Summer Project. *See* Freedom Summer

Mitchell, Daniel, 176

Mize, Sidney C., 155–56

Mobile, AL, 24, 66, 113–14

mobs, 125, 127, 163–64, 179. *See also* lynchings

Monroe, LA, 169–75

Monroe, NC, 57–58

Montgomery, AL, 51–53, 118–25; bus boycott, 1, 7, 14, 52–53, 118, 119, 206; museum, 121–22; public library, 51–53, 118–25

Montgomery Improvement Association (MIA), 119

Montgomery Negro Ministerial Association, 51–52

Moon, Eric, 190–91, 192, 193, 195, 202, 245n29

Moore, Ronnie, 171

Moreau, Joseph, 43

Morgan, Juliette, 53, 147, 202

Moses, Robert, 157

motels and hotels. *See* hotels and motels

Motley, Constance Baker, 8, 71, 136

Mound Bayou, MS, 29

murder of civil rights activists, 1, 11, 12, 146; Chaney, Goodman, and Schwerner, 13, 157, 159, 162, 163, 206

Murray, Samuel C., 59–60

Muse, Andrew, 92

Muse, Benjamin, 168

museums, 121–22

Myrdal, Gunnar, 48

Nashville, TN, 66, 70, 72, 73; public library, 53–54, 72

Nashville Negro Public Library, 29

National Association for the Advancement of Colored People (NAACP), 7–8, 52, 63–64, 72, 186; Albany, GA, 133; Columbus, GA, 143, 145; Greenville, SC, 77, 78, 79, 80; and Ida B. Wells, 20; Legal Defense and Education Fund, 8, 81, 90, 152, 182; Memphis, TN, 67, 68, 69, 75; Mississippi, 146, 148, 150, 151–52; Monroe, NC, 57; Virginia, 82, 83, 84, 90, 92, 94–100

National Guard, 11, 163–64

National Lawyers Guild, 162

National Library Week, 193–94

national media. *See* mass media

Neshoba County, MS: murder of civil rights workers (1964), 13, 146, 157, 159, 162, 163, 206

Newman, Samuel, 97

New Orleans Public Library, 28, 56–57, 70, 168, 197

Newport News, VA, 59, 95

Newsletter on Intellectual Freedom, 194

newspapers and magazines, black. *See* black newspapers and magazines

New York City: school segregation, 200

New York Garrison Literary Association, 18

New York Public Library: Schomburg Center. *See* Schomburg Research Center

Norfolk, VA, 74, 95

North Arkansas Regional Library, 198

North Carolina A&T College, 8

North Carolina Library Association, 188, 190

North Carolina Negro Library Association, 188, 190

northern public libraries, 18–19, 199

Not Free, Not for All: Public Libraries in the Age of Jim Crow (Knott), 15

Oboler, Eli, 195–96

Oklahoma City, OK, 27

Ouachita Parish Public Library, 169–75

Owens, Hugo, 60–61

Oxford, MS, 10

park benches, removal of, 153

park segregation and desegregation, 121; Albany, GA, 137, 144; Birmingham, AL, 115; Danville, VA, 90, 91; Mississippi, 153; Montgomery, AL, 118, 123

Parks, Rosa, 1, 7, 15, 52

Patterson, Catherine, 176

Petersburg, VA, 44, 82–90

Petersburg Improvement Association (PIA), 86–87, 89

Philadelphia, MS, 13, 146, 159, 206
Philadelphia, PA, 199
Philadelphia Library Company of Colored Persons, 18
pickets and picketing, 86, 132, 135, 165–66, 176, 177
Piel, Eleanor Jackson, 162
place (concept), 31, 33–35, 38
Plant City (FL) Public Library, 198
playgrounds, 47, 80, 86, 115, 137, 151, 153, 156
Pleasant, Bertha, 52
Plessy, Homer Adolph, 3
Plessy v. Ferguson, 3–4, 6
Portsmouth, VA, 60–62, 95
Powell, Dalzie M., 37
Powledge, Fred, 8–9, 11, 65–66, 137
Prater, Ruby, 22
presidential orders. *See* executive orders
Pritchett, Laurie, 133, 135, 137, 141, 142
private libraries, 94, 95, 96, 124
Profit, Joseph, 173–74
protests and demonstrations: Alabama, 113–29; Georgia, 131–42; Louisiana, 169–84; Mississippi, 148–67; Virginia, 85, 86, 100. *See also* pickets and picketing
Public Accommodations Act, 2–3
public parks. *See* park segregation and desegregation
public schools. *See* school segregation and desegregation
public transportation, 168. *See also* bus boycotts; bus desegregation
Pullman porters, 19, 39
Purcellville (VA) Public Library, 59

The Rabbits' Wedding (Williams), 63–64
Rachlin, Carl, 181–82
Raleigh, NC, 24
Randolph, A. Philip, 4
Randolph, Wassell, 68, 69–70
Rayfield, W. D., 154–55
Readers' Guide to Periodical Literature, 190
reading rooms, 25, 27, 29, 44, 59, 70, 126; Albany, GA, 134, 140; Anniston, AL, 126;

Danville, VA, 93; and literary societies, 18; Montgomery, AL, 119; Nashville, TN, 54; New Orleans, LA, 28; Petersburg, VA, 83, 85; removal of periodicals from, 123; sit-ins, 73, 85, 134
read-ins, 143–44, 160, 169, 170. *See also* library sit-ins
Reagon, Bernice Johnson, 132
real estate redlining, 15
Reconstruction, 1–3
Reddick, L. D., 45
Reed, Emily, 63–64, 202
Reeves, Katie, 180
referenda, 93, 95–96, 98
Reid, Milton, 86, 87
removal of chairs and tables. *See* chairs and tables, removal of
removal of park benches. *See* park benches, removal of
restaurants and lunch counters: Albany, GA, 132, 139, 141; Birmingham, AL, 117; Danville, VA, 100; Greenville, SC, 79; Hattiesburg, MS, 159–60; Louisiana, 169; Memphis, TN, 75; Petersburg, VA, 87, 89. *See also* lunch counter sit-ins; snack bars
restrooms, 4, 25, 57, 74, 75, 121, 144, 193; at train stations, 133
Reyburn, Samuel W., 30
Reynolds, Quintus, 125, 126–27
Richmond, VA, 86, 90, 187; public library, 55–56, 72, 95
A Right to Read: Segregation and Civil Rights in Alabama's Public Libraries (Graham), 15, 16, 23, 36, 39, 53, 201–2, 204
Riley, Virginia, 133–34, 135, 137, 138
riots, 63, 117, 118, 202
Rives, Richard T., 155
Robertson, Florence, 93, 99
Robey, Mrs. Clarence, 60
Robinson, Anne, 24
Robinson, Jackie, 138
Robinson, Larry, 176, 177
Robinson, Tommy, 173
Rochell, Carlton, 158

Stokes-Jackson, Jimella, 159
Stoner, J. B., 97
story hours for children, 31, 32–33, 38
Stow, Charles E., 81
Stowe, Harriet Beecher: *Uncle Tom's Cabin*, 41
Student Nonviolent Coordinating Committee (SNCC), 9, 10, 55, 132, 150, 159
subscription libraries, 20, 28, 94
Supreme Court. *See* U.S. Supreme Court
Swanson, Paul K., 195
swimming pools, 118, 137, 140, 144, 178

tables and chairs, removal of. *See* chairs and tables, removal of
Talladega College, 20
Talmadge, Herman, 136
television, 10, 65, 117, 119, 122, 138, 175, 198
Temple, T. E., 92–93
Tennessee Valley Authority (TVA), 37–38
Terrell, Mary Church, 27
textbooks, 39, 42–43, 159
theaters, 5, 12, 75, 169, 177; Albany, GA, 137, 141, 142; Birmingham, AL, 115; and Public Accommodations Act, 2
Thirteenth Amendment, 1
Thomas, Clarence, 29, 131
Thomas, Doyle, 92
Thomas, Eddie, 166
Thomas County, GA, 36
Thompson, Roby, 92, 93, 94, 98
Thompson, William Hale, 59
Thornley, Fant, 117, 118
Till, Emmett, 7, 146, 149
Tougaloo Nine, 148–56
Trailways buses, 89
train stations, 124, 133, 142
transportation. *See* interstate transportation; public transportation
trials, 163, 180, 206; Albany, GA, 134, 141; Jackson, MS, 150, 151; Memphis, TN, 72–73; Petersburg, VA, 85–86
Troy, AL, 55, 206
Truman, Harry, 5, 54
Tuck, Stephen, 13

Tucker, Samuel W., 48–50
Tulsa race riot of 1921, 28
Turner, Allegra, 66–67, 68, 75
Turner, Jesse H., 66–71, 73–75
Turner v. City of Memphis, 75
Turner v. Randolph, 71
Tuttle, Elbert Parr, 163–65
Tyson, Cleophas, 143, 144

Ulveling, Ralph, 199
Uncle Tom's Cabin (Stowe), 41
universities, desegregation of. *See* colleges and universities, desegregation of
University of Alabama, 11, 121
University of Georgia, 164
University of Mississippi, 10, 155, 162, 164
U.S. Commission on Civil Rights, 7, 176, 196
U.S. Congress, 2, 12; House Committee on Un-American Activities, 14. *See also* civil rights legislation
U.S. Constitution. *See* constitutional amendments
U.S. Department of Justice, 136, 150, 180
U.S. Supreme Court, 72, 97, 139, 141; *Brown v. Louisiana*, 181–84; bus segregation (intracity), 7, 53; interstate travel segregation, 5, 9; justices, 29; *Loving*, 82; *Plessy*, 3–4; *Turner v. City of Memphis*, 75. See also *Brown v. Board of Education*

Van Jackson, Wallace, 187
"venereal disease" fears, 74, 75, 155
"vertical integration," 97, 124, 128, 140, 153. *See also* chairs and tables, removal of
veterans, black. *See* black veterans
Vicksburg, MS, 166
Virginia State College, 84, 88
voter registration, 13, 58, 68, 98, 132, 146, 157
Voting Rights Act, 157

waiting rooms, 4, 133, 153, 182
Wakeman, John, 190, 191, 197
Walcott, Victoria, 205
Walker, Alice, 46